THE NEWMAN BROTHERS

BY THE SAME AUTHOR

The Ethical Idealism of Matthew Arnold

JOHN HENRY NEWMAN IN 1890
from a portrait by Emmeline Deane

WILLIAM ROBBINS

THE
NEWMAN BROTHERS

AN ESSAY IN
COMPARATIVE INTELLECTUAL BIOGRAPHY

HARVARD UNIVERSITY PRESS

CAMBRIDGE, MASSACHUSETTS

1966

Printed in Great Britain

Contents

248799

Contents

Introduction

IN 1891, members of the English reading public were startled, and according to individual bias shocked or intrigued, by the appearance of a little book entitled *Contributions Chiefly to the Early History of the Late Cardinal Newman*. Casting his ageing memory back over almost seven decades of fraternal conflict, Francis Newman set down every act or utterance of his brother that, to his mind, revealed strains of fanaticism or dishonesty, notably such as seemed to prove that John Henry Newman was a thoroughgoing Papist long before he left the Church of England. The reason he gave for this irascible attack was the danger that many uncritical people, especially young people, might be seduced by the Cardinal's great reputation, by the respect for him as a thinker and the admiration for him as a man, into joining the Roman Catholic Church. The unspoken reason was probably a sense of relief at releasing the accumulated resentments and irritations of a lifetime, which began when 'a most painful breach, through mere religious creed, broke on me in my nineteenth year, and was *unhealable*'. That word 'mere', breaking the surface of the reflective mind, sets up historical ripples, ironic and unending.

Except for a brief *succès de scandale* which took it quickly into a second edition, the book made little impact. Certain anti-Newmanites, religious or rationalist, were confirmed in their suspicions, but a generation of readers had already acclaimed the *Apologia Pro Vita Suâ* as a classic, in which Newman had first pulverized Charles Kingsley and then vindicated himself. Furthermore, the edition of his letters by Anne Mozley also appeared in 1891, and in these two volumes the Cardinal gave his own early history with controlled and documented fulness. Already seen as the greatest religious figure in England in the nineteenth century, growing in stature and importance, internationally renowned, he was not likely to suffer in fame because of his brother's reminiscences, which could be dismissed as the mutterings of an angry old man, in bad taste even where accurate.

In general, the response was one of rebuke. In the *Athenaeum* obituary on Francis himself six years later, the writer referred to the little volume as betraying 'a theological unbrotherliness rarely met with in recent biography'. Later writers have dismissed it as 'that odd little book', as strange or curious or unpleasant. Yet a remark attributed to Cardinal Manning may be worth recalling, before one dismisses the book as hopelessly or malevolently astray on the complex Newman character. 'Francis Newman, he said, had produced a painting which revealed a most unenviable state of mind in a brother. But, he added, "if you ask me whether it is *like* our dear friend, it is a *photograph, a photograph*".'[1]

More important than the question of accuracy in portraiture is the witness to the strength and bitterness of religious differences, and to the powerful currents of thought that carried two brothers, starting from the same background in the early years of the century, in completely opposite directions. In a just and sympathetic essay on Francis Newman which brings this neglected Victorian before us as a good deal more than a figure of fun and frustration, Professor Basil Willey begins with the statement: 'In the history of nineteenth century English thought there is no story more striking, or more full of moral significance, than that of the divergent courses of the brothers Newman.'[2] With this judgment no student

[1] In H. L. Stewart, *A Century of Anglo-Catholicism*, London, 1929, p. 126. The feeling in Manning's remark may of course be explained by his difficult relations with Newman over many years, a relationship in which Manning does not show very well in the view of most biographers. It is true too that Francis Newman spoke warmly of Manning, contrasting his passion for social reform and for working-class improvement with his brother's indifference to such matters. Later extremes in Catholic comment on Francis may be seen in Father Tristram's Newmanolatrous vehemence in *Newman and His Friends* (Francis, 'having dipped his pen in slime, has given a silly and malicious account'), and in E. E. Reynolds's *Three Cardinals* ('It is a pity that so much notice has been taken of Francis Newman's oddities. He was a man of considerable intellectual power.' But his book on his brother 'needs to be read with caution').

[2] Basil Willey, *More Nineteenth Century Studies*, London, 1956. Tempering the virtual neglect of half a century are articles in the *Hibbert Journal* for July, 1925, by J. R. Mozley, and in the *Church Quarterly Review* for July, 1934, by Kenneth N. Ross, both titled "Francis William Newman". Mozley, mainly concerned with the element of suffering in their history, finds an inward similarity in the brothers despite the divergences. Ross gives full play to the eccentricities of Francis and the contrasts with John, but also finds much originality and insight, if much 'perverseness', in this earnest seeker after truth. A full dress treatment, able and appreciative, is that by James R. Bennett, entitled *Francis W. Newman*

of the period can quarrel. Indeed, from 1850 on friends and reviewers commented in a variety of ways on this striking sign of the times. What seemed to me merely an arresting phenomenon many years ago has widened in meaning and interest, stimulated by such shrewd or lively comparisons as those in Maisie Ward's *Young Mr Newman* and Sean O'Faoláin's *Newman's Way*. The contrasting careers of the brothers have prompted this attempt at an essay in comparative biography. Thoroughly explored, in terms of sources and of main movements of thought, they would lead into a history of the age.

Only the dedicated specialist can hope now to bring fresh insight to any aspect of the life or work of the famous Cardinal. In 1945, C. F. Harrold prefaced his study of Newman's 'mind, thought, and art' with the statement: 'Of the making of books on Newman there seems to be no end.' The flood has continued, of attack and defence, of attempts to penetrate the 'mystery of Newman' or to deny that there was any mystery. Or to agree with one of the Cardinal's disciples, who remarked, 'the only mystery about Newman was that he did not give a damn for this world'. So a footnote (p. xvii) tells us in volume 11 of Father Dessain's superbly edited *The Letters and Diaries of John Henry Newman*, a volume which covers the period from October, 1845, to December, 1846. With ten volumes allowed for the earlier 'Anglican' correspondence, this monumental and indispensable edition will total some thirty volumes.

Many writers on Newman have, naturally, focused attention on his role in the Oxford Movement or Anglo-Catholic revival, assessing or expanding Dean W. C. Lake's obituary statement in the *Manchester Guardian* of August 27, 1890. To Newman, he said, 'we owe the establishment of principles which have gone so far to

---

and *Religious Liberalism in Nineteenth Century England* (unpublished doctoral dissertation, Stanford University, 1960). This title reminds us of what Francis was mainly noted for in his own day. Perhaps notorious is the better word. A striking forerunner of Professor Willey's statement, but one expressive of contemporary alarm, appeared in a review of five books, entitled "Forms of Infidelity in the Nineteenth Century" (*North British Review*, May, 1851): 'We know not that this two-fold tendency towards a superstitious Ritualism on the one hand, and a sceptical Rationalism on the other, which seems to be incident to a critical era like the present, has ever been more strikingly or more instructively exemplified, at least in modern times, than in the case of the brothers Newman.'

change the character of the Church of England during the last half century, and of which the fuller development is probably yet to come'. Others have examined the extent of his contribution to the Church he joined. J. A. Froude's remark in 1881, that to Newman, 'if to any one man, the world owes the intellectual recovery of Romanism', is supported by Father Bouyer, the translation of whose *Newman: Sa vie; sa spiritualité* appeared in 1958. He points to a virtually stagnant Catholic theology in the mid-nineteenth century. From this situation, if Tradition was to be preserved, 'there was no escape unless and until some outstanding geniuses came to the rescue. Of these, Newman was one, and probably the greatest.'

To try placing the obscure Francis in any sort of relation to so impressive a reputation and achievement may well seem a wilful attempt to compare a fog-shrouded foothill with a majestic peak. Scholarly critics look puzzled at the mention of his name, or remember him only as the victim of Arnoldian satire for his translation of Homer; in Halévy's *History of the English People in the 19th Century* he is called Frederick Newman, and the translator's note of identification makes no correction; knowledgeable booksellers display invincible ignorance when asked for *The Soul*, a treatise praised by Professor Willey for its 'account of the psychology of religious experience'. Yet though none of his works appears to have been re-published after 1908, a number of them achieved a second or third edition, and both *The Soul* and *Phases of Faith* ran to nine editions by 1874. A writer in *Notes and Queries* for March, 1898, praised the five volumes of *Miscellanies* and regretted that a still larger amount lay buried in periodicals, adding: 'This age has had few, if any, who have excelled Professor Newman in scholarship, in keenness of intellect, or in moral earnestness.' A. W. Benn's *History of English Rationalism in the 19th Century* describes him as, in his time, 'the most influential critic of the traditional theology', and the judgment is echoed by V. F. Storr in *The Development of English Theology in the 19th Century*.

In the light of even these few facts and comments, and many more could be added, it is not enough to say with some writers that Francis Newman passed the whole of his life in the shadow of his famous brother. Nor is it enough to dwell on his oddities of dress and behaviour, his prosaic cast of mind, his lack of a sense of humour, and the faddishness which dissipated his powers, even to the exasperating extent of clothing one of his best essays, "Christianity in Its Cradle", in the eccentric garb of a reformed spelling. All these factors must be taken into account. But a more fundamental reason for his obscurity is, paradoxically, the progressive direction of his mind. Far more than his brother he was a writer of tracts *for* the times (as Elizabeth Barrett Browning observed, John Henry Newman was a writer of tracts *against* the times) and made his contribution to the secular shape of things to come. He did this in such an unsystematic and sporadic fashion that he was a skirmisher rather than a leader in the forces of liberalism, that liberalism against which the Cardinal, with diversified strategy but with a single aim and unwavering purpose, fought a life-long battle. Francis had at least as much of intellectual power, spirituality, and moral earnestness as his brother—some believed he had more—but he spent these in attacking powers already breathed on by the *Zeitgeist*, or in supporting and initiating causes whose triumph would alleviate the human condition without solving the human problem. Rational scepticism towards John's Catholic answer to his age has been matched by a pragmatic scepticism towards such fusions of secular idealism and moral theism as that offered by Francis. His direction and his conflicts, then, lack the drama of the Cardinal's for his own and later generations. To swim against the stream is a more compelling spectacle than to swim with it, whether one is seen as nobly breasting or stubbornly resisting.

Support for this view may be found in the letters of George Eliot. In 1849 she refers to 'our blessed St Francis', and to the inspiring influence upon her of the man and his work. In 1864, she has read the *Apologia* with 'absorbing interest' and with indignant scorn for Kingsley, and is deeply affected by this 'revelation of a life—how different in form from one's own, yet with how close a fellowship in its needs and burthens'. In 1874 she notices 'poor Mr Francis Newman', and feels 'an affectionate sadness' in thinking of the interest which in far-off days she found in his *Soul* and *Phases of Faith*. 'How much work he has done in the world, which has left no deep, conspicuous mark but has probably entered beneficently into many lives.'

At a time of prayers for the beatification of John Henry Newman, it will not be amiss to recall a man whom George Eliot once admired as a saint of rationalism, and to follow the divergent paths of these men through the century spanned by their lives.[1] The Newman scholar will find little to add to his specialized knowledge in these pages; the philosopher and historian will find no challenging reconstruction. But the student of the period and the general reader may, I hope, share my interest in two brothers whose search for religious truth drove them far apart, in spite of a common devotion to spiritual values, and whose response to the claims of the seen and the unseen world was such as to reveal in them perennially different types of humanity.

Note: Footnotes, some with added comment or information, have been held to a minimum. Titles or page numbers likely to be of interest or use have been inserted, wherever possible, in the pages of the text. Decisions made are admittedly arbitrary, and risk inconsistency.

It is a pleasure to record my indebtedness to the Board of Governors of the University of British Columbia for leave of absence on generous terms in 1961–2; to the Canada Council for a scholarship and travel grant; to Father C. S. Dessain of the Birmingham Oratory for making available the unpublished Newman correspondence; to Mr J. H. Mozley of Haslemere, Surrey, for allowing me to read the originals of the Newman letters at the University of London; to the officials of the Bodleian Library for permission to examine collections of letters; to my wife for typing the manuscript and preparing the index.

W.R.

[1] John Henry Newman, 1801–1890; Francis William Newman, 1805–1897.

PART ONE

UP TO 1833

CHAPTER I

A Glimpse of the Background

IF IN a general way the modern age derives from the many-faceted Renaissance, it may be seen on the verge of its later and more striking development during the boyhood of the Newman brothers. Social and political changes, the growth of rationalism and toleration, the triumphs of applied science—these and other trends characterizing the 'age of reform' were apparent or imminent. Hailed with enthusiasm or viewed with alarm, they were soon to gather a momentum steadily increasing into our times, when the weightless encapsuled man, out of the cradle of his genius endlessly orbiting, already continues on his lunar way. To live with and to interpret change (what Julian Huxley called 'living in a revolution') has been the painful demand imposed on whole areas of thought and feeling by the pace of discovery and innovation. We may smile wryly at Matthew Arnold's depressed awareness in 1849, when he wrote:

> Like children bathing on the shore,
> Buried a wave beneath;
> The second wave succeeds, before
> We have had time to breathe.

Yet pace in itself is relative. The implications of a jet plane breaking the sound barrier raise in magnified form the problems that confronted a thoughtful Victorian when a metal monster roared at forty miles per hour through 'six counties overhung with smoke', or when communication was accelerated by the Atlantic telegraph in 1866, caustically described by Arnold as 'that great rope, with a Philistine at each end of it talking inutilities'. Certainly a growing awareness of pace and a sense of possible implications are seen in an essay by W. R. Greg entitled "Realisable Ideals", published in 1872. 'We *remember* light', he said, 'as it was in the days of Solomon, we *see* it as Drummond and Faraday have made it.' So with locomotion and communication. Surely, he went on, mental and moral forces applied to other areas than the material, and fired with enthusiasm for Humanity, could bring us nearer the ideal State. 'Thought has not yet grown feebler than electricity and gases in moulding the destinies of man.'

These moods of pessimism and optimism, elegantly expressed, alike may raise in disillusioned descendants a nostalgic sigh for less complicated days. Yet the pattern is familiar. There is the fact of material progress; the hope (at times the faith) that man's reason will bring about a corresponding moral improvement; the uneasy awareness, or even the profound conviction, that there is no necessary connection.

If we extend this last thought to the fiercely uncompromising belief that no such connection is possible, that faith in a rational and progressive liberalism means spiritual death, and hence moral decay, we have the position of John Henry Newman. The optimistic position, with some reservations, is that of his brother. Both men believed in a personal God, both saw spiritual truth as supreme, both derived their spirituality from, or confirmed it by, the Evangelical experience of conversion. The objects they contemplated as God, truth, and spirit, came to diverge as widely as their paths, to be sure, but one wonders if John's annoyance with Francis is sometimes due to an exasperated feeling that the more fervent utterances of his brother caricatured his own. At all events, their common point of departure suggests that Evangelicalism is the strain in their background that we should look into, rather than the political or social or technological developments leading into and through the nineteenth century.

The wave of religious enthusiasm which stemmed from Wesley and Whitefield in the mid-eighteenth century, and which, as a kind of Puritan revival, added the Methodist drive to Dissent and the Low Church Evangelical zeal to the Establishment, was itself overtaken in the mid-nineteenth century by the growing force of a liberal and rationalistic secularism. Not that its energy was extinguished; rather it was absorbed as a contributory moral strain into the main 'lay current', liberal and social, that Matthew Arnold saw in 1881 as the sign of the times. The abolition of slavery owed a great deal to the Evangelical conscience of Christian men and women, both Nonconformist and Anglican, as did early reforms in prisons, education, and child labour. Halévy analyses the resultant, relatively stable, quality of English life in the nineteenth century.[1]

Why was it that of all the countries of Europe England has been the most free from revolutions, violent crises, and sudden changes? We have sought in vain to find the explanation by an analysis of her political institutions and economic organization. Her political institutions were such that society might easily have lapsed into anarchy had there existed in England a bourgeoisie animated by the spirit of revolution. And a system of economic production that was in fact totally without organization of any kind would have plunged the kingdom into violent revolution had the working class found in the middle class leaders to provide it with a definite ideal, a creed, a practical programme. But the *élite* of the working class, the hardworking and capable bourgeois, had been imbued by the evangelical movement with a spirit from which the established order had nothing to fear.

A religious zeal as much concerned with stricter Sunday observance as with the abolition of slavery could not, however, long compete with a rising spirit of social-scientific humanitarianism, imbued with revolutionary doctrines of the rights of man and seeing the realities of the human lot in terms of economic conditions and political power. The fact that moral and religious reform was yoked to social conservatism meant that the emerging democratic spirit was bound to seek expression outside the Evangelical pattern. Popular education is a case in point. It is not surprising to find Bishop Horsley around 1795 viewing charity schools and Sunday schools with suspicion, as places where 'sedition and atheism are the real objects of instruction', but he was supported even by the scientist Sir Humphrey Gilbert, whose Evangelical fears moved him to attack the principle of compulsion. Education for the labouring classes, he said, would be 'prejudicial to their morals and happiness', making them discontented and enabling them to read 'seditious, licentious, and anti-Christian literature'.[2] A further remark by Halévy, that the spiritual ancestors of the trade union leaders were the founders of Methodism, does indeed remind us

---

[1] Elie Halévy, *A History of the English People in the 19th Century*, (Dent) rev. ed., London, 1949, v. 1, p. 424. Halévy himself notes the changed situation by 1850. For a well-balanced society with a large middle class there was by then no need to look beyond the economic sphere to explain stability. (Vol. 4, 1951.)

[2] In W. L. Mathieson, *England in Transition: 1789–1832*, London, 1920, p. 101.

how much the 'lay current' of change and reform was indebted to the Puritan conscience and concern for souls; at the aristocratic extreme, we have the life-long humanitarian activity of Lord Shaftesbury. Nevertheless, the lack of sympathy with democratic ideals, or the lack of interest in worldly goals, at least as a path of ascent for the under-privileged, was a reason for the decline of Evangelical influence.

Other reasons were the anti-intellectual bias of a narrow pietism, and the too easy equation of success with virtue and failure with vice that could result from applying in the daily round the doctrines of election and reprobation and justification by faith. In short, fervour without tolerance could breed fanaticism, and conformity without conviction could breed hypocrisy. These have been the stock twentieth-century notions of 'Victorianism', largely shaped, be it noted, by Victorian self-criticism, by the angry blasts of Carlyle, the humorous portraits of Dickens, the urbane satire in Arnold's essays, the irreverent wit in, for example, Clough's parody of the Ten Commandments ('No graven images may be/Worshipped, except the currency; At church on Sunday to attend/Will serve to keep the world thy friend.'). An anonymous satirical essay of 1875, titled "Our Insincerity", leaves little to be said on this score. 'People go to Church to propitiate a mother, or to satisfy a father, to pacify their wives or to edify their servants— certainly not to please themselves or their Maker, for they know full well that their motives will not stand his scrutinizing eye.' The writer tells of a little girl who has read of heavenly joys, and asks if she will be allowed to go to Hell on Saturday afternoons if she has been good all week in Heaven. He agrees with 'many others' who break free with relief from 'years enthralled by creeds, dogmas, catechisms, and articles', that the Christ of the Gospels would be amazed at Christendom, and especially at Bibliolatry, and would probably revise the Word of God. This rationalist then zestfully refers to a French Roman Catholic who had never read the Bible till he bought one at the Crystal Palace, and after an hour's read-ing said: 'Je n'ai jamais su qu'il y eût des obscénités dans la Bible!' He concludes: 'Infidels have too high an opinion of God to believe that He had anything to do with the composition of such a volume as the Bible. They hope not—but unfortunately they are not sincere—frequently they act the part of believers so well that they are never found out; and so we go on, wearing our masks, singing our hymns, and denouncing the Jesuits with exemplary zeal, while acting upon their principle that "the end justifies the means", and thinking it best to keep the peace at home—not a bit afraid of God, but in great and abiding awe of Mrs Grundy.'[1]

It is not the satirized and caricatured period of decline that is our concern, however, but the early years of the century, when the powerful influence of Evangelical teaching invaded the comfortably middle-class Anglican home of banker John Newman and, uncomfortably for him, illuminated the lives of two of his sons. Before dealing with this crisis, it may be well to consider further some of the paradoxes and contradictions, latent and dissolvent, in Evangelicalism itself.

Without the 'enthusiasm' that the Restoration had scorned in the earlier Puritans, giving the term connotations of emotionalism and subversion and fanaticism that extended well into the eighteenth century, the religious revival would neither have leavened the drily formalistic service of the Established Church nor strengthened the forces of Nonconformity. Yet feeling exalted over reason, and simple sincerity over knowledge, could not long stand in the nineteenth century against a renewed scholarly appeal to Tradition on the one hand, and a sceptical criticism reinforced by science on the other. Further, the doctrines of election and reprobation, and of justification by faith, are intensely individualistic in nature and stress as the only supreme realities the soul and God, with exclusive attention to the claims of the next world as against this. Yet the sheep had to be fed, and only good works could lessen ignorance and brutality and enable the Message to be received. The resultant amelioration and enlightenment, inevitably, made the sheep restlessly responsive to messages from more worldly sources. Again, these Calvinistic doctrines should have made, and often did make, for a fierce intolerance. But moral and emotional missionary zeal meant a practical rather than a doctrinal application of one's religion. 'By a strange paradox,' says Halévy, 'men who were Protestant to the backbone, zealots for the dogma of justification by faith, were so devoted to philanthropy that on the common ground of good works they were reconciled with the most lukewarm Christians, even with declared enemies of Christianity.'

[1] In Scott's *Controversial Tracts*, London, 1875. (Thomas Scott of Ramsgate published controversial and rationalist writings, including many of Francis Newman's pamphlets.)

The arresting figure in any view of Evangelicalism over the late eighteenth and early nineteenth centuries is William Wilberforce, leading member of the famous Clapham Sect. His advice to his son Samuel, who became Bishop of Oxford in 1845 and took 'the side of the angels' against Huxley in 1860, shows the curious blend of the spiritual and practical marking those mocked as 'peculiars' by their enemies. He said to Sam in 1819: 'We must also [as well as striving to obtain more of the Holy Spirit of God] examine ourselves and recollect, either at night or when we go to bed, or in the morning, as we find best (I am always sleepy at night), what have been the instances in which we have chiefly sinned, and then we shall ourselves discover our besetting sins.'[1] He warns Sam in 1823 not to incur and forget small debts and to 'pay ready money for everything, so far as you can do it with propriety and comfort'. Sunday breakfasts at Oxford are an 'injurious' practice, and 'the less excusable because at that early hour of the day the spirits of young men especially can need no such cordial. . . . For the present let it suffice to say that there are few things not actually sinful (for I do not call this such, but inexpedient) so likely to impair spirituality of mind in the religious exercises of the day.' He urges his son to show sympathy and kindness by intention and feeling before an action, not wait for the occasion of the action itself. His words would repay analysis from many points of view, containing as they do so much of Evangelicalism and the coming Victorian age at their best, and at least a promise to the lurking genius of satire.

Wilberforce did not make his great impact on his contemporaries merely by exhortation to pious exercises, or by his earnest support for Hannah More and others in their educational work and distribution of Bibles and devotional tracts. A wealthy and politically powerful layman, witty and civilized, he influenced statesmen and bishops and made the peculiars seem less peculiar. The full title in 1797 of his book, influential for decades, is *A Practical View of the Prevailing Religious System of Professed Christians in the Higher and Middle Classes in this Country Contrasted with Real Christianity*. The impressive title is matched by the aim recorded in his Journal: 'God Almighty has placed before me two great objects, the suppression of the Slave Trade and the reformation of [my country's] manners.' That the tone of morals and manners, in spite of Regency excesses, did improve, and that there was an awakening of Christian con-

[1] A. R. Ashwell, *Life of Samuel Wilberforce*, London, 1888, v. 1, p. 12.

science, was owing in part to the untiring efforts of Wilberforce in many causes. Of his share in vitalizing the Church Muriel Jaegar declares, in *Before Victoria*, that his refusal to secede to the Methodists 'may well have decided that the Church of England should survive'. If there is exaggeration here, there is none in Ford K. Brown's thoughtful summary.[1]

> No other man of his day, Wesley included, had so great an effect, for better and for worse, on the spiritual life of his country. He attempted a heroic civic task with unyielding courage and as great virtue as a man could have and successfully lead such a cause in such an age. . . . He did it by leading his Evangelicals—and with them very many others—to do as much as could humanly be done of a task that was so heroic as to be impossible: to reform the manners and morals of a society while disturbing no element of its socially immoral structure.

The irony of the dissolvent trends latent in Evangelicalism is evident in the case of Wilberforce. For the practical moral idealism, most strikingly associated with his name in the abolition of slavery, required just that collaboration with non-denominational and even secular bodies noted by Halévy. In itself no safeguard for the doctrinal forms of Evangelical spirituality, it became in time a contributing stream in the 'great lay current', or was used to justify a speculative liberalism in religion. Naturally, many men who were deeply concerned to preserve a doctrinal Christian spirituality saw such collaboration and freedom as a threat. To them, the only safeguard against 'the world' was a restored and strengthened dogmatic authority. This implies a truth in A. W. Benn's view that the Oxford Movement was an offshoot of Evangelicalism. A sufficiently ironic comment, especially in view of his championing of Catholic emancipation, is that three of Wilberforce's sons followed Newman into the Roman Catholic Church.

This brief summary of related but contrasting developments—that of a moral reformism sweeping Evangelical energy into the main lay current of modern times, and that of a resistant religious dogmatism trying to safeguard Evangelical spirituality by a sacramental and sacerdotal system—bears directly on the lives of Francis William and John Henry Newman.

Readers of the *Apologia* will recall Newman saying that in the autumn of 1816 he fell under the influence of a definite creed, and received 'impressions of dogma which, through God's mercy, have

[1] F. K. Brown, *Fathers of the Victorians*, Cambridge, 1961, p. 529.

never been effaced or obscured'. He described the experience more vividly in a letter to John Keble (June 8, 1844), when on the verge of his second conversion, to Rome. He had been led by Providence to this point, from the time when 'a boy of fifteen, and living a life of sin, with a very dark conscience and a very profane spirit, He mercifully touched my heart'. Presumably the life of sin consisted of leading and sharing the musical and dramatic home life of a fairly lively family of two brothers and three sisters, all younger, and the dark conscience arose from reading Paine and Hume and Voltaire with a shocked pleasure in their argument and wit. Or the sin may have been pride in his phenomenal progress through school at Ealing, and a natural desire to excel intellectually. He is not specific on this point. At any rate, the main effect of this experience of conscious inward conversion was in 'confirming me in my mistrust of the reality of material phenomena, and making me rest in the thought of two, and two only, supreme and luminously self-evident beings, myself and my Creator'.

Perhaps the tendency to such mistrust had already been confirmed by the failure of his father's business in March of the same year, the change from banking to brewing, and the move from London to Hampshire. Certainly the mystical tendency was there from the beginning in a lad whose 'imagination ran on unknown influences, magical powers, and talismans', who 'thought life might be a dream, or I an Angel, and all this world a deception', and who readily believed in 'Angels who lived in the world as it were disguised'. The teaching of the Rev. Walter Mayers fell on fertile soil in the summer of 1816. With an imagination predisposed to find reality in the inner self and the unseen world, Newman seized with emotional intensity on the dogmatic assurance offered by the Evangelical creed. He was later to speak disparagingly of the 'peculiars' and their 'enthusiasm', and the extreme Calvinistic doctrines of reprobation and final perseverance were to fade. But from the time of his going up to Oxford in December, 1816, his life was a drive towards securing authority for his intuitions, until his acceptance into the Roman Catholic Church almost thirty years later. The 'rough notes' preserved from the time of the early memoranda and restored in 1874 are worth repeating. 'The reality of conversion:—as cutting at the root of doubt, providing a chain between God and the soul. (i.e. with every link complete) I know I am right. How do I know it? I know I know.'

In the year of John's 'conversion', Francis, as he tells us in *Phases of Faith*, was beginning to read religious books, especially the Bible, and 'commenced a habit of secret prayer'. At the age of fourteen, under the influence of the same Evangelical clergyman, he too became a 'converted person'. Very soon the urge to seek rationality and consistency is apparent. How is the doctrine of election to be reconciled with God's justice? 'I supposed that I should know this in due time if I waited and believed his Word.' Why did the Bishop who confirmed him when he was sixteen, 'a *made-up* man and a mere pageant', not put questions testing his faith rather than his knowledge of religious formulas? Such questions did not as yet demand answers. His faith itself was whole, 'an unhesitating, unconditional acceptance of whatever was found in the Bible'. Not only that, but his creed was 'really operative' on his 'temper, tastes, pursuits and conduct'. The intellectual rigour that was later to subject all verbal authority and historical evidence to the tests of simple logic and common experience was not yet compulsive. Lacking John's imaginative power to translate intuitions into certainties, Francis for the time being found emotional security in an uncompromising piety and in the authority of the Bible Evangelically interpreted.

An instance of this piety appears in his solemn recollection that he 'fell into painful and injurious conflict with a superior kinsman [i.e. had a row with father] by refusing to obey his orders on a Sunday'. The order was to copy out a letter, as we find from John's *Early Journals* for September 30, 1821. Evidently John, home from Oxford and still very much in his own phase of Evangelical strictness (a look at that 'delightful' book, Wilberforce's *Practical Christianity*, put him off going to a play) supported Francis. 'A scene ensued more painful than any I have ever witnessed.' On Monday, 'Father was reconciled to us', and John had the grace to add: 'When I think of the utter persuasion he must entertain of the justice of his views of our apparent disobedience, the seeming folly of our opinions, and the way he is harassed by worldly cares [the brewery business was not a success], I think his forgiveness of us an example of very striking candour, forbearance, and generosity.' We may well agree, and feel sympathy for the decent and kindly Mr Newman faced with these self-righteous young recalcitrants.

Though Francis was probably the more obstinate, the father's warning to John is worth quoting in full, as showing some

shrewdness of prophetic insight and a more widely used Anglican
Via Media than that later projected by his eldest son. The entry in
the *Early Journals* is for January 6, 1822.

> Take care. It is very proper to quote Scripture, but you poured out
> texts in such quantities. Have a guard. You are encouraging a
> nervousness and morbid sensibility, and irritability, which may be
> very serious. I know what it is myself, perfectly well. I know it is a
> disease of mind. Religion, when carried too far, induces a softness of
> mind. You must *exert* yourself and do everything you can. Depend
> upon it, no one's principles can be established at twenty. Your
> opinions in two or three years will certainly, *certainly* change. I have
> seen many instances of the same kind. Take care, I repeat. You are on
> dangerous ground. The temper you are encouraging may lead to
> something alarming. Weak minds are carried into superstition, and
> strong ones into infidelity. Do not commit yourself. Do nothing
> ultra. Men say and do things, when young, which they would fain
> retract when older, but for shame they cannot. I know you write for
> the Christian Observer [Evangelical organ of the Clapham sect].
> My opinion of the Christian Observer is this, that it is a humbug.
> You must use exertions. That letter was more like the composition of
> an old man, than of a youth just entering life with energy and
> aspirations.

A reference clearly showing the difference between the brothers,
and the directions they were to take, is that to the Evangelical
writer Thomas Scott, recalled both in the *Apologia* and in *Phases of
Faith*. John calls him a writer 'to whom (humanly speaking) I
almost owe my soul'. He showed a 'bold unworldliness and vigorous independence of mind. He followed truth wherever it led him,
beginning with Unitarianism and ending in zealous faith in the
Holy Trinity.' Francis, destined to follow truth in the opposite
direction, remembers Scott as 'a rather dull, very unoriginal, half-
educated, but honest, worthy, sensible, strong-minded man', who
explained away seeming contradiction in the three-in-one God-
concept by saying that we hold Him to be three in one sense, and
one in another. 'It crossed my mind very forcibly,' says Francis,
'that, if that was all, the Athanasian Creed had gratuitously in-
vented an enigma.' He accepted the dogma, but 'whatever the
depth of the mystery, if we lay down anything about it *at all*, we
ought to understand our own words'. John accepted completely
this 'fundamental truth of religion', won by Scott's 'unworldliness'

and deeply influenced by the clergyman's 'practical' doctrine: 'Holiness before peace', and 'Growth is the only evidence of life.' In these sayings, which John came to use 'almost as proverbs', his aggressive Tractarian phase and his method of apologetics for Catholic belief are anticipated. Francis, asking that things as far as possible be what they seem, with a one to one correspondence, was already potentially the rationalist.

CHAPTER 2

Oriel and Ireland

WHEN FRANCIS went up to Oxford to live with his brother and to study under his guidance, John was in the midst of an academic career as spectacular in its one collapse as in its distinguished successes. A scholarship at Trinity in 1818 was followed by a failure to get first-class Honours in his B.A. examinations in 1820. Overwork, climaxed by twelve hours reading a day for the last twenty weeks, caused a virtual breakdown. The lack of direction in his studies at a time when 'the very idea of study was new' brought about an element of 'accident or caprice' in allotment of time. Looking back fifty years later, Dr Newman saw himself as 'a type of Protestantism; zeal, earnestness, resolution, without a guide; effort without a result. It was a pattern instance of private judgment and its characteristics.'[1] He was never at a loss in drawing lessons or analogies from experience, especially when these bore on stages of his religious development.

The reactions of his friends ranged through shock at the failure, reassurance that the result was meaningless, later surprise at Newman's temerity when he decided to stand for Oriel, 'the acknowledged centre of Oxford intellectualism', and growing confidence in the final outcome. The confidence matched his own, in spite of prayers and lapses into despair and Evangelical self-reproaches making up many entries in his *Journals* for 1822. On February 5 he has '*very* little chance of succeeding'; on March 7, 'I certainly feel very confident with respect to Oriel'; on April 12, at last: 'I have this morning been elected Fellow of Oriel. Thank God, thank

---

[1] *Autobiographical Writings*, ed. H. Tristram, London, 1956, p. 53. The third person form of the *Memoir* lends a rather detached and impersonal air. The *Journals* on which the reminiscent history is based, in their first person immediacy, have the vivid and emotional quality of the passing fragments of experience. Succeeding references to this volume, unless otherwise specified, will be made to either *Memoir* or *Journals*. These include the *Early Journals*.

God.' He had performed so impressively as virtually to ensure success in the first three days of examinations; he had justified earlier hopes and inspired glowing prophecies; he now entered into a distinguished company and gained a comfortable income, enabling him to help Francis through college and to take the strain off the family resources. That his abilities were generally considered worthy of Oriel's high reputation for scholarship is evident in a congratulatory letter from a fellow-student.[1]

> Behold you now a Fellow of Oriel, the great object of the ambition of half the Bachelors of Oxford. Behold you (to take a peep into futurity) in Holy Orders, taking pupils in college, and having a curacy within a short distance; then Public Tutor, Vicar of ——, Provost, Regius Professor of Divinity, Bishop of ——, Archbishop of Canterbury; or shall we say thus—Student-at-law, Barrister, Lord Chancellor, or at least Lord Chief Justice of the King's Bench? Which of these ladders is it your intention to climb? You now have it in your power to decide.

The first three prophecies were quickly fulfilled. The others might well have been had Newman stayed in the Church of England. The alternative career in law, intended by his father, had been rejected a year before. We can hardly see it as having been a serious possibility, in spite of this note in the *Journals*: 'In 1819 and the beginning of 1820, I hoped great things for myself, not liking to go into the Church, but to the Law.'

In contrast to this dramatic and detailed sequence of events, we hear little of Frank Newman's matter-of-fact progress from a scholarship at Worcester College in November of 1822 to a brilliant double First degree in June of 1826, followed by a Fellowship at Balliol. According to the *Dictionary of National Biography*: 'On his taking his degree, the whole assembly rose to welcome him, an honour paid previously only to Sir Robert Peel on his taking his double first.' His intellectual powers were recognized, and the expected success came. Passages in John's letters home remark on Frank's abilities, most strikingly in a letter to his mother on November 5, 1822. 'I am convinced that he knows much more of Greek as a language than most of those who take first classes, . . . he . . . in fact is a much better Greek scholar than I. . . . Again he

[1] A. Mozley, *Letters and Correspondence*, London, 1891, v. 1, p. 74. Unless otherwise specified, succeeding quotations from Newman's Anglican letters will be from these two volumes.

is a much better mathematician than I am. I mean he reads more mathematically.'

The mother's letters to her favourite son are interesting for another reason, the careful adjusting of the spotlight. In December of 1822: 'I congratulate Francis on his matriculation, and am delighted to anticipate that he will, whenever opportunity occurs, do you credit, and reward all your labours and anxiety for him.' On June 6, 1826: 'I think I must congratulate you equally with Frank on his success, as I suspect your anxiety on the occasion has been much greater than even his.' And a week later: 'It is very delightful about Frank. I am more thankful on your account than on his. He is a piece of adamant. You are such a sensitive being.' To all this we may add John's entry in his *Journals* for June 5, 1826. 'The class list came out on Friday last, and Frank was in both first classes. How I have been led on! how prospered! . . . I went before, failing in the Schools, to punish and humble me. Then, by gaining a fellowship here, I was enabled to take him by the hand. And now he is my τιμωρός φονόυ.'[1]

The young man here revealed, like the old man looking back later in the autobiographical *Memoir*, is the boy who found only two 'supreme and luminously self-evident beings, myself and my Creator'. An intense self-consciousness pervades every detail of experience recorded; a strong sense of drama places other persons and events in relation to the leading character, foreshadowing the decisive alignment of forces in later Tractarian days, and the cry of young Oxford, *Credo in Newmannum*. These qualities explain the zealous care in the composition and revision and preservation of the letters, at least 20,000 in the course of a long life of voluminous production in other kinds of writing. John tells his sister Harriet on August 20, 1828, that he has been sorting the 348 letters written to him over the past two years. On July 28, 1830, he tells Hurrell Froude: 'I wrote out all that correspondence which I mean to be a document to my heirs.' This was not Frank's attitude. 'He had a theory,' his biographer tells us, 'that letters should not be kept, and many people have told me that he asked for his letters back in order to destroy them.'[2] Many of his later correspondents, fortunately, ignored his theory and kept his letters.

---

[1] Avenger of blood (cf. Sophocles, *Electra*, 'Avenger of thy father's bloody death').

[2] I. G. Sieveking, *Memoir and Letters of Francis W. Newman*, London, 1909, p. 162.

This self-absorption of John's is not selfishness. His help to
Francis at college, to his mother and sisters before and after his
father's death in 1824, to his pupils and friends, is the subject of
grateful comment from all, not least from Francis. The *Journals* up
to 1826 make frequent mention of cruelty or ill temper to Francis,
with John seeing himself as a battleground for the contending
forces of arrogance and humility. Yet when he added to his confessions, on entering the Roman Catholic Church in October of 1845,
a *mea culpa* letter to Francis recalling this atrocious behaviour,
Frank mildly replied that he could not remember any cruelties at
school or college. 'It is credible that like other elder brothers you
may have expected and enforced more obedience than the younger
was always willing to yield; but I am certain that for one act of
cruelty there were ten of protection, affection, and generosity.'[1]
Getting into the confessional vein himself, Francis avows that
clashes were as much his fault, and were caused by his harsh and
heartless following of dogmas as axioms; John's was the 'more
refined and tender heart', and 'I fully felt this, even when I most
rudely jarred against you'.

Allowing for the generous impulse to meet gesture with gesture,
it is clear that Frank's dual obstinacy in putting awkward rationalistic questions, and in adhering to Evangelical beliefs as axioms
when his questions had to be left suspended, was productive of
many clashes. He was all the time seeking to clarify beliefs and to
base them upon an inner authority of reason and conscience; John
already had his intuitive certainties and was groping towards
external forms and symbols that would visibly embody authority
of a transcendent kind. Frank demanded that religious dogmas
support moral judgments, but until such time as reason was to
reject these dogmas in the name of morality, he gave them whole-
hearted support. To John, on the other hand, without the dogmatic principle there could be no morality; his mystical certainty
gave priority to objects of faith imaginatively grasped. As early as
April 23, 1823, he wrote to a sceptical young man:

> We find one man of one opinion on religion, another of another; and
> thus may be led hastily to conclude that opinions diametrically
> opposed to each other, may be held without danger to one side or the
> other in a future state. But contradictions can be no more true in

[1] C. S. Dessain, *The Letters and Diaries of John Henry Newman*, London, 1961,
v. 11, p. 310.

religion than in astronomy or chemistry; and there is this more important distinction between scientific and religious opinions, that, whereas errors in the former are unattended with danger to the person who maintains them, he who 'holdeth not the faith' (I am not now determining what that faith is), such a one is said to be incapable of true moral excellence, and so exposed to the displeasure of God.

The mother's description of Frank as 'adamant' beside the 'sensitive' John reads oddly to one who has heard the pathetic cry in *Phases of Faith*. Looking back to the 1830's, when he was ostracized by the narrow Evangelical piety in those he thought his friends, Frank recalls his loneliness. 'My heart was ready to break; I wished for a woman's soul that I might weep in floods. Oh, dogma! dogma! how dost thou trample underfoot love, truth, conscience, justice.' There is ample later testimony to his joy in friendship, to the gentleness and kindness that attracted people to him, people like Martineau and Sterling and Holyoake. His affections, like his tolerance, were moulded by experience.

It is true that in his Oxford days, whether following logic or dogma, Frank must have been a trial to both family and acquaintances. Yet it was John, adjusting both experiences and friendships to demands of his inwardly committed self, who was in a subtler way the really adamant one. With the exception of his almost feminine admiration for Hurrell Froude, he was happiest mainly with those he could help, or mould, as disciples. He could cut friends, like Whately, with whose views he came to differ. With his sister Harriet, a woman of independent mind, affection waned in disagreement, and even his mother was unhappily aware before her death in 1836 of her failure to understand the inflexibility of purpose in him. Jemima, the second sister, questioned his line of action when it became clear where he was going, but her acquiescence in the truth of his vision (for himself) allowed the affectionate relationship to persist. As for Francis, the cold terms of rejection are familiar to all readers of the *Apologia*. Putting his 'conduct upon a syllogism', John said: 'St Paul bids us avoid those who cause divisions; you cause divisions; therefore I must avoid you.'

This is a rhetorical flourish, of course, open to the *tu quoque* retort, and the contacts of the brothers throughout life did not entirely lose the element of affection, even if Frank could only have the last word by a kick at the Cardinal's bier. Nor is anything more striking than the rich admixture of human relations woven into or bearing upon the complex structure of John's personality. The most moving expressions of feeling in the *Journals* are those at the death of his youngest sister Mary, the bright and gay spirit who revered her wise and managing eldest brother even while she teased him. Abandoned to grief at the death of his devoted helper Ambrose St John in 1875, an event described as 'the greatest affliction I have had in my life', he could add: 'What a wonderful mercy it is to me that God has given me so many faithful friends!'

Such evidences of emotional sensitivity abound in John's letters and *Journals*. Yet the test of tolerance invites a contrasting judgment to that of Mrs Newman. John's was the mind that must subordinate friendships, however humanly rewarding, to the demands of dogmatic religion. Francis was to move away from the dogmatic principle, and to find his friendships among those of any belief, or none, provided they measured up to his criterion of moral goodness actively operating in human society.

A brief sketch of the early career of John Henry Newman at Oxford must emphasize three main matters: the nature and scope of his offices and activities, the various influences among which he charted his way, the gradual consolidation of his faith in the direction of Anglo-Catholicism. His appointment as Fellow of Oriel was 'the turning-point' of his life. 'It raised him from obscurity and need to competency and reputation. . . . Nor was it in its secular aspect only that it was so unique an event in his history; it opened upon him a theological career, placing him on the high and broad platform of University society and intelligence, and bringing him across those various schools of ecclesiastical thought whereby the religious sentiment in his mind, which had been his blessing from the time he left school, was gradually developed and formed and brought on to its legitimate issue.' (*Autobiographical Writings*, p. 63.)

Ordained priest in 1824 ('my heart shuddered within me; the words "for ever" are so terrible'), Newman took over the curacy of St Clement's. The parochial duties included composing sermons and caring for parishioners; gaining subscriptions for rebuilding the church ('to recover the parish from meeting houses, and on the other hand alehouses, into which they have been driven for want of convenient Sunday worship'); organizing a Sunday school ('I

find I am called a Methodist'). The sermons went well ('Many
gownsmen attend the Church— . . . and all this puffs me up'). In
1825 he accepted an invitation to become Vice-Principal of St
Alban's Hall under Whately, and was burdened with the clearing
up and keeping of accounts. Made a Tutor of Oriel in 1826, he
surrendered the curacy and Vice-Principalship, and entered upon
a vigorous attempt to purify the College ('filled principally with
men of family . . . of fortune . . . [of] very considerable profli-
gacy'), and, more successfully, to wield direct influence over the
chosen few, his own special pupils (*unless* I find the opportunities
occur of doing spiritual good to those over whom I am placed, it
will be a grave question, whether I *ought* to continue in the Tui-
tion'). To this question, which led to the quarrel with Provost
Hawkins and the subsequent giving up of the Tutorship in 1830,
we must return. In 1828 came the appointment as Vicar of St
Mary's, the University Church, with the village of Littlemore in
its parish. Here, until his retirement to Littlemore in 1843, Newman preached the sermons that did so much to spread his fame. His
active life in the 1820's did not prevent intensive study, with such
tangible fruits as the articles on Cicero and on Appolonius of
Tyana, the "Essay on Miracles" and the essay on "Poetry with
Reference to Aristotle's Poetics", and the book, *The Arians of the
Fourth Century*, that grew from the systematic reading of the early
Church Fathers begun in 1828.

The question of influences upon Newman is a matter for
cautious judgment. Certainly he is explicit enough in the *Apologia*
and elsewhere about the ideas he took over from individuals, and
about the intellectual training he received. From Edward Hawkins, Vicar of St Mary's till 1828 and then Provost of Oriel, he
received the 'quasi-Catholic' doctrine of Tradition and was introduced to that of Baptismal Regeneration; from William James,
another Fellow of Oriel, the doctrine of the Apostolical Succession; from Richard Whately, later Archbishop of Dublin, the idea
of the visible Church as a substantive body of divine appointment,
autonomous even in its State alliance.

These and other 'Oriel Noetics', vigorous and independent
thinkers representing all shades of opinion in the Establishment
from priestly High to evangelical Low, had among them created a
liberal intellectual atmosphere foreshadowing the so-called Broad
Church. They were, Newman recalls, 'a new school . . . char-

acterized by its spirit of moderation and comprehension'. Hawkins was 'the first man who taught me to weigh my words and to be cautious in my statements'. Whately, under whose leadership, it was said, the Oriel Common Room stank of logic, 'taught me to think correctly, and (strange office for an instructor) to rely upon myself'. A result of this instruction was Whately's particular acknowledgment of Newman, in the Preface to his *Elements of Logic*, as one 'who actually composed a considerable portion of the work'. Under this Noetic influence (and that of the ex-Catholic priest Blanco White, en route from atheism through the Church of England to Unitarianism) Newman was, he tells us in the *Apologia*, drifting in 'the direction of liberalism. I was rudely awakened from my dream at the end of 1827 by two great blows—illness and bereavement.' This narrow escape—and some Catholic biographers shiver in horror with him—is not very convincing. What is convincing is the sense of dramatic crisis in his development, the application of personal experience as warning or prophecy.[1]

Newman's very explicitness has led some critics, the admiring Brémond agreeing with the hostile Abbott, to see him as in large measure the sum of his influences. It makes understandable Francis Newman's irritated comment on the *Apologia*, that his brother always tells us who taught him what, but not why he changed. But Maisie Ward is surely right in saying that there was no real change. The need to find dogmatic support for the relationship of the two 'luminously self-evident beings' is there from the beginning. It was the teaching of Bishop Butler on analogy and probability, the study of the early Church Fathers, and the companionship and views of younger men who joined the Oriel ranks, that offered congenial channels for the flow of his thought. He had already, he tells us, found in John Keble's poems and sermons an

---

[1] At the age of fourteen, so Newman tells us in the *Apologia*, he had said of Voltaire's attack on the belief in immortality 'something like "How dreadful, yet how plausible!" ' His biographers still debate whether his faith was based mainly on love or on fear. Certainly the 'dread' added to the conviction ('From the age of fifteen, dogma has been the fundamental principle of my religion') was enough to offset the fascination of liberal ideas, even if occasionally (cf. paragraph 1, Chapter 7) one is reminded of Browning's Bishop Blougram.

> With me, faith means perpetual unbelief
> Kept quiet like the snake 'neath Michael's foot
> Who stands calm just because he feels it writhe.

attractive embodiment of the sacramental system, 'the doctrin
that material phenomena are both the types and the instruments o
real things unseen'.

Here we come to the third matter, the consolidation of ideas an
impulses into the Catholic pattern and the breaking of Evan
gelical ties. The attitude to Pusey, the titular head and to man
the originator of nineteenth-century Anglo-Catholicism, passe
from a touch of Evangelical suspicion ('I fear he is prejudice
against Thy children') to eager admiration of a Christian s
zealous and pure and withal humble, a High Churchman dis
tinguished for his rare combination of learning and spirituality
But the man who made the greatest personal impact was the livel
Hurrell Froude, who delighted in saints and miracles, believed i
hierarchical system and priestly power, and poured scorn on th
Protestant religion of the Bible. 'He made me look with admiratio
towards the Church of Rome, and in the same degree to dislike th
Reformation. He fixed deep in me the idea of devotion to th
Blessed Virgin, and he led me gradually to believe in the Rea
Presence.' It is easy to see why Francis later said of John that
'whether he knew it or not, he was pushing on the Romish lin
while in the garb of an Anglican'. Finally, the study of primitiv
Christianity in the writings of the early Church Fathers, a literar
and historical as well as religious attraction, did most to shape hi
course. 'Some portions of their teaching, magnificent in them
selves, came like music to my inward ear, as if the response t
ideas, which, with little external to encourage them, I ha
cherished for so long.' The first centuries were his *beau idéal* o
Christianity'. Begun in 1816, this renewed and intensive readin
of the Fathers saved him, by his 'imaginative devotion to them an
to their times', from leaving 'the crags and precipices of Luther an
Calvin' only to fall into 'the flats' of the 'cold Arminian doctrine'
a doctrine common both to high and dry Anglicans and, as
'first stage of Liberalism', to the Oriel divines.

It is here, as Newman and his friends moved towards a definin
and proclaiming of Anglo-Catholicism, that affinities with th
Romantic Movement may be seen. In rejecting both legacies fro
the eighteenth century—the unspiritual, too-intellectual high an
dry Anglican, and the unintellectual, too-spiritual fervour of th
Methodist or Low Church Evangelical—there was the excitemen
of rediscovery. The old was again the new; the reactionary coul

e seen as the radical. Further, the phrase 'imaginative devotion'
uggests the strong appeal of Christian history and saintly men to
he feeling for drama and personality. Such men were witnesses to
continuing struggle between a world of spiritual values and a
world of resistant and oppressive materiality. Again, there was the
thrill of mystery, which need never be lost when satisfactory
postulates about irrational experience could establish the unseen
world as the world of reality, and could express timeless truths by
transcendental doctrines and sacramental symbols.

The drift away from Evangelicalism Newman attributed partly
to the influence of associates and books, partly to the growth of his
own religious experience. The doctrine of the Apostolical Succession, and that of Tradition as the means of eliciting Scriptural
truths, undermined the Protestant reliance on the individual's
literal reading of the Bible. Bishop Butler's *Analogy of Religion*
served to place 'doctrinal views on a broad philosophical basis,
with which an emotional religion could have little sympathy'.
Meditating upon imputed righteousness, that ski-lift salvation
process of the Evangelical whereby an inner illumination enabled
him to drop his load of guilt and share in Christ's purity, Newman
came to feel that spiritual regeneration through baptism was more
convincing. 'Forgiveness of sins is conveyed to us, not simply by
imputation, but by the implanting of a habit of grace.' Sudden
conversion, sweeping one from conviction of sin through despair to
good news to joy in Christ to final perseverance in virtue, led to
the rigid division between the elect and the reprobate. In his
parochial duties Newman found many who were 'not altogether
without grace', even if their spiritual feelings were 'weak and uncertain'. And it seemed to him 'more agreeable to the analogy of
God's works, that there should be no harsh line, but degrees of
holiness indefinitely small'. When he gave up the curacy of St
Clement's, he summed it up: 'I am almost convinced against predestination and election in the Calvinistic sense, that is, I see no
proof of them in Scripture. Pusey accused me the other day of
becoming more High Church. I have doubts about the propriety
of the Bible Society.'[1]

---

[1] *Autobiographical Writings*, p. 208. In 1830 Newman was excluded from the
Church Missionary Society, of which he had been secretary, because of his
pamphlet urging Anglican clergymen to join in large numbers and so take over
his comprehensive body. This attempt to achieve a fifth column penetration

It is in his *Memoir* that Newman, looking back, gives us the tw
main reasons for the change. In the first place, he had found tha
'Calvinism was not a key to the phenomena of human nature, a
they occur in the world.' And secondly, he had never really bee
an Evangelical. He had been converted to the spiritual life, bu
'not in that special way laid down as imperative', with its definit
stages of experience illustrated from Biblical texts, experiences tha
marked one with 'the prescribed signs of a secret society'. He hel
on to three great doctrines—the Holy Trinity, the Incarnatior
Predestination—'which are doctrines of the Catholic Church, anc
being such, are true'. The fourth, 'Luther's tenet of justification b
faith only', faded out, at least in its harsh and uncompromisin
form. There is a hint of another reason, in his statement that 'th
peculiarities of the evangelical religion had never been congenia
to him', because 'its emotional and feverish devotion and i
tumultuous experiences were foreign to his nature'.

This last passage, with its suggestion of fastidiousness, of dis
taste for vulgar emotional display, bears on the growing estrang
ment from Francis, who had entered upon a spiritual crisis of h
own. Straining his conscience to sign the Thirty-nine Articles as
condition of getting his B.A. degree, he was unable to repeat th
performance when the time came for taking his M.A., and su
rendered his Balliol Fellowship. He was finding more and mor
that the institutions and documents of the Christian religion cor
flicted with his reason and his moral sense. The more his intelle
rebelled against discrepancies, the more desperately his feelin
sought compensation in the doctrinal simplicities of Evangelic
faith, the warmth of religious friendships, and the activities
parish work and teaching. He acted as curate for the Re
Walter Mayers, or as tutor to pupils in Mayers's home, in Lor
Vacations from 1823 to 1826. A passage from the diary of Cha
lotte Giberne, a visitor, tells us of meeting both John and 'h
brother Frank, who . . . was only twenty, but as bright a specime
of young Oxford student as I had ever met. They had both bee
considered converted in early youth, and so uncommon an ever

by the Establishment was indignantly recalled by Francis in 1891. One frien
who agreed with Newman 'in theory' pointed out to him at the time th
Church indifference had called such (initially sectarian) bodies into being, an
that they might decline if placed under the Church, 'which often seems
paralyse by the frigidity of its touch any institution that comes in its way'.

was it with me to meet with Christian young men [men whose religion was their motive power and not merely a conventional formality] that my admiration knew no bounds. Of course I told my sister Maria.'[1]

Maria came the next summer, and developed a warm attachment to the Newman family. Frank fell in love with her, and 'long talks on scientific and religious subjects passed between them'. He soon proposed marriage, and again five or six years later. The beautiful Maria, however, admired John (a prospective celibate in 1816 and a confirmed one by 1829), and later followed him into the Roman Catholic Church to become Sister Maria Pia. She was much struck by Frank's 'piety, which had nothing affected about it', but she herself was striving to get rid of her 'narrow religion', and furthermore, she found in him even then 'a great tendency to free thought'.

Of the contradictory tendencies noticed by this observant young woman, both of which grated on John in different ways, the first can be seen in two unpublished letters, of the year 1826, in the Oratory at Birmingham.[2] Writing to John from Mayers's home, Frank declares that he has derived the greatest benefit from Mrs Mayers's religious conversation, more effective 'in drawing off my mind from this world and exciting to prayers and meditation, than either discourses from the pulpit or private reading'. He goes on to speak against reserve in communication of feelings. Intimate knowledge of a person's religious feelings enhances pleasure in his company; freer converse helps to bind people together in ties of Christian friendship. He does not blame John, but 'we might with great profit commune much more on such topics'. He had spoken to John about this 'last October', but John's agreement had something discouraging in his manner. So Frank had been silent, unable 'to tell you freely all that had passed in my mind'. For five years he has struggled with sins that almost have reduced him to despair, yet he loves the law of God, and will cling so much more to the cross of Christ. 'Since my last birthday, which I made a sort of era, I have been especially enabled to begin a new life; and

[1] Sieveking, p. 17.
[2] This body of correspondence, quoted from extensively in Chapter 4, and also in Chapters 8 and 9, will be published as Father Dessain's volumes continue to appear. There are fewer from John than from Francis, but the tenor of some may be guessed from the replies.

I am beginning to rejoice, though with trembling, in God m'
Saviour.'

One can imagine the reply John made to this letter, at a tim
when he was moving with Pusey and towards Froude and th
Fathers. Six weeks later Frank wrote again. He apologized fo
being loquacious, but long as the letter is, it is so revealing of th
sincere Evangelical faith, and of the attitudes and relationshiʃ
of the brothers at that time, that it deserves quoting virtually iɪ
full.

I think I see every day more & more, how much individual *tempers* &
habits put on the form of religion or non-religion, with which the
have no necessary connection: and you have given me an admonitio
on this head. I have naturally enough concluded that others felt lik
myself here: you tell me that you do not. . . . whenever I most enjo
peace in religion, I am most disposed to talk of it; not indeed of th
circumstances of my enjoying it, but of the *objects from which it* arises
again, I have always derived the greatest benefit from persons wh
have conferred with me thus most freely; towards such I always fee
the greatest confidence; . . . such I love most. That I may fully ex
plain to what consequences reserve between us seemed to me to hav
a tendency, I add, that at times when I have had most real spirituɑ
comfort myself, I have observed a growing distaste for your society
simply, because I could find others whose conversation was moɪ
free & delightful to me. I struggled against it, and I hope successfully
by recollecting,—not merely all your kindness [which] might ex
cite *gratitude* & *esteem*; but not *love*:—but . . . that we were brethre
in the adopted family of God, as well as by nature, & to look forwar
to the time when we should all join in singing the song of the Lamɪ
. . . under this fear [loss of enjoyment in John's company and henc
of love] I wrote my last letter, hoping to obviate it. But I think I no'
see that it is from difference of *temper* that it arises. If, as you say, yo
are not therefore the more inclined to talk of a benefactor, becaus
you love him the more; it may be so. I pray God that you may enjɑ
the riches of his mercy & everlasting consolation, and indeed do nc
doubt that he thus blesses you: I am sure I do not argue the contraɪ
from your not talking of it. But I am of an opposite temper, . . .
think I bear peculiar love to all whom I believe to love the Loɪ
Jesus; but I see there is the *tendency* in me to love those most, wh
most easily let me see that love:—those who seem to put more coɪ
fidence in me, . . . those between whom & myself I can see mo
feeling in common: this is the χοινον τι[1] of which I spoke . . . . I caɪ

[1] Common ground.

not endure *forced* conversation on spiritual things; . . . I need *plain dealing*: I want someone to be continually saying to me, "Are you watching? Are you daily examining yourself, Are you living for another world?" & other similar questions; . . . These questions I wish to put to myself every hour: but I am apt to forget them, & fall asleep. . . . [This does not mean that] I think you deficient in spiritual affections, though . . . our reserve did not please me.

And now I have to ask that, on your hand you will not suspect me of enthusiasm or any "unsound feeling." Your fears both for my health & spirits are . . . groundless. . . . never in my life [have I had] so stable a peace, at times such real joy, or such confidence in him who is the light & life of our souls, as I have had the last two months. . . . it is nothing in my *religion* that makes me melancholy: but the prevalence of *sin* grievously wounded me. I sought to the cross, & I was eased: I thought that I was pardoned:—But presently I was again lulled in carelessness & fell into *wilful* sin; & then where was my peace! . . . to my shame I confess it, that this round of sinning & repenting . . . continued for 5 years! I cannot at all express the anguish of mind, the despair into which I have often fallen for my horrible iniquity: it is only of the rich and glorious mercy of God that I am now alive to tell of his grace. I cannot & would not tell my surprise & horror on awakening, as at once I did, to my condition; to recollect my prayers & tears & confessions, & longings after true holiness, & after that Spirit which alone could deliver me from the love of sin & support me against my crafty enemy. I just say enough to magnify Jesus, who, I trust, saves me amid much weakness; and to show you that if I spoke strongly of my mental trouble, I had indeed ample cause.—Now nothing has ever strengthened me so much against sin, as the conversations of Christians on *personal* religion; and I think, if I selected anyone, I should say I had gained more good from Mrs Mayers than from anyone on earth. I have learned also . . . that I cannot keep half measures in religion: unless I would be a profligate, I must be a truly devoted Christian; I must not let a single five minutes in the day lie waste; I must give my whole heart to Christ; I must pray for this *One Thing*, that I may know him & the power of his resurrection;—or at once I become a prey to temptation. This retirement is peculiarly delightful; I confess I tremble at the idea of returning to Oxford: but I cannot help seeing that Christ really loves me, & I try to cast all care on him. . . . God knows that I do not think anything in this world to be wished for or regretted, if I can but keep the full assurance of faith, that his almighty arm is with me, and that he will save me to eternal life. Pray for me, dear John; for though I have for some time now been able to rejoice in the strength of Christ, yet I often tremble to recollect the past. I look with gratitude at myself, & cannot believe the change: I have the same temptations . . . but I do know much more the exceeding greatness of the power of God towards us that *believe*, and I think that I practically understand more what faith is. Oh that my whole life might be spent to his glory, who has done such things for me.

Even a sceptic would at this point feel sympathy for John, and, much as the letter deserves a chapter of analysis in itself, approve Frank's 'theory' about not keeping correspondence. Parts of this effusion must have been as irritating to John on aesthetic as on religious grounds. More important, however, is what his experience of the Oriel Common Room had already taught him, that piety and fervour and sincerity cannot in themselves nullify the dangers of free thought. It was almost ten years before he was to tell Frank, 'a clear-headed man like you will unravel the web of self-sufficient inquiry', but Frank had already begun to show the signs of a restless intellect, and to herald the *Zeitgeist* by showing in himself the conflict between piety and rationalism. Of this early estrangement Frank offers a retrospective summary in *Phases of Faith*. He had felt gratitude to his 'warm-hearted and generous brother', whom he admired as a man of 'various culture and peculiar genius'. But[1]

my doctrinal religion impeded my loving him as much as he deserved, and even justified my feeling some distrust of him. He never showed any strong attraction towards those whom I regarded as spiritual persons; on the contrary, I thought him stiff and cold toward them. Moreover, soon after his ordination he had startled and distressed me by adopting the doctrine of baptismal regeneration, and in rapid succession worked out views which I regarded as full-blown "Popery." I speak of the years 1823–26; it is strange to think that twenty years more had to pass before he learnt the place to which his doctrines belonged.

At this stage of his development, Frank's difficulties arose not so much from scholarly criticism, which was not then easily available (he remarked later that German books might have saved him 'long peregrinations of body and mind'), as from a simple-minded desire for candour and consistency. If his 'peculiar' piety irritated John, his moral simplicity led him to questions and judgments that were

[1] F. W. Newman, *Phases of Faith*, London, 1850, p. 11. Unless otherwise specified, succeeding references will be to this edition.

often just as alarming to his Evangelical friends. It was one thing to be shocked by finding that of the young men at Oxford who signed the Articles so nonchalantly, 'not one in five seemed to have any religious convictions at all'. It was quite another thing to argue the difficulty of reconciling the doctrine of imputed righteousness—the belief that the sacrifice of Christ atoned for our sins—with abstract moral right and justice, though he accepted the doctrine, as advised, 'reverentially by an act of faith'. Impressed by a sermon that dissociated Sunday from the Sabbath, and the Sabbath from us, he examined the Scriptures only to find 'how baseless was the tenet for which in fact I had endured a sort of martyrdom'. Most instructive is his rejection of episcopal authority as based on the Apostolic Succession. How could one regard as Apostolic, bishops appointed by civil rulers? Why respect an order which had lagged in opposing 'inhuman and immoral practices' at home or abroad, and which had failed to set 'a higher tone of purity, justice, and truth' in the House of Lords? To Frank theory and practice, appearance and reality, should as far as possible be one. 'That an unspiritual—and, it may be, a wicked—man, who can have no pure insight into devout and penitent hearts, and no communion with the source of holy discernment, could never receive by an outward form the divine power to forgive or retain sins, or the power of bestowing this power, was to me then, as now, as clear and certain as any possible first axiom.'

Unable to accept the man for the sake of the office, Frank was rebuked by John for 'wanting reverence towards bishops'. One wonders whether he also told John that on reading the Fathers he found them, in the main, superficial and fraudulent, and that the sole result of reading them was to exalt his 'sense of the unapproachable greatness of the New Testament'. In sum, Frank by 1826 was rejecting all that John was in process of accepting, and was forced into the extreme Protestant position of complete reliance on the Bible. The Gospels might be full of difficulties to the understanding; they were still, at the end of 'the first period of my Creed', an article of faith. The more he needed the reassurance of the New Testament, the more he exalted it over what he considered the inadequacies or puerilities of other guides.

The moral chasm between it and the very earliest Christian writers seemed to me so vast as only to be accounted for by the doctrine in which all spiritual men (as I thought) unhesitatingly agreed,—that the New Testament was dictated by the immediate action of the Holy Spirit. The infatuation of those who, after this, rested on *the Councils* was to me unintelligible. Thus the Bible in its simplicity became only the more all-ruling to my judgment, because I could find no Articles, no Church Decrees, and no apostolic individual, whose rule over my understanding or conscience I could bear. (*Phases of Faith*, p. 25.)

Dissatisfied as he was with the doctrinal, historical, and apostolical aspects of formal Christianity, it is doubtful that Francis Newman could have held to his faith in the Pure Revealed Word without some powerful influence, some living exemplar of unworldly Christian truth. This he found, in a man whose influence shaped his course for the next six years. He went to Ireland as tutor in the family of Mr John Vesey Parnell, later Lord Congleton, for fifteen months. Though dates here are vague, the period would seem to cover all or most of 1827. In Parnell's home he met 'a young relative of his—a most remarkable man—who rapidly gained an immense sway over me'. This 'Irish clergyman' combined high intellectual powers with a completely fundamentalist Biblical faith, and a fanatical zeal which took him, often half starved and in rags, through the mountains of Wicklow. The poor Irish peasants regarded him as a saint, though Frank does not mention any converts. It is clear that John Nelson Darby, afterwards the founder of the Plymouth Brethren sect, was a born leader of men. In his *History of the Plymouth Brethren*, W. Blair Neatby uses copious quotations from Frank's *Phases of Faith* to show both the power of Darby's personality and the limitations of his mind, and offers as an evidence of his strength that he 'brought into almost servile subjection the mind of one of the most remarkable men of the nineteenth century . . . the younger brother of the more celebrated (not, I think, the abler) J. H. Newman, the Cardinal'.

Francis had come to Ireland with a two-fold view of religion. On 'natural' religion, it was essential to form an independent judgment, 'the real basis of all faith'. With 'revealed' religion, one must judge the credentials of the messenger and, if these prove sound, accept the Message reverently. Before he could work out the implications of this view, he met Darby, who showed complete sincerity and consistency in living by the Scriptures, and who always laid hold of 'the moral side of every controversy'. He was to find that new presbyter was but old priest writ large, but the immediate impact was overwhelming. 'For the first time in my life I saw a man earnestly turning into reality the principles which others confessed with their lips only.'

The blend of power and sincerity in Darby reinforced Frank's conviction that nothing is more pervasive in the New Testament than the expectation of the early return of the Lord, to destroy the earth and raise the elect to glory. He looked with 'mournful pity on a great mind wasting its energies on any distant aim of this earth', even such aims as 'the pursuit of science, knowledge, art, history'. Darby's example, furthermore, stimulated Frank's imagination and revived his earlier desire to be a missionary to the heathen. He was, he felt, cut off by his views from the ministry of Dissenting sects as well as from that of the Church of England, but here was a practical outlet for his energies. With the sceptical intellect subdued for the time being to Darby's influence, he turned away from the question of evidence and logic in the area of Christian doctrine and history. A 'convert' named Anthony N. Groves, a dentist from Devon, had written a tract called *Christian Devotedness*, stressing the Christian's duty to renounce all worldly goods and follow Christ, and was practising what he preached by going to Persia as a teacher of Christianity. 'Inflamed with the greatest admiration', Frank decided to join him, as one of a group of Christians with 'vital affinities'. The rationale of his plan makes clear the practical limits of his religion at the time; it also foreshadows the humanitarian champion of many causes that he was to become.

> I felt distinctly enough that mere talk could bring no convictions, and would be interpreted by the actions and character of the speaker. While nations called Christians are only known to heathens as great conquerors, powerful avengers, sharp traders—often lax in morals, and apparently without religion—the fine theories of a Christian teacher would be as vain to convert a Mohammedan or Hindoo to Christianity as the soundness of Seneca's moral treatises to convert me to Paganism. . . . I imagined a little colony, so animated by primitive faith, love, and disinterestedness that the collective moral influence of all might interpret and enforce the words of the few who preached. (*Phases of Faith*, p. 43.)

A letter to John from Ireland in October, 1827, shows the mixture of evangelical fervour and devotion to personalities that marked Francis in those years, together with a hint of the latent reformer. 'I now see a great error that I have of late run into, which I fear has given offence in more than one quarter: I mean that of taking too vivid an interest in political events. I think I feel more than I did, that these have little to do with the establishment of Christ's kingdom: . . . It is God's part to overrule them . . . to forward that great event; it is ours simply to promote it directly by those means which he has prescribed and to which his promise is annexed.' A eulogy follows of the Christian family he is with, especially of Mrs Parnell. 'The clearness with which she brings the first principles of the Christian temper to bear on the minute actions of daily life' is shown in her gentle advice to her sons—in all, she is 'the most perfect character I have ever seen'. He has gained insight into the meaning of Christians being opposed to the spirit of the world. He has no pleasure in recalling the trifling common room discussions of Oxford: when he is there his 'convictions fade away', and that is 'a very bad symptom'.

The two years between Frank's return to England and his departure for Persia were apparently spent in lending some help to John as a 'visitor' in his parish and in preparing for his journey. There was no open rift as yet between them; they were already collaborating in their long years of sporadic rescue of their wayward brother Charles, and together paid the debts of their enterprising but impractical Aunt Elizabeth—£700 at the end of 1828, according to a note in the *Journals*. Details of the period are scanty, but among the unpublished items at the Oratory are some notes left by Frank on visits to parishioners ('Universally I find the men more difficult to get on with'), with the covering datum: 'F.W.N., given me when he left visiting at Littlemore, perhaps 1828(?) J.H.N.' (This item would seem to discount Maisie Ward's suggestion that Frank's memory was faulty about dates, and that he really recalled helping John in St Clement's parish in 1826.) An exchange of letters, with John's dated 1830, concerns one Mary Birmingham. John fears that Frank's treatment of her has been 'irrelevant' and 'mischievous', in addressing her as 'a child of God, except so far as she has the general privileges of a Christian. To apply high Xtian doctrines as medicines is (in my opinion) but to inflame the disease . . . of mistaking words for things. It is offering for her accepted truths, which require a faith (to understand and receive them) grounded in deep self-knowledge and a long course of self-discipline.' He adds: 'As to M.B., doubtless (as you observe) the forms of society throw a restraint around the educated classes, which is no proof of their greater virtue;—but this does not make her any better.' She may have wishes and views now of a better sort, but 'to me words are no evidence themselves, but works'.[1]

Clearly Frank, though unorthodox and 'peculiar', was not yet a schismatic, and could be used as a part-time labourer in the vineyard. But a growing irritation, as well as a sense of a lost cause, shows through. 'My dear F.,' says John, 'I have written this not as thinking to convince you—nay doubting whether I shall be rightly understood—but resolved not to let any opportunity slip of declaring to you my sentiments, since you do not often give me an opening. Let me hope you will not answer this, if the answer is to contain a *second explanation of your meaning*. . . .' Nothing daunted, Frank again explains at great length what he said and why, and how M.B. reacted, and concludes: 'But I neither had nor have the least doubt that she is really a child of God, and shall deeply repent, though thro much suffering; and be restored for his mercy's sake. Are we not often kept from sin as much by forms of society as by fear of God? I think great allowances must be made for those in lower life: as indeed for persons in a heathen country, in all ranks.'

The exchange of family letters over this period is both revealing and entertaining. In 1827 John wrote to his mother, apparently as a result of a social gathering where a friend displayed a turn for interpreting handwriting:[2]

R. [Rickards?] has given some most admirable characters of Froude, B. White, S. Wilberforce, and others. He has given Francis in a most marvellous way—I transcribe it—"This is a hand of very great talent—great versatility, i.e. for example, great elegance of scholarship with powers of abstract reasoning. Skilful in the niceties of Greek plays. Talent for Mathematics . . . Enterprising mind, wh. is giving considerable trouble and unsettles him—a great deal of pertinacity, very great deal, yet arising rather from a very clear view

[1] The degree to which John had cooled towards Evangelical fervour in two years is suggested by a footnote to a letter of 1840. Looking back to his curacy of St Clement's, he recalls a visitor whose manner disturbed an invalid but seemed to him then to be a mark of spirituality. 'I took things on faith, *i.e.* I had faith that God's presence ever was where people spoke in a certain way.' (A. Mozley, *Letters*, v. 2, p. 317.)

[2] MS Letters in the Bodleian Library. Hereafter referred to as *Bod. Lett.*

of what he considers to be the truth, than from any other cause; for
he is very amiable . . . he will be of great usefulness hereafter. He has
not gained much from society; but it would have been much better
if he had gained more from others—In consequence of this defect he
has many crude notions—He does not pay sufficient attention to the
opinions of others. The hand bears a considerable resemblance to
Arnold's, a resemblance which I have made much of in giving his
character.

The reference to Thomas Arnold is significant, in view of Frank's
later visits to Arnold, and his admiration as opposed to John's distrust. Nor was graphology, apparently, the only parlour game of
the time. In his 1826 letter to John from Mayers's home, Frank had
described Maria Giberne's preference for sacred music over profane, and had added: 'Miss M.G. is very anxious for the development of her organs (she has a taste of phrenology).'

On the verge of Frank's departure for Persia in 1830, the family
letters (*Bod. Lett.*) show a mixture of concern, annoyance, and
relief. Harriet writes to John on May 25 that she is not surprised at
Frank's views—'I think I should feel as he does in his case'—but
she is distressed at the conflict of the brothers and at John's trials.
To Jemima on May 27, John says that missionary work involves
self-denial, 'tho' from F.'s great dissatisfaction with everything as
it is, I doubt not that it will be a great relief to his mind to be free
from the irritation which I believe the sight of everything around
him occasions'. Perhaps, he adds, it would be good for the Church
to employ such men, of true Christian feeling but of untrue vision,
abroad. His one scruple is that Frank, lacking the authority of the
Church in his venture, may be '(abstractedly) committing a sin'. A
very human outburst follows, at Frank offering Froude his books.
'*He has made no such offer to me.* One would think I had a prior
claim.'

A letter to Frank from his mother on June 22 shares John's
scruple. She is distressed at his staying outside the Church and its
system of doctrine and discipline, and believes he needs both a
'call' and authority in order to be a missionary. Two days later she
writes John that Frank's is 'a fearful wild plan'. He seems to think
people differ with him 'because they are so far behind him in
Faith, and the influences of the Spirit'. We should show confidence in our religion, but 'we have no right to *assume the privilege*
of being martyrs'. In August she writes more affectionately, stress-

ing Frank's own regret at misunderstandings and strains, hoping
for harmony between the brothers, and concluding in an almost
obituary tone that John can use Frank's writing-desk: 'It would
have increased value for having been dear F.'s.'

It was in September of 1830 that Frank's little band of 'vital
affinities' sailed from Dublin to Bordeaux en route to Bagdad. The
letters in that month from Mrs Newman to John sum up the
family situation. She has had letters from her 'three dear sons', all
exciting different feelings. Poor Charles is 'at present quite out of
reach of human assistance' with his successive deviations (over the
years he quarrelled with both his brothers, tried to set them against
each other, sneered at his sisters, turned atheist, was reclaimed,
turned Socialist, turned again, got into debt, showed contrition,
lived in slums, wrote insulting letters right and left, and generally
acted in a way to make his family doubt his sanity). 'We can only
pray to bring him to a right mind.' Frank, once referred to as her
'other anxiety', is having his trials, but 'it is a great gift when trials
prove blessings'. John is her comfort and her stay, as the head of
the family. True, there was mutual benefit, in that when successive
moves finally brought his womenfolk to Iffley near Oxford, John
had their valuable help in the work of his parish. Yet as the rest of
the letter makes clear, it was indeed the eldest son who took a close
and affectionate interest in their welfare, advising and assisting in
even the smallest domestic matters, in spite of the press of work and
the growing conflict with authorities at Oxford.

Newman's election as Fellow of Oriel was, in his own words, 'the
turning-point of his life'. The phrase is better applied, however, to
the outcome of his quarrel with Hawkins, which showed him the
'radical' element in his position. As he grew away from the Evangelicals, disliking their 'peculiarity' and finding them helpless to
cope with 'Liberalism', he aligned himself with High Church
principles, only to find that these principles were too often sacri-
ficed to political expediency or time-serving compromise. The loss
of the Tutorship was only one of the factors involved, but it was the
most personal, and so important to Newman even in recollection
that the whole of the *Memoir*, Part IV, is given to it.

The nub of the matter was that Newman (and his fellow tutors
followed him) regarded the Tutorship as a pastoral office, 'feeling
that, unless he could make his educational engagements a fulfilment of his ordination vow, he could have no part in them'. This

meant giving priority to a select few pupils, and attending to their moral and spiritual welfare as well as offering them intellectual nourishment. The traditional view (Newman could reject tradition when it conflicted with his own views) was that public responsibility as a lecturer to all undergraduates came first. Possibly too, the Provost feared the growth of a cult or cults as he noted the strengthening influence of his energetic and dedicated young tutors. If so, the irony of Hawkins being elected over Keble partly by Newman's support is compounded in the larger irony that he helped bring about the very thing he sought to avoid. Newman had preferred Hawkins for the office of Provost as a more 'practical' man. Had Keble been elected, he would have been sympathetic to the aims of the young rebels, and the energies later to take shape as the Oxford Movement might have found adequate expression. Newman himself says that, in such a case, 'humanly speaking, that movement never would have been'. But a larger conflict, as outside forces threatened the Church, already was beginning to engage Newman's attention, and another occasion might well have started him on his course of protecting his unfolding vision of the Church, of proclaiming Divine Authority by challenging established authority.

The break with Hawkins did not come quickly. Relations were easy until 1829, when the tutors drew up their own Lecture Table in such a way as to implement their views. Hawkins declared that they were sacrificing the many to the few and upsetting 'a received system' which had worked well. A long correspondence on the matter ended in 1830, when Hawkins finally wrote: 'I shall not feel justified in committing any other pupils to your care.' Newman kept the pupils he had till the summer of 1832, when he 'gave over into the hands of the Provost' the two or three remaining, and terminated his College Tutorship.

It was the political issue of 1829, with ecclesiastical and religious overtones, that had sharpened the conflict between Hawkins and Newman. The pressure to emancipate Roman Catholics from their political disabilities had become irresistible. An article on "Civil and Religious Liberty" in the *Edinburgh Review* as early as February, 1816, had noted the decline of animosity and persecution, with even the Test and Corporation Acts in abeyance, so that *in fact* Dissenters suffered no liabilities. Only the Catholics were 'actually molested and degraded on account of their religion', even though they were one-fifth of the population and, as figures quoted in Parliament in 1810 had shown, composed half the army and navy. But foolishness and bigotry were in process of weakening, the reviewer thought. 'To a layman, the religion of his neighbours is of no consequence, if their moral conduct is good; to government, the religion of its subjects is of no consequence, if they live like good subjects; and it is notorious, that good morals and good citizenship are not monopolized by any sect whatever.' The great 'lay current' was at work on behalf of tolerance to Catholics, that current which Newman was to identify as liberalism and to fight all his life. By 1829 it had gathered sufficient strength to push through emancipation, assisted, according to an article of that year in the *Edinburgh Review,* by a feeling in some quarters that England appeared out of date and absurd to a liberal-minded and tolerant continent.

It is an arresting comment on the alignment of forces in 1829 to find the High Church and Tory John opposing the move, and the Evangelical but liberal Frank supporting it. Robert Peel, the University Tory representative but a supporter of emancipation, had resigned his seat over the matter, and was now seeking re-election. The tutors actively campaigned against him, and he was defeated, in spite of an 'insolent faction' of non-resident voters. (Peel was soon returned for Westbury.) Hawkins was angry enough to refer to the tutors as a 'Tory cabal'. John's position is a curious one, yet typical of him. After the 'glorious victory' over Peel, he admits in a letter to Harriet that emancipation is now necessary, but that it might endanger the Irish Protestant Church. He is '*in principle* an anti-Catholic', but he will be for emancipation so that he may take a stand 'against the foes of the Church on better ground, instead of fighting at a disadvantage'. After this explanation, an earlier letter to Jemima is crystal clear. 'You know I have no opinion about the Catholic question, . . . but still, its passing is one of the signs of the times, of the encroachment of Philosophism and Indifferentism in the Church.' In short, what was to other men a question of justice was to John a question of State interference, motivated not by religious zeal but by the hated liberalism of reform. A letter to his mother on March 13 has a significant paragraph.[1]

---

[1] A. Mozley, *Letters,* v. 1, p. 205. In this letter John summed up the enemies of the Church as being '(1) the uneducated or partially educated mass in towns

And now I come to another phenomenon: the talent of the day is against the Church. The Church party (visibly at least, for there may be latent talent, and great times give birth to great men) is poor in mental endowments. It has not activity, shrewdness, dexterity, eloquence, practical power. On what, then, does it depend? On prejudice and bigotry.

Bigotry and prejudice were then to be his allies (he had for these terms a 'good meaning and one honourable to the Church') against the secular pride of intellect and the Jacobinical spirit that, proceeding from the corrupted nature of man, comprised 'the talent of the day'. Of the pending Reform Bill of 1832 John asks, in a letter of 1831, why should the Church act? 'Society is rotten', and mere political change is of little interest. There are some good men in high place, but the majority one meets are 'Liberals, and in saying this I conceive I am saying almost as bad of them as can be said of anyone'. A letter to Samuel Rickards of July 4, 1831, best sums up John's disgust with the age. These are times of trouble and blasphemy, he says, with men in the ministry professing irreligion on principle. 'When statesmen are bad men, as private characters, we must in private society deal with them as such and avoid them in private—yet professing good principles in their public capacity, we may recognize them in public as men after God's heart and co-operate with them as "religious and gracious"—but what shall be said when they openly support bad principles, uphold institutions adverse to the Church, and (tho' in the general calling themselves Churchmen) yet in detail avowing heathen sentiments. O my soul, come not into their desert! It is with inexpressible grief I hear that the Primate has dined at Lord Brougham's at a party of 6 or 7.'[1]

Such grief at archiepiscopal dalliance with sinister powers over the port suggests agreement with Samuel Johnson that the devil was the first Whig. To the frustrating loss of the Tutorship we must add, then, the sad spectacle of reform rampant in the nineteenth

---

. . . professedly deistical or worse. (2) The Utilitarians, political economists, useful knowledge people. . . . (3) The Schismatics, in and out of the Church, . . . (4) The Baptists, whose system is consistent Calvinism— . . . (5) The high circles in London. (6) I might add the political indifferentists, . . . like men who join Roman Catholics on the one hand and Socinians on the other.'

[1] J. H. Mozley collection of Newman letters in the University of London Library. Hereafter referred to as *Lond. Lett.*

century, and the physical exhaustion caused by the strenuous concluding weeks of writing *The Arians of the Fourth Century*. By December, 1832, Newman was more than ready to accept Archdeacon Froude's invitation to accompany him and his son Hurrell on their Mediterranean cruise.

CHAPTER 3

Two Travellers

WHEN JOHN HENRY NEWMAN set out on his six months' journey, Francis had already been almost two years in Syria and Persia, after four months spent in travelling from Dublin to Aleppo. By coincidence they both arrived back in England on July 9, 1833. The records kept are characteristic. Each, for example, had a near-fatal illness. For John this was another turning-point, dramatic and prophetic, an experience which transcended all others and gave him a fresh sense of dedication and destiny. Of Frank's illness we hear little. What we do read about are peoples and customs and incidents and circumstances that press upon him and move him to speculate and to compare. Both men, to be sure, observe and describe. But John resists the pressures of experience until a personal crisis, personally interpreted, reactivates a faith whose unchanged elements are in a temporary state of quiescence. Frank, empirically responding to facts and discoveries, finds the very basis of his beliefs undergoing a process of attrition.

Frank's account of his travels, revealing at least one departure from his theory that correspondence should not be kept, was published in 1856 under the title, *A Personal Narrative in Letters Principally from Turkey in the Years 1830–3.* (The word 'Turkey' is here used for the large and rambling Ottoman empire.) Some changes were made, those he felt to be right and proper in personal letters to 'kinsfolk and to intimate friends'. Frank describes the little book as a private journal with free corrections but with no facts altered. In one respect, he admits, it is not a true picture of his mind at the time, as 'the phraseology, especially when religious subjects are approached, is chastened to suit the writer's maturer taste'. Presumably he refers to the pious hopes and fears of Evangelical utterance that marked his earlier phases. To the older man looking back, the significant feature of the whole experience was the beginning of a new freedom of thought, of the break from Darby's influence. 'The dear companions of my travels no more aimed to guide my thoughts than I theirs; neither ambition nor suspicion found place in our hearts; and my mind was thus able again without disturbance to develop its own tendencies.'

The 'dear companions' were an odd lot of missionaries to embark on this quixotic journey, with all its discomforts and hardships. Lord Congleton (Mr Parnell as he continued to be called), a young man of Frank's age, gave all his fortune to finance the trip, with its masses of luggage including a small library of books, a lithographic press for printing tracts, and a large medicine chest. A doctor, Edward Cronin, brought along his old mother and his sister Nancy, to whom Parnell was engaged and whom he married at Aleppo. Cronin's wife had died in Dublin before the party left, and his infant daughter was an added responsibility. A man named Hamilton, later to abandon the venture, completed the group. The guiding spirit, Groves, had already gone out to Bagdad in 1829, and was awaiting their arrival. The light by which he guided the intrepid band of evangelists, the truths they shared, we find in his *Memoir of Lord Congleton*: 'The oneness of the Church of God, involving a fellowship large enough to embrace all saints, and narrow enough to exclude the world. The completeness and sufficiency of the written Word in all matters of faith, and preeminently in things affecting our Church life and walk—the speedy pre-millennial advent of the Lord Jesus.'[1]

Oddly assorted as the little group was, and bizarre as their enterprise may appear, there is something heroic in their serene confidence and in the courage with which they faced not only hardship but tragedy. Old Mrs Cronin, worn out by the journey, died in Bagdad, where Mrs Groves had succumbed to the plague before the party arrived. Young Mrs Parnell died in Latakia, ill and exhausted after an extra trip back to the coast from Aleppo with her husband to help Hamilton on his way home. The 'unspeakable loss' of 'this meek and quiet spirit' moved Francis to his one comment on his illness. 'Two months back she was hanging over my pillow weeping and kissing me as a dying man; now am I in youthful vigour, and she is in her grave.' En route to Bagdad, Cronin was beaten and stoned unconscious at Aintab by a mob of angry Muslims, after the party was peremptorily ordered by the Turkish governor to move on for selling four Turkish Testaments.

[1] Quoted in Sieveking, p. 29.

The gravity of the last episode is lightened a little by Newman's part in it. When a mounted Muslim galloped up and tried to seize his horse's bridle, Francis 'beat him off with an umbrella'.

Comedy, at times farcical, is plentiful throughout the narrative. 'Think of us,' Frank writes on landing in Bordeaux, 'at the top of a hotel and an army of porters carrying up the height of three stories many hundredweight of trunks, chests, hampers, bags, baskets to stow into our bedrooms *for the night*! And this misery is to be repeated everywhere.' The prospect, he says gloomily, is 'frightful'. Finding fruit delicious and cheap in France, he decided to live on it, with the result that diarrhoea made him almost miss the 'diligence' one morning, and so 'cancel out' his savings. On a canal trip nearing Marseilles, high waters had made the bridges dangerously low. A cry of 'A bas!' brought a mass flying tackle from the men in the party, just in time to drag the dozing Mrs Cronin and Miss Cronin from their seats on deck into a tangled heap of men and women, so saving a couple of cracked heads. A sardonic touch enters on the voyage from Marseilles to Cyprus (from whence an aged and uncertain Turkish craft took the party to Latakia) in the form of a Jewish fellow-passenger on his way to propagate the faith. This coincidence, Frank admits, the captain found 'highly diverting'. In Syria, among their other troubles was the broad native saddle, like a table across the horse's back. Getting up without help was almost impossible. Mr Parnell's 'most successful way was to make a run from behind and *divaricate* on to the horse's tail, like a boy playing at leap-frog; but the beast was always frightened, and bolted before he was well on. You will imagine the rest! . . . but we were all equally ludicrous.' Perhaps it was as well that the Syrian stay had some elements of comic relief; they had to remain there from January 14, 1831, to April 18, 1832, held up by the dangers of civil war and banditry in the shaky Ottoman empire and by the difficulties of arranging transport.

No tourist could be more attentive than Frank to the details of life and living in the lands he visited, whether of food, prices, accommodation, transportation, climate, social customs, or political institutions. He remarks on the Bactrian camel, hairy and two-humped, a beast of all work and a mainstay of the economy. He wore the native costume of Syrian gown and slippers, though the gown 'is ridiculously feminine', being puffed out above the

girdle into 'two *bosoms,* which are used as pockets'. He took up
smoking on a 'when in Rome' basis, and gives pages to pipes and
tobaccos and the complicated ritual of the hookah. Even at the
end of the narrative the wealth of descriptive detail is there, on the
grim and dispirited winter trip to Constantinople through Turkey
proper, over snow-covered mountain paths and swamps with cor-
duroy bridges. Frank became in his misery 'a mere animal', and
could 'think only of two things—my horse's feet and my horse's
footing'.

Over the Syrian period and the five months in Bagdad, three
main impressions of Francis Newman emerge from the mass of
detailed observations. The first is of his special linguistic interest,
foreshadowing his later reputation as a teacher and scholar of
languages, classical and exotic. Secondly, there is his growing
concern with justice and decency and sanity in human affairs,
pointing to the later champion of reform in many fields. Finally
one notices, of course, the changes in his religious views, as he
considers the reasons why the Christian message made so little
impact on the Mohammedan mind.

The long stay in Syria gave Frank a chance to study Arabic in-
tensively, and to find that his grammar bought in Soho Square was
useless. 'I myself distrust the literary men, as too fond of the old
bookish language. I wish, if I can, to learn from the people themselves, as children do.' His teaching experience later in Bagdad
confirmed his belief that children can learn two languages as
easily as one, but only as living languages, not from dictionaries
and classical texts. The texts put out in Arabic by Bible Societies
were simply unintelligible. But let a child from the school turn a
few sentences into the vernacular, and the parents and neighbours
'make him read it again and again'. Part of the difficulty, to
Frank, was that Arabic seemed rich in specific terms, poor in
generic; partly it was the strangeness of literal and metaphorical
usage. How, he asks plaintively, is he to get his message over to a
Muslim to whom the Lamb means only meat, or 'a piece of paste
with a lamb stamped on it'? His problem of steering between the
vulgar and the pedantic on sacred subjects moves him to observe
that Arabic needs its Dante. Reading the Koran is no help to him
in understanding people and language; it is a 'tedious and shallow'
book, clearly prized for tinkle and epigram and age. 'How wonderful is the power of tradition!'

This larger difficulty, of a whole way of life to which language is the index, Frank's literal mind was slow to grasp, though even in Syria he had recognized that when his little party was accepted it was for certain qualities of character and mind rather than for Christian doctrine, and had made the depressed admission, 'I am apt to faint into unbelief of heart as to their ever adopting what is here called *English religion.*' A much-quoted reminiscence from *Phases of Faith* tells of a Mohammedan carpenter who listened patiently to Frank's exposition of Gospel authenticity, and then said: 'God has given to you English a great many good gifts. . . . But there is one thing that God has withheld from you, and has revealed to us, and that is the knowledge of the true religion by which one may be saved.' This, Frank says, made a 'lasting impression' on him.

It was a Colonel Taylor, however, resident in Bagdad with a Persian wife, a master of Persian and Arabic after twenty-eight years, who compelled Frank to face the facts. 'Our religion, poetry, philosophy, science, are so opposed to everything here that, he says, nothing but long time in the country can make an Englishman intelligible on religious subjects.' A people with 'habits and principles ingrained for three or four thousand years' is almost 'a special humanity'. Taylor's reasoning led to the conclusion Frank was reluctant to accept, that such a gap causes special difficulty in religious discussion, discussion 'which, he says, presupposes a *common* religious *philosophy* between the parties. I find it disagreeable to admit this; it seems to prove too much.' Frank was to propound his own 'common religious philosophy' in the moral theism which he developed after 1850. But in the word 'disagreeable' we see the disturbing sense of failure that, when his imagination caught up with his honesty, decided him against staying on in Bagdad.

Frank's logical mind, his persistent search for reasons and analogies, is evident in his comments on the social and political scene. Struck by the indifference and apathy and decay around him, he tries to analyse the nature of Turkish despotism. He likes the Turks as a 'John Bullish' sort of people—worthy, neighbourly, good-humoured, and unintellectual. But they have not known how to govern. 'They have crushed material prosperity, but not national spirit. The Romans crushed national spirit, but, for a while, fostered material prosperity.' Irresponsible Pashas spend no taxes locally, have no care for domestic economy. A native centralized despotism may be a good form of government, Frank concludes, when it rests on the good will of the people, 'but when it is foreign, and imposed on an unwilling people, history seems to pass a stern vote against it'. It would be best if the empire fell, but the kingdom stood. 'We know what Ireland is. There are ten Irelands here.'

The tendency to such observation and comparison, and a lively interest in events at home, was clearly irresistible to Frank, even at a time when he held on New Testament authority 'that Christians are *non-political* beings'. For instance, in September, 1831, he wrote a letter home about bread riots in England. He has no faith in political reform, he says, but it may be a needed preliminary. If it is sudden and convulsive, those are to blame who resist innovation and gradual change. On another front, he hopes that the present agitation will break up both East and West Indian interests, 'which hinder the negroes from getting freedom or the Indians good government'. The letter probably was written to John ('I fear you cannot see this'); it concludes with the cry of a man in whom a this-worldly concern for the human lot is already struggling with the other-worldliness of Darbyite evangelicalism: 'Woe be to the aristocracy which founds its strength on popular starvation.'

Frank's observations on social morality among Turks and Arabs are interesting. He finds them kind to lunatics and animals (especially cats); free of petty theft (though given to robbery and extortion in the wide open spaces); not addicted to drink, prostitution, nor the passions of high ambition. Whether all this is due to morality or inertia he is not sure. Two experiences show him in the difficult process of adjusting his ideas. A laundress refused extra money for extra washing, asking why she should earn more pieces of coin and go to bed with a backache. 'Who can confute this philosophy?' Thinking of England, where many labour through long and severe hours merely to exist, Frank decided to talk less of 'Oriental indolence'. More perplexing to him was the blend of refinement and 'coarseness'. When a child of five, wanting to know whether Frank came from France or England, asked him, 'Where did you come out of your mother's belly?', the first reaction was shock. He decided, however, that he had confused coarseness with plainness, with a 'Biblical' simplicity. Brooding over the question of whether 'such phraseology in a nation' revealed a state of mind 'more or less conducive to mental purity than our state', Frank concludes: 'I incline to think that this is a more wholesome state of mind than ours.'

Several writers have remarked that Frank's narrative says little of missionary activity, the purpose of the journey. The fact is that the party achieved little beyond distributing Bibles and tracts, and in his later selection of letters he could hardly have wished to dwell upon the details of a depressing failure. But he did learn something about religion. One discovery has been noted, the awareness, rein-forced by the cheerful realism of Colonel Taylor, that a different language and tradition can be an almost impassable barrier to the communication of doctrine or philosophy. The other discovery was that divergent and sectarian religious views have a paralysing, even destructive, effect upon the moral and social relations of human beings. Observing a society 'cut to bits by religions', Frank thought that 'Roman Catholic jealousy', leaving the minds of the people in 'secular darkness', was as bad as Turkish apathy. The worst form of enmity was that shown between Christians before the Muslims they were trying to convert. He felt no hostility to those who, like a Greek Orthodox bishop he met and talked to, 'concede equal rights of conscience to others. But the Romanists everywhere, like the established church in England, *take* and will not *give*. They have no notion of reciprocity or mutual equality, but they claim *dominion*. It is not we, but they, that make peace impossible.'

The honesty of Francis Newman emerges here, when he recog-nizes his own intolerance in this outburst and says, 'do I not bear my part in this enmity?' His last disillusioned comment embraces Protestant activity as well as Catholic. Meeting some American missionaries on his way through Constantinople, Frank feels he 'must approve', but painfully foresees schism and controversy. 'I am faithless,' he sadly concludes, 'and see too many difficulties.' Even sadder for the earnest young Evangelical was an experience in Aleppo. Commenting on the uncertain prices and the lack of trust in money matters among Christian, Jews, and Muslims, Frank says: 'A Piedmontese, unhappily a secret disciple of Vol-taire, seems to me the honestest man we know.'

That Frank's theological doctrines had not yet suffered a sea change is evident in a late letter referring to the Irving controversy in England, more exciting to him 'just now' than 'any other religious or mental speculation'. Irving or Darby—he had not yet abandoned hope of finding the perfect exemplar of evangelical Christian teaching, leading a little band of the faithful who would know each other by certain signs, and whose illuminated lives would awaken the conscience of the Christian world. But in the light of his own experiences and meditations doubts and questions were crowding in upon him. Increasingly he gave priority to purity of life over purity of doctrine, to morality over religion, to rational acceptance over obedient adherence. It was only a question of time before he would break with Darby and the brethren and proceed on his lonely and rigorous way. Meanwhile he clung to his belief in a spiritual invisible church and an inspired, infallible Bible, even as his brother, refreshed and purposive, moved towards the ideal of an Infallible Church, inspired in its interpretation of the Revealed Word.

The word 'refreshed', as used here of John, does not refer to physical fitness. He had just come through a dangerous illness, shaky on his legs and with his hair fallen out from fever, and was probably less fit than when he left England. The refreshment was spiritual, the sense of a need for action, the eager and impatient desire to meet a challenging crisis in Church affairs. In the *Apologia*, it is true, he speaks of the 'exuberant and joyous energy' with which he returned from abroad, 'the exultation of health restored', but it was 'amid familiar scenes and faces' that 'my health and strength came back to me'. Of no man is it truer than of Newman, that his physical condition reflected his state of mind. Defeat or discouragement could induce exhaustion or illness; even more strikingly, a call to action—and Newman was essentially a man of action—would see a resurgence of physical resources that had merely been quiescent. If the action was not forthcoming, and the drama, he created them.

Throughout John's letters home from his Mediterranean tour, no interest is as intense as that in English affairs. He awaits with torturing anxiety the news about Oriel Fellowships, and rapturously kisses the newspaper which tells of the election of his friend Frederic Rogers. He waxes sarcastic over Thomas Arnold's plan for a comprehensive Church of England, and fulminates against the arrogance of statesmen who propose to suppress ten Irish bishoprics and so slightly lessen the burden of the English Church on Irish Catholics. As causes for excitement, such events may strike the modern reader as tempests in a teapot that was soon to be put on the shelf. But they were to Newman symptoms of the triumph of the hated liberalism, threats to the very life of the Church. In 1831, Thomas Mozley tells us, 'every party, every interest, political or religious, in this country was pushing its claim to universal acceptance, with the single exception of the Church of England, which was folding its robes to die with what dignity it could'.[1] But the Church would not die if Newman could help it. When he and Froude visited Wiseman in Rome, the invitation to come again brought the grave reply, 'we have a work to do in England'. The growing sense of urgency came to a climax in his illness and recovery, which convinced him that God had saved him for a purpose, and he hurried home to join Froude in the Homeric slogan, 'You shall know the difference, now that I am back again.'

In spite of the great amount of descriptive detail (the journey from Oxford and back again takes almost one-third of Anne Mozley's first volume) Newman gives the impression of a deliberate detachment from experience. He is aware of this himself, even as he communicates his pleasures and reflections in a concrete and vivid style. A month after leaving England he tells Harriet: 'No description can give you any idea of what I have seen, but I will not weary you with my delight; yet does it not seem a strange paradox to say that, though I am so much pleased, I am not interested?' One reason for this 'paradox' is a sense of constraint, almost at times of fear, at the disturbing influence of the passing show. Of the brief call at Gibraltar, he wrote to Harriet on December 18, 1832:

> I no longer wonder at younger persons being carried away with travelling, and corrupted; for certainly the illusions of the world's magic can hardly be fancied while one remains at home. I never felt any pleasure or danger from the common routine of pleasures, which most persons desire and suffer from—balls, or pleasure parties, or sights—but I think it does require strength of mind to keep the thoughts where they should be while the variety of strange sights— political, moral, and physical—are passed before the eyes, as in a tour like this.

It is striking to find the words 'corrupted' and 'danger' and 'strength of mind' at the very outset of the journey. Both John and Francis sought the truth, but in John's case the kindly light, already

---

[1] T. Mozley, *Reminiscences Chiefly of Oriel College and the Oxford Movement*, London, 1882, v. 1, p. 273.

luminously and self-evidently his, must resist not only the encircling gloom but also the contamination of the prismatic hues of experience.

The conflict revealed, in the repression of the natural man, is an element in the complex Newman personality that is apparent in a number of ways for most of his life. Jealousy, ambition, contemptuous distaste—such emotions and attitudes, and the prayers and tears and discipline needed to exorcise them, recur noticeably in the earlier *Journals*, to a degree indeed that makes one suspect Newman of exaggerating faults in an unconscious heightening of inner drama. The extremes of self-absorption and aggressiveness are there at all times; they are repented only when they cannot be interpreted as serving the holy cause of religion. There is sometimes, too, the need to resist the appeals of history and Nature, of sensuous beauty and the pagan dream. Of the ancient road to Taurominium in Sicily, he says, in words which explain his fascinated return there after leaving the home-bound Froudes in Rome:

I never saw anything more enchanting than this spot. It realised all one had read in books about scenery—a deep valley, brawling streams, beautiful trees, the sea (heard) in the distance. But when, after breakfast, on a bright day, we mounted to the theatre, and saw the famous view, what shall I say? I never knew that Nature could be so beautiful; and to see that view was the nearest approach to seeing Eden. O happy I! It was worth coming all the way, to endure sadness, loneliness, weariness, to see it. I felt, for the first time in my life, that I should be a better and more religious man if I lived there. . . . And so I went off to Giarre. There first I went through the river-beds. The hills receded—Etna was magnificent. The scene was sombre with clouds, when suddenly, as the sun descended upon the cone, its rays shot out between the clouds and the snow, turning the clouds into royal curtains, while on one side there was a sort of Jacob's ladder. I understood why the poets made the abode of the gods on Mount Olympus. (Mozley, *Letters*, v. 1, p. 397.)

Dangerous sentiments indeed, convincingly if rarely expressed, and revealing more of the poet than most of the verses composed for the *Lyra Apostolica* with almost scheduled regularity on shipboard. They recall letters of July, 1831, written while on a holiday visit to the Froudes in Devon. The first to his mother is full of the richness of colours and scents, and concludes, 'Let me enjoy what I

feel.' The second, to Harriet, begins with 'some lines that came into
my head':

> There stray'd awhile amid the woods of Dart
>   One who could love them, but who durst not love;
> A vow had bound him, ne'er to give his heart
>   To streamlet bright, or soft secluded grove.

Four years later, a letter to Jemima from Devon sums up neatly the
conflict and the awareness. 'This country is certainly overpower-
ingly beautiful and enchanting, except to those who are resolved
not to be enchanted.'

Nostalgia for Oxford, anxiety about English affairs, and a
conscious resistance to the excitements of beauty and the passing
show, are then three of the restraining notes in Newman's record
of his travels. A fourth is the need to preserve intact his anti-
Romanism. There are interesting variants in the tone of his comments as he moves from Malta to Zante and Patras in Greece
and back to quarantine in Malta, to Sicily and Naples and Rome
and back to Naples. Distaste at popular pleasure in the gaudy
externals of worship, at 'the solemn reception of [superstitions] as
an essential part of Christianity', and at dirt and slovenly habits
(at one time even the priest spitting during the service), alternates
with thrilled admiration of magnificent churches and the monuments of historical Christianity. At Malta the 'exciting religion' of
Madonna and Saints in the streets, 'a more poetical but not less
jading stimulus than a pouring forth in a Baptist chapel', makes
him think with joy and longing of the 'quiet and calm' of services
at St Mary's and Littlemore. 'We do not know how great our
privileges are.' Naples Newman finds 'unbearably filthy', full of
fleas and beggars and poverty, and so over-rated for scenic beauty
that he acidly compares the more attractive features with Brighton;
it is 'a watering-place for watering-place people'. Bad weather and
a cold no doubt help to explain the irritation, but even 'the state of
the Church is deplorable. It seems as if Satan was let out of prison
to range the whole earth again.' Most of the condition is blamed on
the neglect and confiscation which impoverished the priesthood,
to be sure, yet the spectacle of 'infidelity and profaneness' makes
Newman declare: 'I begin to hope that England after all is to be
the "Land of Saints" in this dark hour, and her Church the salt of
the earth.'

It is in Rome that the tone changes, as the struggle develops between the emotional and imaginative appeal of tradition and beauty, and the intellectual rejection of doctrine and dogma, of Virgin worship and purgatory and the Mass and Papal supremacy. As Hurrell Froude recalls in the *Remains*, their joint visit to Wiseman in Rome to discuss possible terms of union between the Churches brought the dismaying discovery that 'not one step could be gained without swallowing the Council of Trent as a whole'. The time was too soon for such a step; yet a letter of April 5, 1833, shows both the distinction Newman is holding and the direction in which he is moving.

> As to the *Roman* Catholic system, I have ever detested it so much that I cannot detest it more by seeing it; but to the Catholic system I am more attached than ever, and quite love the little monks [seminarists] of Rome; they look so innocent and bright, poor boys! . . . I fear there are very grave and far-spreading scandals among the Italian priesthood, and there is mummery in abundance; yet there is a deep substratum of true Christianity; and I think they may be as near truth at the least as that Mr B., whom I like less and less every day. [Mr B. was a 'semi-evangelical' chaplain in Rome.]

An early letter from Rome, and two written after his return alone to Naples, are the most revealing. In the early one, Newman gives his impressions of Rome in sequence. 'The first thought one has of the place is awful—that you see the great enemy of God—the Fourth Monarchy, the Beast dreadful and terrible.' Then the world of art and history, Christian and pagan, exerts its power. 'Next, when you enter the museums, galleries, and libraries, a fresh world is opened to you—that of imagination and taste.' Finally the conflict appears. 'As to the third view of Rome, here pain and pleasure go together.' It is the city of the Apostles, of the saints and martyrs. The clergy are decorous, and most things are 'very different from Naples', with nothing of the trumpery or absurd 'profaning the most sacred subjects'. But 'there are (seemingly) timidity, indolence, and that secular spirit which creeps on established religion everywhere'. The conflict can only be expressed in verses whose questions, far from being merely rhetorical, suggest the weakening hold on earlier anti-Roman bias.

> Far sadder musing on the traveller falls
> At sight of thee, O Rome!

> Than when he views the rough sea-beaten walls
>   Of Greece, thought's early home;
> For thou wast of the hateful four whose doom
>   Burdens the Prophet's scroll;
> But Greece was clean till in her history's gloom
>   Her name and sword a Macedonian stole.
>
> And next a mingled throng besets the breast
>   Of bitter thoughts and sweet;
> How shall I name thee, Light of the wide West,
>   Or heinous error-seat?
> O Mother, erst close tracing Jesus' feet,
>   Do not thy titles glow
> In those stern Judgment-fires which shall complete
>   Earth's strife with Heaven, and ope the eternal woe?

More personal than these balanced verses is the confession to Jemima from Naples. 'How shall I describe the sadness with which I left the tomb of the Apostles? Rome, not as a city, but as the scene of sacred history, has a part of my heart, and in going from it I am as if tearing it in twain.' The next letter, to Samuel Rickards, attempts to analyse the 'mixture of good and evil' in Rome, passing from prophecies of Babylonian doom for idolatry to a hope that the captive Church will break its dual bonds of corrupted Christianity and secular tyranny. It ends with the cry of reproach, 'O Rome! that thou wert not Rome!', a cry welling from powerful and positive feelings that are already threatening to sap the force of theoretical and doctrinal negations. Looking back on the distinction he was trying to make in 1833, Newman tells us in the *Apologia*: 'This was my first advance in rescuing, on an intelligible, intellectual basis, the Roman Church from the designation of Antichrist; it was not the Church, but the old dethroned Pagan monster, still living in the ruined city, that was the Antichrist.'

The 'most wonderful city in the world' made even Naples more endurable on second look. 'I have been too hard on it,' Newman says. The colours are 'certainly indescribably beautiful', and the people are 'very civil and good-natured, though they are knaves'. But it was Sicily that was calling him, compelling him to undertake his strange and lonely pilgrimage, with all its hardships. It was not merely the appeal of historical ruins and natural beauty, though at his first visit he had said: 'Little as I have seen of Sicily, it has filled me with inexpressible delight and (in spite of dirt and

other inconveniences) I am drawn to it as by a loadstone.' It was
rather that on this whole voyage Newman was in search of himself.
He had shared experiences with the Froudes, he had felt the conflict of emotion and judgment in Rome, he was to yield temporarily,
as the Taurominium letter shows, to the beauty of a view that was
'the nearest approach to seeing Eden'. What he had to find, however, was a meaning for himself, a sign from that Other of the two
'luminously self-evident beings'. This he could only experience
alone, in an act of supremely egotistic awareness. Five years later
he was to tell Jemima not to worry about his being lonely. 'God
intends me to be lonely; He has so framed my mind that I am in
great measure beyond the sympathies of other people and thrown
upon Himself.' And on his journey God did not let him down. A
Sicilian fever re-charged his spiritual batteries, and set him off on
the Oxford Movement.

The importance of this crisis to Newman is evident, even without
his own estimate, in the meticulous care with which in the years up
to 1840 he recorded and arranged his memories and notes, and the
attached comment of 1874: 'I wonder I have not mentioned how I
simply lost my memory as to *how* I came to be ill and in bed—and
how strangely by little and little first one fact came back to me,
then another, till at length I realized my journey and my illness
in continuity.' The autobiographical account of his Sicilian illness
is absorbing reading, governed as it is by a shaping and selective
art, an art that could not have marked Frank's treatment of any
episode in his own narrative, had he similarly selected one for
development. There is the wealth of concrete detail: the loving
care shown by the Neapolitan servant Gennaro; the need to
communicate with the doctor (providentially there) in Latin; the
drastic treatment, including bleeding and Epsom salts; the aroma-
tic bitter flavour of oranges; annoying noises, including a daily
mass bell; the post-fever effects of peeling lips and darkening nails.
There is at times the vivid effect of broken recollections ('my
account may be confused, running to and fro'), realistically conveying the state of mind. 'I had some miserable nights—the dreamy
confusion of delirium—sitting on a staircase, wanting something,
or with some difficulty—very wretched—& something about my
Mother & Sisters.' And finally, there are the insights and recurring thoughts that weave the whole together into a pattern of
significance, conveyed in the sentence, 'Now in all this seems

c

something remarkable & providential.' Remorse and humility are
strong notes at the beginning. God is fighting against him for his
'self will'; he is a hollow man, with 'little love, little self denial'; his
whole course is one of 'presumption'; he even dictates a letter to
himself of apology to the Provost (in his delirium) for being 'dis-
respectful & insulting'. Yet these notes remain subordinate. For
running throughout are the dominant themes, 'I have not sinned
against the light', and 'God has still work for me to do'.

Recovery gave re-assurance on both these scores. The effect was
tonic, a call to battle on behalf of the Church Catholic and Apostolic against both Tory betrayals and what Keble had called 'the
stifling and corrupting embraces of Whiggery'. Full of 'fierce
thoughts against the Liberals', Newman fretted in Palermo for
three weeks, partly calmed by visits to churches there. Off to
Marseilles on an orange boat, he wrote "Lead, Kindly Light"
while becalmed in the Straits of Bonifacio, and refused even to
glance at the tricolour of a vessel in Algiers. How the surge of
renewed energy carried him on, after a break at Lyons caused by
fatigue, he tells us at the end of the first part of the *Apologia*. 'At last
I got off again, and did not stop night or day till I reached
England, and my mother's house. My brother had arrived from
Persia only a few hours before. . . . The following Sunday, July
14th, Mr Keble preached the Assize Sermon . . . published under
the title of *National Apostasy*. I have ever considered, and kept the
day, as the start of the religious movement of 1833.'

PART TWO

1833–1850

CHAPTER 4

Three Blows and a Third Period

In the summer of 1841 I found myself at Littlemore, without any harass or anxiety on my mind. I had determined to put aside all controversy, and I set myself down to my translation of St Athanasius; but, between July and November, I received three blows which broke me. (*Apologia Pro Vita Suâ*)

... towards the end of what I will call my Third Period ... the authority of the Scriptures as to some details had begun to be questioned, ... but hitherto this was quite secondary to the momentous revolution which lay Calvinism prostrate in my mind, which opened my heart to Unitarians, and, I may say, unbelievers; which enlarged all my sympathies, and soon set me to practise free moral thought, at least as a necessity, if not as a duty. (*Phases of Faith*)

FOR BOTH Newman brothers, the years following their return to England were a time of clinging with loosening hold, in John's case to the Church of England, in the case of Francis to Christianity itself. It was a period of almost total obscurity for Francis, as he plodded a lonely and painful road from Scriptural Evangelicalism towards moral theism. It was a period of growing reputation for John, as his talents found full expression in the movement to make the Church of England synonymous with Anglo-Catholicism. A few letters, among the unpublished correspondence at the Oratory, bracket the period effectively, if not exactly. They offer a frame in which to set the events of those years.

Though the first pair here selected were written over a year apart, and make tantalizing reference to other letters, they are full enough and coherent enough to mark the inevitability of the break. It is the break between the Catholic and Protestant principles, between the appeal to historical witness and the appeal to private judgment, between an emotional need which safeguards its truth, if need be by submission, and an intellectual need which seeks its

57

truth at the risk of isolation. With Frank still the text-quoting Evangelical, the break is not yet complete, but John has no doubt of where his brother will end. The *odium theologicum* is evident as each, alarmed for the other's spiritual safety, accuses him of betraying the true Christian faith. Nor were John's feelings likely to be soothed by Frank's earnest prayer that 'if in the midst of much trash I drop some truth wholesome to you, you may get the benefit of it', or by the terms of his pious meekness: 'I desire to be humbled far below you. I hide my head in confusion at my numberless iniquities, & can only look to the blood of Jesus Xt for daily washing.'

Frank's letter, written from Bristol in 1834, is his fourth attempt to set down his views after reading John's first volume of *Parochial Sermons*. These sermons show John in danger of losing 'the marrow of all religion'. Frank is not writing as 'Dissenter vs. Churchman' but 'for brotherly love's sake', and 'for the vital truth in which the peace and spirituality of the soul is concerned'. Then follow twenty-one pages of commentary on selected passages from the sermons, passages which reject sudden conversion, which stress salvation by works and holiness as the gift of a whole life. 'To say that faith means a life of persevering obedience makes absolute nonsense of every passage in which Paul speaks of our being justified *not* by works *but* by faith.' Pouncing indignantly on a later passage, Frank then accuses John of inconsistency in believing Infant Baptism to be a channel of grace, so letting the Church clothe those of 'no faith in glory from the first. And what Church? One of conflicting doctrines, not one of the community of Christians. 'Paul never says, "Depend on me"; but "Follow me, as I follow Christ." '

John, Frank continues, has destroyed real (Pauline) Christianity, of the simple faith and sudden conversion which show Christ's power and love. Furthermore, by saying that texts expressing joy are beyond us, by stressing suffering and self-denial as the only 'evidence', John has denied the connection between faith and joy as well as that between faith and a change of heart. Frank goes on to quote texts showing that conscience, love, inwardness, are the true religion, and alone can make one's actions good. If this is 'mere feeling', it is 'a feeling more precious in God's eyes than all the privations or sufferings and all the services of all the saints; for the last are only valuable in so far as they imply real love'. John's teaching is like scolding a sick man for laziness. A man must first gain strength, which comes from the gospel, not the law. As for a

JOHN HENRY NEWMAN IN 1847
from an engraving after a portrait by W. C. Ross

F W Newman
Ætatis 46

FRANCIS NEWMAN IN 1851
from a photo by John Davies

body of men calling themselves 'Church, Mother of Saints, and other swelling words of vanity', this can give none of the grace that comes by inward strength. The emptiness of gifts from such a body is shown in the rite of Infant Baptism, taking us at a time when we cannot discriminate good from evil more than does 'a dog or a stone', when we are quite capable of growing up profligate, and without any consciousness of righteous joy in Christian fellowship.

In a letter of November 23, 1835, John makes reference to recent rumours that Frank has denied the Trinity, justifying his fears that 'latitudinarianism *is* a secret Socinianizing'. With some hope that Frank's silence indicates shame, on this point, he then goes right to the main issue. The letter is worth quoting almost entire, not only for the attitude to Frank, but also for the clear statement of the larger conflict in which that attitude is only a part, and for the insistent appeal to probabilities.

That wretched, nay (I may say) cursed Protestant principle, (not a principle in which our Church has any share, but the low arrogant cruel ultra-Protestant principle)—your last letter showed me you had so imbibed it as to be in great peril—but I had no notion you had gone so far . . . On what ground of reason or Scripture do you say that everyone may gain the true doctrines of the gospel for himself from the Bible? where is illumination promised the *individual* for the purpose? where is it any where hinted that the aid of teachers is to be superseded? where that the universal testimony of the Church is not a principle of belief as sure and satisfactory as the word of Scripture? This is the πρῶτον ψεῦδος[1] of your notions. Till you give it up, till you see that the unanimous witness of the whole Church, (as being a witness to an historical fact, viz. that the Apostles so taught), where attainable, is as much the voice of God (I do not say as sacredly & immediately so, but as really) as Scripture itself, there is no hope for a clear-headed man like you. You will unravel the web of self-sufficient inquiry.

You will tell me perhaps that you must pursue truth without looking to consequences. Yet I cannot help begging you to contemplate *whither* you are going. Is it possible you are approaching Charles's notions? There will be this difference that you will admit the being of God—though this, I verily think, would be an inconsistency in you —but, admitting it, what else at least will you retain? Indeed, my dear F., you are in a net which I do not like to think of. I do feel it to be a snare of the devil.

Why should you object, as you take Scripture to be from God, and

[1] First falsehood.

to be an external bond upon you, to take the universal teaching of
the Church also? What antecedent probability is there against it?
You cannot say the Scripture *cannot possibly* mean what the Church
says it means—only that it need not. Why may it not have been
God's intention that the Church should be, as the keeper, so the
interpreter of Scripture?

As to you holding regeneration etc., I value it not a rush. Such
doctrines have no substantive existence. They may remain on your
mind awhile after you have given up the High Mysteries of Faith—
but will not last longer than the warmth of a corpse.

P.S. Observe I am not urging the testimony of the Church as if
the opinion of a number of persons of the meaning of Scripture, but
as an independent source of truth, viz. an historical testimony to a
fact, viz. the Apostles' having taught such and such doctrines. I hope
you understand, that decidedly as I might object to meet you in a
familiar way, or to sit at the table with you, yet should you be
coming here and wish to have any talk with me (not disputation)
or in like manner of course to write to me, I shall be most happy.
If I can be your servant in any way, so that I do not countenance
your errors, you really may command me—at least I trust so.

It was characteristic of John to ask for the return of this letter,
written as much to a lapsed heretic as to a brother, together with
the one written 'the other day'.

The two letters could not be plainer on the split between the
Protestant religion of the Bible and the Catholic religion of Church
and Creed, between a reliance on private judgment and a reliance
on authoritative interpretation. It was undoubtedly the correspondence of this period that Frank had in mind when he spoke of his
brother as sacrificing 'private love to ecclesiastical dogma', and
himself as slighting 'relationship in comparison with Christian
brotherhood'. Not that there was unkindness, but the practical
mischief lay in cutting 'me off from other members of my family,
who were living in his house, and whose state of feeling towards me,
through separations and my own agitations of mind, I for some
time totally mistook'. (*Phases of Faith*, p. 55.)

The next group of letters, in 1840, shows both men much further
along the roads they were travelling, and, now that plea and warning are futile, desirous of reconciliation. John is moving nearer to
the view that there is no half-way house between Rome and rationalism (or pantheism or atheism—the terms vary). His resigned
acceptance of the split between them probably reflects a feeling

that Frank might as well stray with the Unitarian black sheep as persist in Evangelical bleatings about the Lamb. A letter to Jemima on February 25, 1840, shows his state of mind. He is sluggish and miserable, expecting a great attack upon the Bible. The 'wretched Socialists', the 'geologists, giving up parts of the Old Testament', Milman 'clenching his "History of the Jews" by a "History of Christianity" which they say is worse', the school of Arnold 'giving up the inspiration of the Old Testament, or of all Scripture', the 'political Economists, who *cannot* accept (it is impossible) the Scripture rules about alms giving, renunciation of wealth, self-denial, &c.,'—all this makes him feel that no religious body but the Roman Church can 'withstand the league of evil', as it withstood Satan at the end of the first millenary. And now the end of the second draws near. Of the 'good principles' developed at Oxford, 'I am not clear that they are not tending to Rome.' In short, the high Tractarian hopes have dimmed, and the wilfulness of an erring younger brother merges with the looming triumph of the forces of liberalism.

In Frank's case, suffering and persecution bred tolerance, even of Roman Catholics, capable as individuals of spirituality in spite of the system. His brother 'surely was struggling after truth, fighting for freedom to his own heart and mind. . . . I therefore wrote him a letter of contrition.' (*Phases of Faith*, p. 119.) This letter, presumably the one sent from Bristol in April of 1840, accepts the 'overtures of friendship' in a letter from John of April 11, dwells on their common loss of a mother who was 'a promoter of their love', and confesses to an erring judgment and a misled conscience that made him 'a less dutiful son to her' and 'a more wilful brother towards you'.

All this sweetness and light is somewhat misleading. There were many sharp exchanges to come between the brothers, though they never ceased to sign themselves 'affectionately'. Yet the desire to live and let live is evident, in recognizing that they are alike in holding 'principles which we perhaps think dearer than life itself'. Their tastes differ, Frank admits. For 'these 6 years' John has offered everything '*but* friendly and familiar intercourse', which to Frank is more painful than none at all. 'Men such as we are,—for this at least we have in common, the entering with great ardour into the highest interests of man, in this world and the next—naturally find chief sympathy from agreement as to religious & political

sentiments.' With some who disagree with him, Frank can talk
on literature and science. But John is 'opposed to science', and his
literature and history are all religious. Only domestic and social
topics are left, not much to fill 'a brother's sphere between men of
earnest mind'. He must be free to disagree, even with an elder
brother, otherwise there would be no equality. As for the preaching
John has criticized, to Frank every Baptist or Independent meeting
is as true a Church as the Established, which is as much a sect as
they. Something larger is needed. 'If anything reconciles me to
your party, it is the hope that they are God's appointed instruments for overturning & unsettling far & wide, preparatory to a
better building up.' Frank ends by saying that he dreads renewed
intercourse, knowing that his views may provoke censure, and
that he has avoided old friends whose zeal grows more intense,
more bitter, every day.

John's reply to this, on April 16, welcomes Frank's affection, and
argues that even restrained intercourse is not valueless, if there is a
will to seek agreement and diminish differences. Perhaps he has
not borne opposition as he ought, but 'there are degrees of bearing
it'. Frank is not to suppose, he quickly adds, that he is pleading for
a renewal of close relations. Their differences, he fears, would
simplify to 'one or two very deep & great ones', but 'there might be
much cordiality in our opinions of men and measures'. Meeting
Frank half-way, John agrees that no ordination is needed to preach
in church at the request of authorities; that sectarianism may exist
without outward separation; that the Established Church is (inter-
nally) a sect; that the Church has power to abolish episcopacy. He
denies that he is opposed to science. 'And yet, if I had to explain
definitely what I meant, and was probed to the bottom, doubtless
you would think me more like the Roman Catholics than you do
at present.'

Answering on April 29, Frank, who could never leave well
enough alone, declares that he has long thought John to be one
with the Roman Catholics in main principles, and has had to wait
until a larger mind has enabled him to admit them in Christian
charity before he can admit John. For his own part, he must either
hold to the principle he was reared in and demand agreement in a
creed as being essential to Christian faith, or he must cast this off and
judge men by 'their sincerity, their reverential spirit, and practical
benevolence & purity'. The latter course has been his choice, for

exclusion is odious and opposed to the spirit of Christianity. So he receives, as Christians, 'Romanists, Quakers, Unitarians & Sweden-borgians', if they are 'not wanting in the moral peculiarities of a Christian'. Far deeper than what is 'theologically prominent' is 'an inner element of the moral and spiritual' which 'may suffice to make us love one another'. He amiably concludes by hoping to see John at Oxford, and invites him to Bristol. On the back of this letter John, a week later, wrote a few sentences saying that Frank would be surprised to know of how many different schools and views his own friends were, and that though it would distress him to fraternize with Unitarians, he was willing to abide by Frank's test of religious truth, 'the moral peculiarities of Christians'. Estimates of these will differ, however, as of creeds.

That their relations remained touchy, an armistice subject to lapses rather than a peace, is suggested by John's letter of October 22, following what was evidently a sharp exchange—or more likely, an exchange stubborn on Frank's part and sharp on John's. He is pained by Frank's letter, but not surprised. Without 'divine grace you must go further still—your principles lead to scepticism on all points whatever, and this circumstance is to my mind a reductio ad absurdum of them. . . . Man is made for religion: and your principles make religion impossible. I am not attempting to prove this: but I state my opinion for your information, as you have stated yours for mine.' Frank's reasoning is irresistible, given Frank's principles, and John anticipates that they will be general in the coming age, causing a downfall of Christianity for a time. The assumed (and undeniable) irrationality of the Church religion used as a principle, on the other hand, exemplifies the Apostle's meaning that worldly wisdom knows not God. 'Latitudinarianism is an unnatural state; the mind cannot long rest in it.' The outcome is scepticism, and the more of this, the more chance of a revival of ecclesiastical authority. Averse as Englishmen are to Romanism, they will embrace this rather than absolute uncertainty, given only the two. The letter concludes with an eight-point statement as to why Unitarians cannot be admitted into a Christian Church.

Referring the whole debate between them to the fundamental issue of private judgment, Frank evidently had asked for a clear statement of John's position. For himself, believing the principle essential to all religion as a guard against superstition, he declares the great question between Christians to be whether there is *any external authority* for deciding controversies. In a long letter of November 10, John discusses the nature of authority, the Anglican principle, the Higher Criticism, and his own doctrine of development, and finally apologizes for not replying to specific observations. He returns to the attack on November 15. He had already suggested that 'God may have granted the Church a power of speaking truth within certain limits', outside of which private judgment may range, that 'there would be no inconsistency in upholding the authority of the Church, and yet, when she did not speak or could not be heard, going by private judgment'. It would seem as if primitive times were happiest, as being too near the event for doubt; but again, perhaps this certainty was not most beneficial, for 'as Bishop Butler tells us, the judging of truth under difficulties is a moral trial'.

This last letter (there are no more in this batch of unpublished exchanges with Francis until 1854) is less that of a man setting out to vanquish or to convince his correspondent than that of a man setting down his thoughts for himself in a somewhat tentative way. They had not much more to say to each other. On the issue of private judgment the impasse was reached. Thoughts were already crystallizing in John's mind, around the principle of probability, that were to emerge five years later in *The Development of Christian Doctrine*. Meanwhile he was in something of a state of suspension; the 'three blows' that were to break his hold on the Anglican *Via Media* were imminent. It is time to consider the events which took place in the period covered by the two groups of letters, the period following the return of the brothers to England.

Of Francis there is not much to tell. In 1834 he received an appointment as classical tutor and lecturer in mathematics at Bristol College, a non-sectarian institution which was founded in 1831 and closed ten years later, unable to meet the competition of a Church of England college set up in part through the hostility of the clergy. Among his pupils there was Walter Bagehot, the distinguished social and political writer of the later Victorian era. In 1835 he married Maria Kennaway, daughter of Sir John Kennaway, whose meritorious services in India had brought him a pension from the East India Company. She was a young woman of some beauty, of simple and devout faith, a Plymouth Sister given to good works among the poor and to religious instruction in neighbouring village schools. Perhaps the rumours of Frank's unsoundness in certain doctrines had not penetrated to Ottery St Mary in Devonshire, or his intellectual attainments and missionary travels to Persia may have invested him with a degree of glamour. Neither the remoteness of his academic interests nor his growing scepticism seems to have affected her devotion, or his, through the years marked by her recurring and increasing ill health. The restrictions imposed on him over the years may be seen, though he does not complain, in certain letters which show 'the unfailing unselfishness with which he constantly gives up his own plans of seeing his friends, in order that his wife may go to those places for which she has a special affection. Not infrequently he gives up a journey much further afield for the purpose of pursuing antiquarian researches because he knows how great would be her ennui were she to accompany him, and he is ever full of a tender concern that she shall suffer no unnecessary discomfort or trouble.'[1] Her illness prevented Frank's attendance at the funeral of his mother in 1836. He had, however, managed a meeting of his bride with his mother and sisters at Oxford. His mother remarks in a letter of 1835 to John that she suspects Sir John Kennaway would prefer to have his daughter married to a good churchman, and adds her hope that the marriage will 'lead to improvement in poor dear Frank'. (*Bod. Lett.*)

There is a paucity of reference to Frank in letters over these years, reflecting the estrangement mentioned in *Phases of Faith*. The occasional use of 'poor Frank' and 'poor Charles' in the mother's letters moves one to pity 'poor Mrs Newman', especially as her favourite John was by then expressing views which puzzled and alarmed her. That she still tried to be the peacemaker is evident two months before her death. A recent letter from Frank speaks of an intended visit from him and his wife, and a willingness to accompany her at Easter to her place of worship. It also admits an altered view of the Hampden controversy (*q.v.*) in the light of

---

[1] Sieveking, p. 172. On her death in July, 1876, he wrote to his friend Dr John Nicholson: 'For more than forty years I have been in possession of a heart that loved me ardently: that happiness is no more. But I kept my treasure ten years longer than I had any reason to expect. . . . Of course I feel very desolate, and to live quite alone in declining years seems unnatural and unhealthful; but I cannot form any decisions at present. I am conscious of excellent health and unbroken strength, and after forty years of happy love should be very ungrateful to repine.' Some years later he married his wife's friend and companion, Miss Williams, who had lived with them for eleven years, and who outlived him.

developments at Oxford, and discusses a possible division between
Church and State. 'I hope all this,' she says to John, 'may give you
some satisfaction. I leave it to you whether you shall like to come
while they are with us. Your time is occupied, I know it could only
be a call.' There is no sign of a peaceful interlude, however.
Writing to Jemima (*Lond. Lett.*) on February 1, 1837, John
describes a long, trouble-making letter from Charles, in which
Frank is quoted as accusing John of setting up a schism in the
Church. This is uncharitable of Frank, as well as odd, but 'I judge
him in no way. I only say that God tells me to avoid persons who
make divisions—and he makes a division.' Frank here 'imputes
motives', and this John always deplores. The pot-and-kettle retort
shows that the accusation rankled, and a letter of 1843 quoted in
the *Apologia*, on the decline of the Oxford Movement, in effect
allows its justice: 'Men of Catholic views are too truly but a party
in our Church.'

Frank admits in *Phases of Faith* that he was partly responsible,
in this 'time of deep and critical trial', for the estrangement,
'slighting relationship' in a search for 'Christian brotherhood—
sectarian brotherhood, some may call it.' The search failed. He
found himself rejected for heresy, though 'not one who met me face
to face had a word to reply to the plain Scriptures which I quoted'.
Unable to accept Darby's 'irrational' dictum that the Father
meant the Trinity, Frank found that 'the Irish clergyman' had
written friends and acquaintances to spurn him on pain of being
'cut off from Christian communion and recognition'. Such treatment from a man who had declared that 'intellectual dogma was
not the test of spirituality', and whom he 'had looked up to as an
apostle', together with the 'social persecution' that followed, led
Frank to a resolution 'to love all good men from a distance, but
never again to count on permanent friendship with anyone who
was not himself cast out as a heretic'. He was finding that his ideal
of a spiritual church compatible with intellectual freedom and
moral truth was difficult to achieve. 'I had been charged with a
proud and vain determination to pry into divine mysteries, barely
because I would not confess to propositions the meaning of which
was to me doubtful, or say and unsay in consecutive breaths.'

Fundamentally, Frank was opposed to the idea of mystery, at
least as a basis of dogmatic utterance, and the ancient and continuing disputes over nature and number in the concept of the

Christian Deity were to him so much word-shuffling. He managed for a time to believe in Christ, the Son of God, as a being of 'superior nature', but there could be only one God the Father, and the Holy Spirit could only be 'God in the hearts of the faithful'. Scriptural authority was intact as yet, but only as interpreted by his own reason. On this basis, and by an appeal to his own conscience and sense of justice, he rejected the dogma of Original Sin, with the Calvinistic corollary of eternal punishment for the many, as he already had rejected belief in vicarious atonement. 'I was conscious that in dropping Calvinism I had lost nothing Evangelical; on the contrary, the gospel which I retained was as spiritual and deep-hearted as before, only more merciful.'

Frank became sorrowfully aware that he had been contemptuous of 'mere moral men', and that common-sense morality, though it may lack the high excellence of a spiritual morality of which God is the embodiment, is yet necessary to balance the unworldly intensity of the saints. He also, near the end of this period, made his first acquaintance with a Unitarian, and was both surprised by his sweet and charitable temper, and astonished at his holding Jesus to be a mere man yet sinless. Frank's rigorously logical mind could make no such compromise. When he surrendered belief in the divinity of Christ he would go the human limit; as yet, 'I held fast an unabated reverence for the moral and spiritual teaching of the New Testament, and had not the most remote conception that anything could ever shatter my belief in its great miracles.' He thought many times of going to India to help his friend Groves, but fear of fresh bigotry, and his new ties at home, stopped him. He went instead to Manchester, in 1840, as Classical Professor in Manchester New College. James Martineau came the same year as Professor of Mental and Moral Philosophy, and a friendship began between the two men which lasted throughout life. The great Unitarian thinker watched with sympathetic, if sometimes pained interest, as Frank, his Christianity going the way of his Calvinism, developed through the 'forties his independent and startling religious views. He began the period with a total rejection of dogma and doctrine as making for un-Christian sectarian intolerance, and, asking only that a man show the 'moral peculiarities of a Christian', he was able to extend the hand of friendship to Unitarians. He ended the period accepting even atheists, provided they were men of moral goodness, and with a critical view of Jesus as man and teacher that made most Unitarians unwilling to extend the hand of friendship to him.

The phrase 'loosening hold' used at the beginning of this chapter is obvious in Frank's case. It may seem odd when applied to John's Anglicanism, in view of his aggressive leadership of the Oxford Movement, with its aim of restoring authority and independence to the Established Church. Yet he was going against the temper and historical development of the Church. This was latitudinarian and comprehensive, coming to terms with the spirit of the age, and destined to seek its salvation in an awakened social conscience rather than in a revival of primitive mysteries. In his efforts to change the course of things, he was fully aware of the strength of the forces, secular and religious, that he was attacking. Indeed, it gave zest and drama to the Movement as ministers of the Crown became alarmed at the defiance of the Oxford rebels, as startled bishops found themselves pressured into reluctant approval, or acquiescence, and as the Evangelical *Christian Observer* voiced its suspicions of Romeward tendencies.

'I expect to be called a Papist when my opinions are known,' Newman cheerfully admitted as early as November 22, 1833. And well he might. The whole anti-Roman strain, even before the 'three blows' in 1841, has an air of shadow-boxing about it. In August of 1833 he had sent home an essay in dialogue form to Hurrell Froude, published in 1836 as "Home Thoughts Abroad". Arising from his passionate desire to separate idolatrous from Christian Rome, the essay is ostensibly a first attempt at defining the Anglican *Via Media*, as a Catholic alternative to Romish corruption. It is so presented in the *Apologia*. But when the spokesmen for this point of view, Cyril and Basil, have made their case, Ambrose (Hurrell Froude?) sums it up: 'I have been watching with some interest how near, with all your protestations against Popery, you would advance toward it in the course of your speculations.' The title of 1872, "How To Accomplish It", aligned the essay more precisely with the account in the *Apologia*, but the voice of Ambrose was the prophetic one. If the ground, like Bishop Blougram's, should break away, there was a firmer yet beneath it, as yet dim-descried and seemingly inhospitable.

The Oxford or Tractarian Movement, and Newman's part in it, have been treated exhaustively in many full-length studies. Com-

pression runs inevitable risks. Yet it is possible to sketch briefly
Newman's course from confident action to disillusioned defeat.

Broadly summarized in a letter of August 13, 1833, the objects
of the Movement were 'to make the clergy alive to their situation,
to enforce the Apostolical Succession, and to defend the Liturgy'.
One would think that certain of the clergy were alive to their
situation, when three-quarters of the curates received less than
£100 a year, and some less than £40, a scandalous situation
reflecting the abuses of plural livings, non-residence, and absentee-
ism. (*Edinburgh Review*, October, 1832.) But it was another kind of
scandal, the threat of government interference going beyond a
reforming of such abuses, that alarmed the high-minded Oxford
Apostolicals. With the repeal of the Test and Corporation Acts,
the emancipation of the Roman Catholics, and the passage of the
Reform Bill, they saw the prospect of a radically changed House of
Commons influencing episcopal appointments, attacking the university requirement of subscription to the 39 Articles, and tamper-
ing further, after the dissolution of the ten Irish bishoprics, with
the forms and practices as well as the privileges of the Established
Church.

To save the Church Catholic and Apostolic, societies were set up
all over the kingdom, lay and clerical petitions were organized,
and the famous *Tracts for the Times* were started and circulated,
with Newman as the earliest and chief contributor. It was a sound
instinct that made Newman oppose the idea of an Association as
long as he could, in his desire to reach and influence conservative
minds of radical temper, like his own. For one thing, societies were
suspect. One thinks of Tennyson's metrical threat, written that
year, to leave England and 'seek a warmer sky',

> Should banded unions persecute
> Opinion, and induce a time
> When single thought is civil crime,
> And individual freedom mute.

For another, they were too apt to suggest the activities of the Evangelical peculiars, or even of the Dissenters. Furthermore, in Newman's view 'no great work was ever done by a system, whereas
systems rise out of individual exertions. Luther was an individual.
The very faults of an individual excite attention; he loses, but his
cause, if good, and he powerful-minded, gains. This is the way of
things; we promote truths by a self-sacrifice.'

The tracts were successful from the start in drawing attention, sympathetic or hostile, to neglected points of Church discipline or Catholic doctrine. Even more successful were the sermons, especially the *Parochial Sermons*, which from 1834 spread Newman's fame to larger than university audiences. In the words of Thomas Mozley they were 'a trumpet through the land'. To J. C. Shairp they were, with Keble's *Christian Year*, one of the two permanent monuments of genius from the Oxford Movement. In them, to use Newman's own motto, *Cor ad cor loquitur*. Doctrinal matters were in abeyance, or implied only. 'He laid his finger,' says Shairp, '—how gently, yet how powerfully,—on some inner place in the hearer's heart, and told him things about himself he had never known till then.'[1]

This intense and sincere religious feeling, this personal witness to the reality of religious experience, is one source of Newman's power as the key figure in the Movement which made such an impact at Oxford and throughout England. (The impact was made, H. L. Stewart caustically observes, at a time when the realities of the condition of England question were expressed in Chartism and *Hard Times* and *The Song of the Shirt* rather than in an obsession with the niceties of the Nicene Creed.) The negative response to the Movement may be attributed in the main to the 'No Popery' nerve that was still quivering just below the surface of English consciousness. The positive response was due to a variety of elements in the complex Newman personality, at least as much as it was due to intellectual excitement over tracts on apostolic antiquity or ecclesiastical autonomy. Besides the *cor ad cor* eloquence, there were the dramatic sense and the flair for strategy and tactics that marked the man of action and made him the natural leader of the Movement, motivated as he was by his 'fierce hatred of the Liberals'.[2]

[1] J. C. Shairp, *Studies in Poetry and Philosophy*, Edinburgh, 1872, p. 248. Keble's pious poems are little known today, and a more recent verdict is Geoffrey Faber's, that he was 'the Ella Wheeler Wilcox of his time'.

[2] The most hated liberal was Renn Dickson Hampden, former Oriel Noetic, whose Bampton Lectures in 1832 advanced the daring thesis that the formularies of the Church, including the Creeds, were of human not divine origin. He was made Professor of Moral Philosophy in 1833, defeating Newman, and in 1834 supported a proposal (not realized until 1858) to broaden admission of students to the universities of Oxford and Cambridge by relaxing subscription to the 39 Articles. He was appointed Regius Professor of Divinity

Urged not to go too far too fast, Newman wrote on November 22, 1833, 'We are as men climbing a rock, who tear clothes and flesh, and slip now and then, and yet make progress (so be it!), and are careless that bystanders criticize, so that their cause gains while they lose.' Energy is what gives the edge to any understanding, 'and energy is ever incautious and exaggerated'. This is not to excuse himself, but to console his friends. 'It is well to fall if you kill your adversary.' He concludes on the note that Anne Mozley finds 'to be instinct with the spirit of the Movement', as Newman led it. 'Let it be the lot of those I love to live in the heart of one or two in each succeeding generation, or to be altogether forgotten, while they have helped forward the truth.'

To do battle with the foe, to endure even to martyrdom in the cause of Truth, to join the ranks of the great ones who, the observed of all observers, flung the torch while falling—such tried and militant metaphors may have disgusted the rationalist and liberal antipathetic to the Movement. But they helped to kindle the enthusiasm of the young, even temporarily of some young sceptics and of Arnoldians up from Rugby, who, in Clough's later description of himself, were 'like a straw drawn up the draught of a chimney'. Newman summed up the psychology of the situation, in which the excitement of a High Church revival could offset the enthusiasm of the Low Church Evangelicals, in a letter of April 10, 1836. 'The Roman Church stops the safety-valve of excitement of Reason; we, that of the excitement of Feeling. In consequence Romanists turn infidels, and Anglicans turn Wesleyans.' Even enthusiasm, that hall-mark of the 'peculiars', could be defended in the right cause. 'I am pleased to find we are called enthusiasts—pleased, for when did a cause which could be so designated fail of success?'

Here the tactical sense comes in to reinforce the dramatic. There

at Oxford in 1836 by the Whig government of Lord Melbourne, a case of State action justifying to the Anglo-Catholic party their worst fears. A storm of petitions and pamphlets blew up around him, with Newman's *Elucidations of Dr Hampden's Theological Statements* the most damaging attack, and Thomas Arnold's angry article in the *Edinburgh Review*, entitled "The Oxford Malignants", the most powerful counter-attack. The orthodox largely supported the Tractarians, and by statute deprived Hampden of his vote in nominating Select Preachers to the University. His appointment in 1847 as Bishop of Hereford, also violently opposed, perhaps was some compensation for his unhappy time at Oxford.

is much of studied effect about the recklessness and fine careless rapture. 'Success is the test of sagacity or rashness,' said Newman in 1833 of certain 'offensive' tracts, and in 1837 he defended a sermon of Keble's on these grounds. 'The age is so very sluggish, that it will not hear unless you bawl—you must first tread on its toes, and then apologize.' Nor is the ruthless note absent. His old friend and tutor Whately, now Archbishop of Dublin, was a liberal and Erastian beyond the pale. 'To know him now is quite impossible.' As for men offended by his views, they are 'made of glass: the sooner we break them and get it over the better'.

Practical soundness of judgment shows itself in comments on the length and style of tracts, if they are to reach the average clerical reader. A larger insight is also apparent, into the dangers attendant upon such a religious movement. In his *Reminiscences*, Thomas Mozley observed in 1882 that the Oxford Movement, unforeseen by the chief movers, was to produce a generation of ecclesiologists, ritualists, and religious poets. Newman, preparing extracts from Froude's letters, had said to Frederic Rogers in 1837: 'I have much to say on the danger which (I think) at present besets the Apostolical movement of getting *peculiar* in externals, *i.e.* formal, manneristic, etc. Now, Froude disdained all *show* of religion. In losing him we have lost an important correction. I fear our fasting, etc., may get ostentatious.'

Not only did Newman compose sermons and tracts, and offer inspirational influence and practical guidance, but he also wrote the manifesto of the Movement. *Lectures on the Prophetical Office of the Church Viewed Relatively to Romanism and Popular Protestantism*, later collected with other writings of the period 1830–41 and published in two volumes as the *Via Media of the Anglican Church*, was 'a hard snowball' made from the earlier drifting snow. 'I cannot conceal from myself,' Newman said in a letter of January 7, 1837, 'that it is neither more or less than hitting Protestantism a hard blow in the face.' Expanded from a tract of 1834 called *Via Media*, it was Newman's attempt to preserve the primitive Catholicity of Anglicanism from 'the flood of Puritanism pouring over the Church, as Liberalism over the world'.

A letter to his sister Jemima on April 25 sums up his position in a notably defensive tone. 'I call the notion of my being a Papist absurd, for it argues an utter ignorance of theology. We have all fallen back from the time of the Restoration in a wonderful way.

... However, I frankly own that if, in some important points, our Anglican ἦθος differs from Popery, in others it is like it, and on the whole far more like it than like Protestantism. So one must expect a revival of the slander or misapprehension in some shape or other.' He had written to Rickards almost three years earlier: 'We are a "Reformed" Church, not a "Protestant". . . . the Puritanic spirit spread in Elizabeth's and James's time, and . . . has been succeeded by the Methodistic. . . . We, the while, children of the Holy Church, whencesoever brought into it, whether by early training or afterthought, have had one voice, that one voice which the Church has had from the beginning.'

Admitting that the *Via Media* is a theory, while Popery and Protestantism are 'real religions', Newman's *Prophetical Office* would avoid the 'corruptions' of the former and the political compromises of the latter. He would go back to the Anglo-Catholicism of the seventeenth century, of such men as Andrewes and Laud, the true heirs of primitive Christianity, so restoring to the English a service that would be 'Catholic and Apostolic, yet not Roman'. Judgment would be needed, in order to interpret the true doctrine for a viable and authoritative visible Church, but not the wilful private judgment of the Protestant interpreting the Bible for himself. For 'the essence of religion is the submission of the reason and heart to a positive system, the acquiescence in doctrines which cannot be proved or explained'. The doctrine is in the Book of Common Prayer, the discipline in the 39 Articles. Guided in interpretation by prayer and by the witness of 'our great masters', holy and reverential minds 'imbued with ancient Truth' and 'well versed in the writings of the Fathers', there will emerge an English theology 'with its characteristic calmness and caution, clear and decided in its view, giving no encouragement to lukewarmness and liberalism, but withholding all absolute anathemas on errors of opinion, except where the primitive Church sanctions the use of them'. This final clause, late in the Introduction, perhaps echoes the wistful note near the beginning, where Newman contemplates the demand by modern reasoners for free debate on every truth. 'Such troublers of the Christian community would in a healthy state of things be silenced or put out of it, as disturbers of the king's peace are restrained in civil matters.'[1]

---

[1] The sinister implications of this view did not escape Frank, who comments on another hint of it almost twenty years later. 'We observe that Dr Newman,

In the lengthy preface to the third edition of 1877, as part of his later Roman Catholic commentary on his earlier Anglo-Catholic theory, Newman was to describe this elaborate proposal of a *Via Media* as an insubstantial pageant. Yet at the time he could not, or would not, foresee the inevitable outcome. The skirmishing against Rome went on until, in the Spring of 1839, he tells us in the *Apologia*, 'my position in the Anglican Church was at its height'. It is true that his own study of the Monophysite heresy and his reading of Wiseman's article on the Donatists made him say in October of that year: 'I cannot conceal from myself that, for the first time since I began the study of theology, a vista has been opened before me, to the end of which I do not see.' The accommodation of the Anglican position to Catholic doctrine was enlarged, however, until the outcry over the famous *Tract 90*, of which Newman said in a letter of March 15, 1841: 'I have asserted a great principle, and I ought to suffer for it: that the Articles are to be interpreted, not according to the meaning of the writers, but (as far as the wording will admit) according to the sense of the Catholic Church.'

The 'three blows' which broke him soon followed. Translating St Athanasius, he found that his 'old trouble' about the Anglican position came back upon him. The Anglicans were 'semi-Arians'; the truth lay not with the *Via Media* but with the extreme party of Rome, before whose Catholicity and continuity the claim to an uncorrupted primitive antiquity crumbled. Then came the condemnation of *Tract 90* and the charges against him by the bishops, leading to the discontinuance of the tracts. The third blow, which 'finally shattered my faith in the Anglican Church', was the proposal to consecrate a bishop to serve jointly with Lutherans in Jerusalem, allowing 'intercommunion with Protestant Prussia, and with the heresy of the Orientals'. The promoters of the scheme undoubtedly saw it as an act of Christian brotherhood as well as of expediency. 'I confess I feel furious,' Samuel Wilberforce said of it on February 2, 1842, 'at the craving of men for union with idolatrous, material, sensual, domineering Rome, and their squeamish anathematizing hatred of Protestant Reformed men.' To Newman

---

in his *Apologia*, while declaring that he believes it would kill him to see an *auto-da-fé*, does not breathe a suggestion that such deeds were not righteous and acceptable to God.' ("Toleration—the Pope's Encyclical", *Fraser's Magazine*, August, 1865.)

the proposal was a declaration of the bankruptcy of Catholic principles in the English Church, a measure which 'will do more to unchurch us than any event for the last three hundred years'. More revealing than the formal protest he made is a letter of October 10, 1841. 'Have you heard of this fearful business of the Bishop of Jerusalem? . . . It seems we are *in the way* to fraternise with Protestants of all sorts—Monophysites, half-converted Jews and even Druses. If any such event should take place, I shall not be able to keep a single man from Rome. They will all be trooping off sooner or later.'

It may be that this blatantly Protestant and liberal move (a failure, but realized in 1887 as a purely Anglican bishopric) furnished Newman with the excuse for which he had been unconsciously waiting. He had already written to Rogers in Rome reproaching him for being 'unfair to those unhappy Romanists'. Certainly a remark made a week later hardly suggests a man totally unprepared. 'I fear I must say that I am beginning to think that the only way to keep in the English Church is steadily to contemplate and act upon the possibility of leaving it.' For all the prominence given them, the three blows did not break him—they helped him to follow his bent.[1]

---

[1] It is proper to insert at this point a post-conversion letter which Newman in 1876 considered an important account of his last few years in the Anglican Church. The letter is also of interest for its reference to Frank. It was no supernatural call which moved him, Newman tells Henry Wilberforce on November 30, 1848, 'it was a mere conviction, however flickered with doubts, *which were no parts* of it, any more than motes are part of the sunbeam, but a simple conviction, growing through years, the more I read and thought, that the Roman Church was the Catholic Church, and that the Anglican Church was no Church. It came to me first in reading the Monophysite controversy, and then the Donatist. When the affair of No 90 happened, Manning said "Shut up your controversy, and go to the *Fathers*, which is your *line*." Well *they* had been the beginning of my doubts, but I did so. I began to translate St Athanasius. The truth kept pouring in upon me. I saw in the Semi-arians the Viamedians, I saw in the Catholic Church of the day the identical [[image the]] self of the Catholic Church now;—as you know a friend by his words and deeds, or see an author in his works. Well then I fled back to one's inward experiences—and said that after all I felt the Anglican Church had done me so much good, that, in spite of all outward forebodings, it must be God's minister. But in time this would not stand, it was no sure footing—and would lead to the veriest liberalism. Curious enough I have lately read some words of Pusey's (I tell you in confidence) in argument, which parallel with some late words in a letter to me of my poor dear Brother, (who thinks that it is a moral fault to

say a man may not be as religious who denies the *existence* of Christ as one who confesses it), in the most marvellous way. Pusey says that to deny the Catholicity of the English Church, Frank that to deny the acceptableness of such an unbeliever, is (the ipsissima verba of *each*) "blasphemy against the Holy Ghost." To return:—then I fled to the notion that perhaps I was in a dream—I had muddled and heated myself with reading, and was no fair judge—so I waited. All along I trust I acted as in God's sight, but neither expecting nor experiencing any thing supernatural. At length I felt I dared not wait longer—and I acted—and from that day to this I bless God for it—for here is truth, and all else is shadow, and I have had (what might, had God so pleased, been otherwise, though I *know of no such case*), not even the *temptation* to doubt. Yes, I believe that God's grace so accompanies that great act, whereby we unite ourselves to His visible dwelling place, that the devil does not touch us.' (*The Letters and Diaries of John Henry Newman*, ed. C. S. Dessain, v. 12, pp. 356–7. Unless otherwise indicated, quotations from Newman's letters after October 9, 1845, will be from Dessain.)

CHAPTER 5

Rome and London

THE DRAMA of action was followed by the drama of suspense as
Newman, the centre of attention, abandoned the *Via Media* for the
route to Rome. Having decided that the Church of Rome could
justly claim to be the one truly Catholic Christian Church, he
spent four more years in coming to the decision to join it, an in-
finitesimal progress marked by infinite variations of the blend of
'subtilty and candour' seen by Keble as the distinguishing mark of
Newman's thought. The external moves were few—the retirement
from Oxford to Littlemore in February, 1842; the resignation from
St Mary's in September, 1843; the rearguard action of four sermons claiming the single Note of Sanctity for the English Church
now that Antiquity had to be surrendered, and of several essays
protesting too much against scandalous shortcomings in Rome;
the austere diet and exhausting monastic regimen observed at
Littlemore with a few disciples, exciting suspicion in the authorities
and hallucinations in the inmates (the *Journals* for 1843 make
reference to 'wandering thoughts' and to 'dreaming, which is a
kind of momentary illusion or scene'); the surrender of the Oriel
Fellowship in October, 1845.

It is perhaps whimsical to measure the pace of those years by the
last and longest chapter of the *Apologia*, which begins, 'From the
end of 1841, I was on my death-bed as regards my membership
with the Anglican Church,' and five pages from the end quotes
from a letter of November 7, 1844: 'I am still where I was; I am
not moving.' There was plenty of *internal* drama, a scrupulously
minute examination of motives carried on with the aid of faithful
correspondents, especially Keble and Jemima Mozley, put quivering through an emotional wringer. The next sentence in the same
letter also shows the consciousness of an audience. 'Two things,
however, seem plain, that every one is prepared for such an event
[his conversion], next, that every one expects it of me.' A notable

77

example of the strained attention focused upon the hermit of Littlemore is Gladstone's alarm at the threatened 'apostasy of a man whose intellectual stature is among the very first of his age', a man who has headed 'the most powerful movement the Church has known, at least for centuries'.[1] If his alarm is histrionic at times ('I stagger to and fro like a drunken man,' he wrote to Manning, 'I am at my wit's end'), we may note the gloomy prediction of Thomas Arnold's old pupil Arthur Stanley. In a letter written on the day of Newman's conversion, he found it less sensational than it would have been a year before, but still a melancholy fact. 'After an Anglican Newman has done so much, there is no saying, if he lives, what a Roman Newman may not do, both to the Roman Catholics and to us.'[2]

The fascination for us in watching Newman over these years lies not, of course, in sharing the suspense of some of his contemporaries as to the outcome, but rather in the psychological and semantic refinements by which he prolonged the last few steps. (The tempting if bizarre figure of an intuitive hare yoked to a rationalizing tortoise must be firmly rejected, recalling as it does Carlyle's grotesquely unjust growl that Newman had the intellect of a moderate-sized rabbit.) One explanation for the delay, already noted, lies in the drama of the situation, when, in Keble's words, 'so many are thinking of you all day long'. The allusive imagery used in a letter to Jemima in December, 1844, ('It is like drinking a cup out'), is reinforced later in the same letter: 'How St Paul must have unsettled quiet Jews who were serving God, and heard nothing but ill of our Lord as a Samaritan and "deceiver"!' Another explanation lies in the fine-drawn, hair-splitting nicety of definition in conveying delicately discriminated states of mind, which carried him from 'conviction' in 1841 to 'certitude' in 1845. A month after his conversion Newman wrote to a friend that Antiquity and the Apostolical Succession were the only grounds against Rome, '*if they can be held*'. He said: 'For myself, I found *I could not* hold them. I left them. From the time I began to suspect their unsoundness, I ceased to put them forward. When I was fairly sure of their unsoundness, I gave up my Living. When I was

[1] W. E. Gladstone, *Correspondence on Church and Religion*, ed. Lothbury, London, 1910, v. 1, p. 284. Written, ironically, to Manning.

[2] R. E. Prothero and G. G. Bradley, *The Life and Correspondence of Arthur Penrhyn Stanley*, London, 1893, v. 1, p. 343.

fully confident that the Church of Rome was the only true Church, I joined her.' This retrospective summary suggests with great precision a slow but sure movement. Yet a letter of July, 1845, had said, 'it is morally certain I shall join' the Roman Catholic Church, and added: 'It has been the conviction of six years from which I have never receded.' Quoting this letter, even Maisie Ward admits it is difficult to plot the progress of Newman's mind.

The main explanation for the delay, reflected in this verbal chess, is Newman's intense, at times morbid, preoccupation with self-analysis. His correspondence with the affectionate and long-suffering Keble is full of discriminations and hesitations and reservations. That some are purely hypothetical is suggested when Keble says, 'Your letters, as you may suppose, make me rather giddy, and put me out of breath; but I wish I felt the distress more keenly than I do.' A characteristic letter to Keble on June 8, 1844, begins with Newman declaring that he has a repugnance to writing, as it is about himself. 'But you should know my state of mind.' He goes on to a five-page summary of his life from Evangelical conversion at fifteen, through the Sicilian journey and sense of a work in store, up to the present time of trial ('Am I deceiving myself? Has He led me thus far to destroy me in the wilderness?'), and concludes: 'How this letter will distress you! I am ever thinking of you, my dear Keble!' The Anglican death-bed had become a psychiatrist's couch, with the patient conducting the analysis and ultimately prescribing the cure. Though expressions of remorse punctuate these demands on Keble to serve as confidant and sounding-board, a further year of such correspondence left Keble, one feels, well qualified for sainthood, especially as a final letter on November 14, 1845, gives him the credit for Newman's conversion. Except Hurrell Froude, no one had so clearly indicated 'that special direction which has led me to my present inestimable gain'.[1]

It is too simple to take at face value a letter to Keble of May 4, 1843, in which Newman said, 'I have enough consciousness in me of insincerity and double dealing, which I know you abhor, to doubt about the correctness of what I shall tell you of myself.'[2]

[1] Dessain, v. 11, p. 34. Father Dessain says, 'The friendship was renewed in August, 1863.' So it was, but only as a moment of pale and passing nostalgia.

[2] *Correspondence of John Henry Newman with John Keble and Others*, London, 1917. Hereafter referred to as *Keble Lett.*

Keble replied that he had never found 'wilful insincerity' in his friend. One may agree, and yet also agree with E. A. Abbott that Newman was 'portentously self-deceptive'. For example, he frequently denied having any influence, or knowing the nature of it, yet when the Jerusalem Bishopric was proposed, he wrote: 'If any such event takes place, I shall not be able to keep a single man from Rome.' Four years earlier he had told the Rev. W. Dodsworth, who became a Roman Catholic in 1851: 'I have from the first thought that nothing but a *quasi* miracle would carry us through with no proselytes whatever to Rome—and, though I shall fairly have to bear my share in them, shall not feel surprise, nor I trust self-reproach at what is not my doing.' (*Keble Lett.*) A trivial instance of this sort of thing—whether one is to call it self-deception, inconsistency, or sheer forgetfulness—occurs in the post-conversion correspondence. When he tells R. W. Church on May 22, 1846, 'I expect to go to Rome for a year in the course of a month or so—*but this is a secret*—you may tell C. Marriott' (having already told Mrs Bowden and Hope on April 18, with Hope on April 30 allowed to tell Badeley, who is to 'keep it to himself'), and then on May 29 tells Henry Wilberforce, who is to 'keep this secret', one begins to wonder if Newman is not the original master of the inspired leak. Perhaps the whole question is best referred to Keble's description of Newman's thought processes as a blend of 'subtilty and candour', with the proportions left to the discretion of the individual reader.

The operation of these processes is, however, intriguing. In the *Apologia*, with reference to the period 1841–5, Newman says, 'All the logic in the world would not have made me move faster towards Rome than I did.' He then quotes from a letter he wrote on May 5, 1841: 'For myself, persons must be well acquainted with what I have written, before they venture to say whether I have much changed my main opinions and cardinal views in the course of the last eight years. That my *sympathies* have grown towards the religion of Rome I do not deny; that my *reasons* for *shunning* her communion have lessened or altered, it would be difficult perhaps to prove. And I wish to go by reason, not by feeling.' To see how this reasoning works, we may consider a passage in *Tract 85*, "Holy Scripture in Relation to the Catholic Creed." Proving that faith, not scepticism, is conducive to happiness, Newman says: 'To follow after truth can never be a subject of regret; free inquiry does lead man to regret the days of his child-like faith; therefore, it is not following after truth.' Logic, then, or at least syllogistic form, can be employed to prove the superiority of feeling over reason, even if the recipe for arriving at truth may remind some sceptics of Lady Teazle's retort to Joseph Surface in the screen scene.

On Newman's view of the nature and place of reasoning more needs to be said. Here it is enough to say that to him thinking in-volves the whole man, with reasoning and feeling and imagining at times coalescing, at times differentiated sharply, at times dis-placing one another. The change in the *Apologia* from 'reason' to 'imagination', Newman first having written that he tried to make 'the doctrine of eternal punishment less terrible to the reason', reflects an attempt at precision characteristic of him.[1] It is a precision proper to his personal and realistic view of the psycho-logy of faith, not a precision controlled by intellectual usage. He describes the mental processes in his development, 'the concatena-tion of argument by which the mind ascends from its first to its final religious idea', and the conclusion he came to that 'there was no medium, in true philosophy, between Atheism and Catholic-ism'. He admits that he may not have expressed himself 'with philosophical correctness', but adds, 'I think I have a strong true meaning in what I say which will stand examination.'

Certainly Newman's reason was informed by the intensity of his feeling, by the need to clothe with authority his early intuition of the two 'luminously self-evident beings'. In a warm review of Keble's *Lyra Innocentium* in 1846, concluding with a prayer for Keble to join him, he praised the 'happy magic' of poetry, as some-times helping Anglo-Catholics to perceive that they ought to be plain Catholics. He also warned that it could as easily lead to Rationalism, because there is not in Anglicanism a power of 'abso-lutely determining the truth in religious matters'. The demands

---

[1] E. A. Abbott rebukes R. H. Hutton for finding this change unimportant. He is right, though in Newman a contempt for the inadequacy of words co-exists with an anxiety to find the right word. Surely 'imagination' is here the right word. And anxiety would seem to be the mood, judging from the variants in three well-known editions, all described as the 1865 (revised) version of the *Apologia*. In a popular edition (London, Routledge, n.d., p. 7) we have 'reason'; in the C. F. Harrold edition (Longmans, New York, 1947, p. 6) we have 'imagination'; in *Newman—Prose and Poetry*, ed. G. Tillotson (London, Hart-Davis, 1957, p. 583) we have 'intellect'.

of his own nature, pre-eminently for mystery and authority, were what shaped his actions, often in the name of reason. He declared to Jemima on December 22, 1844, 'If God gives me certain light, supposing it to be such, this is a reason for *me* to act.' Self-persuaded by the cogency of his 'reasoning' in his *Essay on the Development of Christian Doctrine*, in which cumulative probabilities bring the original intuition to ultimate certitude, he laid down the pen and finally acted. On October 9, 1845, he was received into the Roman Catholic Church by Father Dominic the Passionist, and 'the long gestation was accomplished'. It was the day sacred to St Denis, the beheaded martyr who walked with his head underneath his arm. That the association with the miraculous pleased him is evident in a letter of October 9, 1852, to the editor of *Univers*, referring to the 'glorious St Denis, who presided over my reception into the bosom of Catholicism'. Wilfred Meynell, in *Cardinal Newman: A Monograph*, recounted in 1890 the 'almost comic incident' of Father Dominic skipping the miracle of St Denis with his catechumens [Newman, Bowles, Stanton] because of its possible difficulty. 'But he did not know his men; . . . In truth, the neophytes were rather scandalized at *him*, and not at it.'[1]

In reply to anguished protests from Jemima over the 'pain and grief' of separation by his own sentence, Newman showed in a letter of March, 1845, that he was not indifferent to the sacrifices involved. He was losing a life of ease at Littlemore and of ade-

---

[1] Newman's reading in the early Fathers was a powerful stimulus, through the imagination, to his belief in miracles and in the greater reality of the invisible world, the world of Living Truth, over the world of nature and history. Not only did their teaching come 'like music to my inward ear'; they fostered his belief in angels and evil spirits as 'a middle race' of 'unseen intelligences', who 'gave a sort of inspiration or intelligence to races, nations, and classes of men'. It was this strain in Newman's writing which provoked a sarcastic comment from Connop Thirlwall in 1868. Admitting the sincerity of Newman's 'professed all-absorbing credulity', the liberal-minded Bishop of St David's remarked: 'The conception that all the work of the universe, all mechanical, physical, chemical, and physiological movements, from planetary and sidereal rotations to the dislocations of the molecules of an atom, are carried on by the agency of an order of personal beings, is one which my mind utterly rejects, and I believe that no mind could attempt to realise it without feeling itself in danger of losing its senses. Surely it is one thing to believe that all is regulated by a Supreme Will, and quite another to believe that this Will employs a machinery like that of the "Rape of the Lock".' (*Letters Literary and Theological*, ed. Perowne, London, 1881, p. 269.)

quacy in his Fellowship, perhaps the large income from his sermons, certainly his good name among many. 'I am distressing all I love, unsettling all I have instructed or aided. I am going to those I do not know, and of whom I expect very little. I am making myself an outcast, and that at my age. . . . Pity me, my dear Jemima!' She did pity, and try to understand, and her love remained with him. Yet inevitably there was estrangement, more especially from those friends and followers who neither preceded nor followed him into the Roman Church but remained in the Church of England. In the *Journals* for 1847 Newman speaks in a sadly reminiscent mood: 'On becoming a Catholic I lost not a few of my friends, and that at a time when by death I had lost others most dear to me.'

That Newman felt such separation keenly, as indeed his greatest sacrifice, there is ample evidence. On the nature of some of these friendships there has been speculation, prompted by the intimate language of endearment employed with a few such as Hurrell Froude and Ambrose St John, the occasional hurt reproaches followed by tender reconciliation, and the references to Newman as having almost a feminine charm. 'His friends', says Wilfrid Ward, 'loved his very faults as one may love those of a fascinating woman.' His early dedication to celibacy and the ideal of virginity, and his annoyance at the marriage of disciples, together with the anguish in passages of the *Journals* and in Froude's *Remains* over unnamed sins, are used by Geoffrey Faber in *The Oxford Apostles* to suggest a homosexual strain in Tractarian friendships, a suggestion qualified by the reminder of the idealizing of masculine affinities in both Classical and Biblical times. The reply is made that the exalted spiritual life conceived of by Newman and his friends could only be realized in monastic terms.

The physical aspect of marriage was at any rate repugnant to Newman, as Faber says. A passage in his semi-autobiographical novel of 1848, *Loss and Gain*, has the potential convert Charles Reding looking at some Catholic books in a shop. He hides when he sees a familiar face. 'It was that of a young clergyman, with a very pretty girl on his arm, whom her dress pronounced to be a bride. Love was in their eyes, joy in their voice, and affluence in their gait and bearing. Charles had a faintish feeling come over him; somewhat such as might beset a man on hearing a call for pork-chops when he was sea-sick.' The bridegroom's name is Henry, and one cannot help relating this scene to a marriage fourteen years before, when young Henry Wilberforce was afraid to tell Newman of his fall from grace. Those who, like Meriol Trevor, cannot bear a flaw in the idol, point to Newman's forgiveness, his becoming godfather to Henry's first child, and his (rather acrid) epigram: 'Marriage, when a crime, is a crime it is criminal to repent of.' In fact, friendship with Newman usually involved a complete surrender to his personality and exalted ideals, though it is true too that he missed and longed to renew relations with some men of independent mind who held their own course. One falls back again on the term 'complexity'. There is no doubting the richness and depth of Newman's friendships, but psychological speculation on their nature and quality can evoke as violent disagreement as opinions of his mind, his character, his very manner and appearance.

The next five years were years of relative obscurity, as Newman left Littlemore for Maryvale (Old Oscott), underwent his noviciate in Rome to become an Oratorian, was ordained a Roman Catholic priest, and returned to England to establish the English Oratory of St Philip Neri. The Roman sojourn was a happy one, free of the painful conflict of his earlier visit. His reading and thinking having brought him to acceptance of Roman Catholicity and Papal Supremacy, his feelings and imagination could respond to the records and relics in the heart of Christendom, nourishing his 'simple faith'. From the Pope he had already received a silver crucifix, 'with a particle of the True Cross enclosed in the beam of it—Indulgences too are attached to the use of it.' The enthusiasm of the convert marks a letter to Henry Wilberforce on January 18, 1848, written soon after Newman's return to England, concerning the Holy House of Loreto and the sacred Roman *depositum*.[1]

I went to Loreto with a simple faith, believing what I still more believed when I saw it. I have no doubt now. If you ask me why I believe, it is because *every one* believes it at Rome, cautious as they are and sceptical about some *other* things—I believe it then as I believe that there is a new planet called Neptune, or that Chloriform destroys the sense of pain. *I have no antecedent difficulty* in the matter. He who floated the Ark on the surges of a world-wide sea, and inclosed in it all living things, who has hidden the terrestrial paradise, who said that faith might remove mountains, who sustained thousands for forty years in a sterile wilderness, who transported

[1] Dessain, v. 12, p. 156.

Elias and keeps him hidden till the end, could do this wonder also. And in matter of fact we see all other records [[memorials]] of our Lord and His Saints gathered up in the heart of Christendom from the ends of the earth as Paganism encroached on it. St Augustine (i.e. his relics) leaves Hippo [[for Padua]], the Prophet Samuel and St Stephen Jerusalem, the crib in which our Lord lay leaves Bethlehem with St Jerome, the Cross is dug up, St Athanasius goes to Venice, there is a general μεταβαίνωμεν εντευθεν[1]—In short I feel no *difficulty* in believing it, though it may be often difficult to *realize*.

One sees here the attempt at semantic precision which dictated the change from 'reason' to 'imagination' in the *Apologia*, the index of a mind that could not remain acquiescent and uncritical. For Newman was to some degree fooling himself. His was not a 'simple faith', nor could a willed credulity offset the working of a restless intellect. Peace of a kind he found, but controversy and even bitterness were to mark much of his career as a Roman Catholic.

Even now, with the Roman honeymoon over, differences developed among the Oratorians. Father Frederic (now Wilfrid) Faber exhibited an 'Italianate' extravagance and enthusiasm that Newman found both distasteful and likely to shock conservative English Catholics. The result was that Faber and his band went off to conduct the new London Oratory, where they made many converts, especially among the poor. Newman stayed in Birmingham, both encouraging and criticizing. That the differences between them did not prevent friendly co-operation is evident from the playful humour of a letter to Faber on the possible future of St Wilfrid's in Cheadle, where the Oratorians had stayed prior to the Birmingham move. 'I should like St Wilfrid's to be the Eton of the Oratory—a place where Fathers would turn with warm associations of boyhood or at least youth—a place where they wish to be buried—(where their relics would be kept)—a gin bottle or cayenne phial of the Venerabile servo di Dio, il Padre Wilfride Faber, an old red biretta of his Eminence C. Robert Coffin, and a double tooth and knuckle bone of St Aloysius of Birmingham.'[2]

These years were marked by two volumes of addresses, the Catholic sermons which make up *Discourses to Mixed Congregations* (1849), and the twelve *Lectures on Certain Difficulties Felt by Anglicans*

---

[1] Passing from one place to another.
[2] Wilfrid Ward, *The Life of John Henry Cardinal Newman*, London, 1912, v. 1, p. 222.

D

(1850). The occasion for the latter (as Newman himself points out, much of his writing was 'occasional') was the celebrated Gorham case, when the Privy Council overruled a decision of the Bishop of Exeter to withhold appointment from G. C. Gorham on the ground that he had denied the doctrine of baptismal regeneration. Here, to Anglo-Catholics, was secular interference at its worst, recalling the 'Liberal' excesses which had sparked the Oxford Movement. Any reluctance to intrude on Anglican controversy yielded to Newman's tactical sense of opportunity.

The lectures were frankly addressed to those in or influenced by the Oxford Movement, urging them to follow the logical path to Rome (advice long since given in his own case by his brother Francis). He was well equipped to attack what he had once led. Arguing in great detail through seven lectures that the Catholic life of the Movement could find no expression in the Establishment ('a mere wreck'), or in a party or sect or branch church, he went on in five more lectures to remove the grounds for prejudice against the Roman Catholic Church and to destroy the *Via Media*. He eloquently concluded: 'You are born to be Catholics; refuse not the unmerited grace of your bountiful God; throw off for good and all the illusions of your intellect, the bondage of your affections, and stand upright in that freedom which is your true inheritance.' The arguments and the eloquence were effective, and a number of conversions followed.

Two matters of interest here are the proselytizing activity, and the fate of the Oxford Movement. In his book *Cardinal Newman*, Bertram Newman maintains that 'a sensitive dislike of proselytizing remained with him all his life'. If so, it was controlled with remarkable success. A letter of December 10, 1845, tells Dalgairns that Pusey is pained to find that 'we really do mean to proselyte [sic], instead of considering ourselves transferred to another part of the vineyard'. We also find frequent reference to individuals who may follow him for love, or be persuaded. Three cases will serve to illustrate Newman's tenacity in converting and his extraordinary subtlety and variety of method—those of Mrs John Bowden, Henry Wilberforce, and Mrs William Froude.

With Mrs Bowden, the widow of his old college mate, a man so intimate with him that after marriage he sometimes called 'me Elizabeth and her Newman', the task was easy. A long letter of March 22, 1846, sympathizes fully with her state of mind in the

process of 'moving'; it counsels caution yet points out that we cannot anticipate certainty, and must in a sense 'act in the dark'; it
gives an example from his own experience, concluding: 'Sometimes too I have known at the very morning of acting, a letter has
come, saying for instance, that the step will be the death of some
near relative of his, with strong representations of the recklessness
of his conduct; so that he is like some hero in a romance who has to
make his way to the object of his search amid magical terrors.'
When Newman apologizes for this 'abrupt and stiff letter', one
wonders whether he is being disingenuous, or is really unaware of
the effect of his own moods and styles. Later he reminds her that
'dear John' showed a tendency towards the True Faith, warns
that the 'full consequence' of any act we must leave 'to Him who
makes them', and firmly counsels her to join. After she has joined,
he enlists her aid with the children. She must be reserved, not
urgent, with young John, and 'leave nature to itself'. Yet 'there is
the influence of his sisters and his home', provided one is careful. 'I
do not mean *eagerly* to propose . . . you must show *eagerness* about
nothing.'

Henry Wilberforce was a hard case, long as Newman had
known him. Poor Henry seems to have been one of those people of
wandering attention allegedly so frustrating to hypnotists. The
utmost patience was needed, as Newman alternated endearments
('Carissime') to his old friend, with lectures on doctrine and tradition to his old pupil. Annoyance at Henry's procrastination (he
felt difficulty in moving 'as long as Pusey and Keble are un-
shaken') sharpened into a blast at Henry for hypocrisy. 'Your
dread of my influence is humbug—no one can tell "*what* you
believe", nor "can you say".' Henry had, after all, put it pretty
strongly, saying, 'I feel that if you had turned Quaker I would have
felt you *must* be right.' By 1850 the struggle was over, and the
Wilberforces were safely landed.

A greater challenge lay in winning over the wife and children of
William Froude, younger brother of Hurrell, who had turned to
science and become an engineer and naval architect. Starting
from the same philosophical proposition of Bishop Butler, that
probability is the guide to life, Froude had followed a contrary line
of reasoning. 'And yet a careful examination of the progress of each
one,' says G. H. Harper, 'would probably reveal no error in logic,
proving what Newman had always maintained, that from a single

source two logical minds might nevertheless diverge.'[1] Froude kept his friendship for Newman, but it must have been painful to him to watch the slow process move to fruition as he held to his own standard, that of objective truth decided by the individual for himself. It says much for the power of his sceptical arguments, too, that the process took ten years. Harper maintains that Newman was 'scrupulous never to urge his position too strongly', leaving Mrs Froude, with delicacy, to draw her own conclusions. That is one view. Newman begins a letter, 'This is one thing that keeps me silent, dear friend, because I don't know what to say to you,' then goes on to exclaim, 'Oh that you were safe in the True Fold. I think you will be one day.' Another letter ends, 'O my dear Mrs Froude, are you content to live and die without faith?' True, Newman always insists that she must use her own judgment. But he had already told William that 'persons may have very good reasons, which they cannot bring out into words'. It is not judgment that is appealed to when he writes on May 5, 1854 (having told William on April 10, 'I shall not write to her'), 'Are you sure that, whatever *speculative* doubts or difficulties you may have, you have not a secret feeling that you ought to be a Catholic?'

Harper justifies this 'humble' and 'gentle' pressure as anxiety for her salvation. Certainly its psychological insight and skill are suggested in Mrs Froude's letter of thanks after her conversion. 'Other Catholics always seemed "making a case" . . . you always contrived to say exactly what suited my mind.' Newman replies that he is happy, and adds: 'You must gain your husband by your prayers.' William was not won over. There is pathos and dignity in a letter of his in 1854, as the outcome of the struggle for his wife and children was becoming clear. Her judgment of Catholicism, her feeling in its favour, are 'partly her entire love and admiration for the Catholics she has known—a love and admiration which goes entirely beyond that which she feels for any other persons whatever'.

The gulf between the two men is plain in Newman's definition of faith to Mrs Froude in 1848, ('Faith then is not a conclusion from premises, but the result of an act of the *will*, following upon a *conviction* that to believe is a *duty*'), and in William's statement in

[1] G. H. Harper, *Cardinal Newman and William Froude, F.R.S., A Correspondence*, Baltimore, 1933, p. 227. Letters in this and the next two paragraphs are from Harper.

1859, when his son Hurrell was converted, on the intellectual impasse between science and religion. Below the level of opinions, he said, is the main source of disagreement, 'seated in the very principle of "thinking" and "concluding" and in the very nature of thoughts and conclusions—and pervading the laws which govern the various senses of the term "belief" '. This letter Newman promised to keep. Together with Froude's generous concession that there is in some men a 'spiritual insight' as a psychological factor, a power of mind (though he does not concede that their conclusions may be certitudes), it pointed the way, in Harper's view, to the 'illative sense' developed in Newman's last major work, *An Essay in Aid of a Grammar of Assent*. If so, the man of religion was doubly triumphant. He gained from the man of science a family for his Church, and an argument for his theory.

The lectures addressed to old friends in the Oxford Movement raise the question of its influence and course. To some it was a wave that spent itself; to others it spread beyond Oxford under Pusey's leadership to act as a spiritual leaven in the English Church, through 'preaching, organisation, greater attention to the meaning, the solemnities, and the fitnesses of worship'.[1] According to William Palmer's 1883 Supplement to his Tractarian history, *A Narrative of Events*, the revived life of the Church is shown in the multiplicity of practical good works under Bishop Samuel Wilberforce, with clergymen adding to their regular duties a busy round of beneficial social activities (26 are listed). Apparently Palmer, a High Church zealot, author of *Origines Liturgicae*, and collaborator in the Oxford Movement, saw no irony in his summary: 'Newman laid the foundation, but Wilberforce built up the temple.' The temple was more in keeping with the spirit of the age, but it was a strange structure to rear on the ideas of the Tractarians. The irony is enriched by Isaac Williams's remark in his *Autobiography*, that the only writer of tracts who went to Rome was their leader, and he the only one who had been an Evangelical.

The general effect at the time, Dean Lake said, was to raise 'the tone of religious feeling which pervaded all the higher type of young men'. But the spirit of the Movement was dependent on doctrinal purity and on exalted religious ideals difficult to realize outside a monastic type of life. The defeat of the Tractarians left Oxford at the mercy of a newer, more vigorous liberalism than

[1] R. W. Church, *The Oxford Movement*, London, 1891, p. 348.

that of 1833, with Mill's *Logic* a marked intellectual influence
from 1843 on. This change was no matter of regret to Mark Pattison, who recovered from his period of 'Tractarian infatuation'
and could speak caustically in his *Memoirs* of the 'desolation' of
Oxford life by the Newmanites. He is supported by W. Tuckwell,
recalling the anguish of many at the loss of Newman, but 'the
relief of many more, who thought that Humanism and Science
might reassert themselves as subject matter of education against
the polemic which had for fifteen years forced Oxford back into
the barren word-war of the seventeenth century'.[1] Nor was it
secular learning only that brought the outside world to Oxford. A
satirical remark of Pattison's, referring to the railway construction
mania of 1847, is quoted in G. V. Cox's *Recollections of Oxford*.
'Instead of High, Low, and Broad Church, they talked of high
embankments, the broad gauge, and low dividends. Brunel and
Stephenson were in men's mouths instead of Dr Pusey or Mr
Golightly; and speculative theology gave way to speculation in
railway shares.'

Cox himself, a reasonably detached observer, summed up in
1868 the impact of the Movement on most religious people.[2]

> Without being a "Tractarian" I always thought we were under an
> obligation to the writers of the Tracts, for having maintained (and
> indeed effected) a greater reverence for our Liturgy, our Creeds, our
> Sacraments, and our Bishops; and that they wasted the great oppor-
> tunity, brought about by themselves, of raising our low notion of
> what is meant by "The Church"—by shooting *beyond the mark*, and
> by forcing things (in some respects desirable) too far, too fast, and
> in too arrogant a tone.

The *Via Media*, in short, was a happy term for the Church of
England, but less on the line of Catholic exclusiveness and doctrinal definition, with its concomitant passion for Ritualistic observance, than on the lines of compromise and comprehensiveness

---

[1] Rev. W. Tuckwell, *Reminiscences of Oxford*, London, 1900, p. 183.
[2] G. V. Cox, *Recollections of Oxford*, London, 1868, pp. 302–3. The curt reply
of the Evangelical Lord Shaftesbury to Bishop Wilberforce, when that peace-
making prelate pleaded against driving earnest-minded men out of the Church
as Romanizers, was that he did not mind men of the Hooker and Beveridge
school, but was against Popery. 'You are not aware how many Church of
England people are attending regularly Independent congregations, driven to
them from a whole district by mummeries and Tractarian Dogmas.' (R. W.
Wilberforce, *Life of Samuel Wilberforce*, London, 1888, p. 123.)

followed by the liberal Broad Church, represented by men as diverse as Thomas Arnold and F. D. Maurice.

While John over the 'forties was justifying the fears (or hopes) of those who earlier saw him as a Romanizing extremist, Frank was heading for the opposite extreme of Rationalism. Each brother was fulfilling the other's prophecy; one moved towards an infallible Pope, the other away from an infallible Book. Frank's early view of a mystery, that 'if we lay down anything about it *at all*, we ought to understand our own words', had brought him to reject the dogma of the Trinity. Reasoning from his own principle of justice, he had rejected the grim Calvinistic doctrine of pre-destined eternal punishment for sins. Now his views of moral goodness and his demand for clarity and consistency of statement drove him on to a rigorous criticism of miracle and prophecy, of the integrity and authenticity of the Scriptures, and finally, of the moral authority and perfection of Jesus. Certain German scholars receive mention—Michaelis, de Wette, Neander, and later Strauss —but only de Wette 'produced any strong impression on me'. The main lines of Frank's Biblical criticism and views on supernatural-ism he seems to have already worked out for himself. A visit to Dr Arnold in 1838, and a second visit in 1842, had re-assured him that freedom of interpretation, a refusal to bind historical scholarship and scientific method by a religion of the letter, could co-exist with Christian belief. His final position in *Phases of Faith* would have horrified Dr Arnold, but questions of interpretation and evidence were a ground on which liberal critics could meet. It is probable that Frank was ready around 1839 with materials for his first major work, *A History of the Hebrew Monarchy*. Certainly he was in the mood. 'I was possessed with indignation. Oh sham science! Oh false-named Theology! . . . Yet I waited some eight years longer, lest I should on so grave a subject write any thing premature.' (*Phases of Faith*, p. 138.)

Over this decade Frank's reputation grew, as scholar and teacher and lecturer, and as a writer on religion. His name was not as well known as his brother's, nor did anything he wrote gain widespread recognition of the kind later accorded the *Apologia*. But if we except the more general appeal of the *Parochial and Plain Sermons*, it is probably fair to say that *The Soul* and *Phases of Faith* made at least as much impact on readers of controversial religious literature as anything John had written to that date, other than a few of the Tracts. Frederic Harrison, for example, recalls the year 1849 in his *Memories and Thoughts* (1906). 'I read not a little theology, both orthodox and unorthodox. . . . John Henry Newman, the cardinal, and Francis Newman, the theist, interested me almost equally.' Henry Sidgwick, referring rather playfully in a letter of 1862 to his 'converted' phase, says: 'I was thrown back on myself to ponder whether I could possibly believe that God had (*salvâ reverentiâ*) shoved a book into the world, & left men to squabble about it *in aeternum*. In this state I fell in with F. Newman's books, *Phases* and *The Soul*, devoured them: & felt that I was really only wishing to be a spiritual theist (and a Christian if necessary).'[1] In the *Life of R. W. Dale*, the Congregationalist preacher is described as most influenced in his student days by the Evangelical publicist Henry Rogers, who was in an equal degree, 'the opponent of the catholicism which John Henry Newman represented, and of the rationalism which had found its most gifted spokesman in his brother Francis'. In 1854 George Moberly, Headmaster of Winchester and later Bishop of Salisbury, examined at length, in *The Law of the Love of God*, the threat to the life of the English Church posed by the diverse courses of the Newman brothers, and gave more space to Francis than to John.

The social and political reformer, the man of many causes, began to emerge in Francis in the troubled 'forties.[2] An increasing concern with contemporary issues is apparent as he ranged from a moralist's attack on Plato in 1839 for authoritarian dogmatizing and for the 'foul absurdities' of the *Republic*, to *An Appeal to the Middle Classes* in 1848 to work for reform in taxation through changes in political representation. The Chartists, he thought, had a genuine grievance. Very noticeable is Frank's grafting of a belief in secular progress on to his moral theism. In "Four Lectures on the Contrasts of Ancient and Modern History", given in 1846,

---

[1] A. Sidgwick and E. M. Sidgwick, *Henry Sidgwick—A Memoir*, London, 1900, p. 81.

[2] An entry in the Greville *Memoirs* for November 2, 1842, quoted by Halévy, paints a gloomy picture of the period. 'There is an immense and continually increasing population, deep distress and privation, no adequate demand for labour, no demand for anything, no confidence, but a universal alarm, disquietude and discontent. . . . Certainly I have never seen in the course of my life so serious a state of things as that which now stares us in the face.' What a humiliation for a nation which, 'according to our own ideas', is 'not only the most free and powerful, but the most moral and the wisest people in the world'.

advances are claimed on every front, and commerce is praised as the bond of amity among nations, bringing peace as well as prosperity. Alongside naïve optimism ('ferocious power like that of the old Caesars can never again disgrace the leading civilisations of the world') are realistic reminders. ('It is not pretended that any progress in Art and Science can supersede Moral Energies. But on the other hand, to the support of moral energies certain material conditions are required. . . . the mellow fruits of benevolence and mercy ill ripen under a wintry sky.') The main theme of these lectures is exactly what attracted John's withering satire, in "The Tamworth Reading Room", on Sir Robert Peel's opening address at that institution in 1841. 'It is to the advances already attained by Art and Science,' Frank declares, 'far more than to moral and religious influences, that I believe we must look as our human guarantee for the permanence of civilisation, nay, of morals and religion itself.'

A characteristic production of these years, revealing the humanitarian direction of Frank's religiosity, is his 1844 booklet titled *Catholic Union: Essays Towards a Church of the Future*. The attractive idea of catholicity, divorced from sectarian dogma, is to be based on the principle that 'the moral is higher than the ecclesiastical'. The flame of humanitarian sympathy must be 'the altar-blaze for the Church of the Future; which will be truly catholic, that is, commensurate with human virtue'. Even Communism, though Frank is for private property and against enforced partnership, is sympathetically regarded as 'one mode in which human nature is crying out for a new and better union than has yet been achieved'. It is 'the shriek of outraged humanity, protesting against the doctrine that man was made for landed property, and not the land for man'.

The way in which Frank's spirituality sought expression in a social and political context, a not uncommon nineteenth-century transformation, whether as ethical idealism or as moral theism, is clear in his stress on the importance to humanity of an ideal for man's moral nature. 'Our highest ideal is (whether we know it or not) a God to us; and if we devote ourselves to it, we are practical Theists, whatever our creed. He who worships no ideal at all, but lives for self, is the real atheist.' A Church of some kind is needed to embody and inculcate this ideal, for 'Whatever the personal goodness of individual statesmen, the political affairs of every free and enlightened nation will, on the whole, be conducted by a morality decidedly lower than the best of the day.' To this undogmatic Church, itself a free and voluntary association, a discriminating use of Hebrew and Christian Scriptures will supply 'a valuable storehouse of meditative and devotional thoughts', along with other sources such as the Greek and Chinese and Arabian. For we must not cut ourselves off from the past, from 'the roots which feed our moral life'. Administrative patterns of the new Church, and its social work of reform and organized philanthropy, lead Frank into some repetitious detail, of the kind that always threatens to reduce such humanitarian religions to social trivia (he would, for example, allow children to play on Sunday and eliminate night work for bakers). But the larger theme of mankind unified on 'necessary moral grounds' returns, in a passage which gives his summary of the past and his vision of the future. In place of 'an unholy Earth, an incorrigible World, an absent and offended God, an external mode of Reconciliation to him, a distant and future sphere of Affection, and the evidence of Hearsay . . . the new Religion will teach a venerable Earth, an improvable World, a present and unchangingly benevolent God, inward Reconciliation of the human heart in Him, a present sphere of Affection, and the evidence of personal Insight'.

A letter of the same year as *Catholic Union* shows Frank's awareness of the changes taking place in his interests. It is written to his friend Dr John Nicholson, scholar of classical and Oriental languages and translator of Ewald's *Hebrew Grammar*. 'I shall be more at rest,' he says, 'whenever circumstances put me into that direct conflict with current opinion, which I dare not go out of my way to provoke, and yet feel it to be my natural element. My antagonism to "things as they are"—politically, scientifically, and theologically—grows with my growth; and I believe that every year that delays change more and more endangers destruction to our social framework.'[1] Although some of the correspondence with Nicholson concerns the Berber translation on which Frank was working at this time, and other scholarly matters, much of it then and later is taken up with this growing social consciousness. The Anti-Corn Law League gains his support ('I think I shall be as fanatical as anyone about it'); he is opposed to the 'sinecure' Church in Ireland, though not in favour of supporting Romanism out of com-

[1] Sieveking, p. 139.

mon funds; he writes a paper urging fixity of tenure for cotters in Ireland, a question 'of even more interest than the ecclesiastical one'; he is upset over the news of Ireland's potato famine, which 'rings through our ears'.

Nor was Frank's humanitarianism of that theoretical kind restricted to general causes. In 1844 his old friend of Bristol days, the poet and essayist John Sterling, died, leaving six orphan children. Frank took charge of Edward, the eldest son, and for a time of his 'little brother, aged five and a half'. Reference to this act is made by Carlyle.[1]

Of new friends acquired [at Clifton in 1839] the principal was Francis Newman, then and still an ardently inquiring soul, of fine University and other attainments, of sharp-cutting, restlessly advancing intellect, and the mildest pious enthusiasm; whose worth, since better known to all the world, Sterling highly estimated;—and indeed practically testified the same; having by will appointed him, some years hence, guardian to his eldest son, which pious function Mr Newman now successfully discharges.

Frank's move to London in 1846, as Latin Professor in University College, a position he was to hold for seventeen years, extended the range of his acquaintances and activities. The breadth of his scholarship and the brilliance of his lectures ('We all felt that we had secured for the college an intellectual giant'),[2] at least until his controversial writings absorbed his attention, is testified to in the memoirs of former students. At the same time his somewhat nervous and formal manner held him aloof from them, in spite of patience and generous help in teaching. His humourless response to class-room situations and his eccentricities of dress and behaviour made him a bit of a butt to the non-studious, and

---

[1] Thomas Carlyle, *Life of John Sterling*, London, 1851, p. 226.

[2] Sir Alfred Wills, quoted in Sieveking, p. 108. Further evidence of Frank's reputation at the time of his move to London is a letter to Allingham, editor of *Fraser's Magazine*, in 1875, about some articles on universities. These were prepared as lectures in 1846, Franks says, when John Bright called on him to say that the Anti-Corn Law Leaguers were now free to work at another task, the founding of a great University at Manchester. Bright regarded him as 'one of those to whom they should look to give an elaborate and well-reasoned opinion concerning the curriculum of study and other important topics'. Nothing came of this approach by Bright, as the sudden death and bequest of John Owens led to the founding of Owens College, in later years part of Manchester University. (*Letters to William Allingham*, London, 1911, p. 244.)

tended to restrict his influence to the scholarly few. We hear from many sources of his rug with a hole in the middle pulled over his head for an overcoat, his odd hats, his trousers edged at the cuff with several inches of leather; also of such social gaucheries as inviting a few boys for breakfast on a cold winter morning with a Hungarian dignitary present, then, without introducing them to the visitor, plunging into conversation with an abrupt, 'I have never been able to understand, Herr Vukovich, how it is that you have never introduced the Bactrian camel into Hungary.'

The appointment to 'the godless institution of Gower Street', the non-sectarian college founded as the University of London in 1828, is a comment on Frank's growing reputation as a rationalist as well as a scholar. The feeling raised over this major break-through in freeing higher education from religious control is revealed in a *Quarterly Review* article. 'Every mode of instruction which so teaches learning, science or art as to make them seem all in all and fails to connect them with the higher object of all education, the fitting man for his ultimate destiny, we consider to be both incomplete and pernicious.'[1] Even the liberal Dr Arnold resigned in 1838 because, while approving the admission of Dissenters, he could not tolerate the lack of formal Christian in-struction and the admission of Jews, Unitarians, and other 'in-fidels'. Such comprehensiveness had for Frank become the sign of the truly religious person. He also helped promote Bedford College for Women; according to Margaret Tuke, the College historian, he was the most important influence after the pioneer founder, Mrs Elizabeth Reid. But the storm he raised over the dismissal of a colleague with unorthodox views, and the notoriety the publica-tion of *Phases of Faith* brought him, made the College Board accept his letter of resignation with relief. Conscious of the double pre-judice of the public against a non-sectarian college for women, the Board wished to keep a balance among the members of its staff. An advertisement on this subject by Frank shows a rare vein of irony. 'Wanted, a Professor of Physical Geography . . . who must not be a Deist, nor a Puseyite, nor a Unitarian, nor a Roman Catholic. A liberal Churchman or Quaker will be acceptable, if not too deep in Rationalism.'

Frank's interest in education was keen, and productive of definite and original views. 'I hope,' he said to Nicholson, 'you

[1] In W. L. Mathieson, *English Church Reform, 1815–40*, London, 1923, p. 209.

will not bother your little boy with any foreign language too soon. *Soak* him well and long in his native English, or he will never come to any good, I fear. If he sees a father in love with German, he will of himself quite early take to it.' Latin and Greek, he came to believe, were better taken at a later stage of a student's development than the current practice dictated, and then dealt with as spoken languages. To interest the boys, he added in a paper on "Modern Latin" in 1862, 'we want what I may call a Latin novel or romance—that is, a pleasing *tale of fiction* which shall convey numerous Latin words which do not easily find a place in poetry, history, or philosophy. Nothing has struck me as being so much to the purpose as an imitation of the story of Robinson Crusoe, which brings in much that is technical to special occupations—as in nautical affairs—carpentering, fowling, pottery, basket-weaving, agriculture, etc.' Frank did not get around to this project until 1884, a comment at least on undiminished energy, but he tried his hand at a Latin version of Hiawatha in 1862. (See Appendix A.)

Keenness of intellect, purity of character, and kindliness of disposition—these qualities in Frank were offset by the lack of a sense of humour, or of proportion, and by a deficiency in imagination that explains phrases like 'curious literalness' used of him even by his friend Martineau. Such a blended judgment is seen in a note for May 22, 1847, in Caroline Fox's *Memories of Old Friends*. 'Called on Frank Newman, and were soon in the presence of a thin, acute-looking man, oddly simple, almost quaint in his manner, but with a sweetness in his expression which I had not at all expected. He was as cordial as possible, but in a curiously measured way.'

There is little in the way of family reference in this period, beyond a brief mention of a visit to Harriet in 1843, and a sarcastic comment by John in a letter of July 11, 1846. 'My brother is coming to see me at Maryvale. I saw him yesterday. Why should he come? I think he has some obscure idea he can decide whether there are thumb-screws and the like at Maryvale.' A correspondence with Arthur Hugh Clough in 1847 is of some interest, in view of Clough's coming appointment, in October of 1849, as Principal of University Hall in London.[1] Frank reproaches Clough

---

[1] MS Letters to Clough, at the Bodleian Library. Clough held the appointment for only two years. Frank was himself Principal of University Hall from February to November of 1848.

for a certain Oxford condescension towards the institution known
to its enemies as 'the Gower Street Lecture Rooms'. From a
fellow sceptic, who had also surrendered an Oxford Fellowship for
conscience's sake, he expects more sympathy with the aims and
nature of University College. Religious bigotries as well as ex-
pense made it difficult to establish residences. And Frank is not so
sure that he agrees with Clough as to the moral training they give.
'For myself I must confess, (what I have not dared to put down in
print,) that I look back to my mother, grandmother, and sisters
for my moral training, and to a certain clerical friend for spiritual
benefit (wholly unconnected with my college), but that I am unconscious of any good of this sort I got from my college tutors,
though two of them were highly respectable men, and with one I
often had religious talk.' There is some hope of having a residence.
'At this moment, liberal Unitarians have subscribed £9000 . . .
towards a Hall in which all shall be admissible without respect of
creed, but where there shall be domestic worship, but not compulsory, and lectures on Ecclesiastical history and other subjects
which are inadmissible into the general course.'

But the attitude of Churchmen and Dissenters alike made co-
operation seem further off than ever. Frank dismisses the 'idle
janglings which . . . will vanish with the progress of knowledge',
and turns from the matter of residences to the larger issue raised.
'The great reason why bigots deprecate worldly co-operation with
heretics, is *because* such co-operation softens animosity and begets
friendly feeling. Among ourselves, I believe we could easily effect
compromise sufficient for religious union; but each has to propitiate the opinion of his own sect without, and so it will be until a
great intellectual revolution, already begun, has been consum-
mated.'

On this note, of bigots rejecting co-operation with heretics, and
an intellectual revolution hopefully envisaged, we may turn to a
brief discussion of the religious views of the two Newmans as
revealed in a selection of their works. For a few major contrasts,
three books by each writer will suffice: in John's case, *The Arians
of the Fourth Century, An Essay on the Development of Christian Doctrine*,
and the *Apologia Pro Vita Suâ* (written in 1864 but confined to his
life up to 1845); in Frank's case, *A History of the Hebrew Monarchy,
The Soul*, and *Phases of Faith*.

CHAPTER 6

Catholic and Rationalist

THEIR STUDY of historical religious materials resulted in two rather dull and virtually forgotten books, but the compulsive inner drives that sent the brothers on such divergent courses could not be better shown. In his *Arians of the Fourth Century* (1833), John set himself, by exploring the writings of the early Fathers, to explain the origin and necessity of dogma and creed, and to help the Church resist the modern flood of scepticism by showing how it had preserved Christian truth against heresy in earliest times. 'Every word of Scripture is inspired and available,' he tells Froude. When heresies arose, however, the Church in Council decided interpretation by authority and by the witness of tradition. The modern clergy are ignorant of the value of authoritative doctrine. 'We have no *theological* education,' he writes in August, 1835, 'and instead of profiting by the example of past times, we attempt to decide the most intricate questions, whether of doctrine or conduct, by our blind and erring reason.' Frank too complains about the lack of theological education, but rather with respect to the ignorance in English universities of German advances in the Higher Criticism of the Old Testament. In the course of his *History of the Hebrew Monarchy*, he makes two assumptions diametrically opposed to John's. 'We have no choice,' he says, 'but to proceed by those laws of thought and reasoning, which in all the sciences have now received currency.' Phenomena are to be explained by human causes, not by inventing unknown ones. 'True Religion consists in elevated notions of God, right affections, and a pure conscience towards Him, but certainly not in prostrating the mind to a system of dogmatic History. Those who call *this* religion are (in the writer's belief) as much in the dark as those who place it in magical sacraments and outward purifications.'

Applying historical analysis to the Old Testament in a spirit of 'free, critical inquiry', Frank finds the Pentateuch an assembling of piecemeal fragments, Deuteronomy a composition from mixed sources, and the prophecies a tangled web, especially those of 'Elijah and Elisha, whose adventures and exploits have come down to us in such a halo of romance, not unmingled with poetry of a high genius, that it is impossible to disentangle the truth'.[1] He is not indifferent to other qualities. A hymn of David is 'of such eminent beauty, that for the sake of it we can almost pardon the fabulous history in which it has been embedded'. As for the prophets in general, 'the most important and most honourable peculiarity' of their prophecies 'is their purely *moral* character'. But the truth he seeks is the truth apparent to unaided human reason, even if such truth will distress English readers, who still hold to 'current notions as to the immaculate character of the entire and indivisible Old Testament; as if it were a book defined and guaranteed to us by God himself'. The book did distress many readers. A writer in the *British Quarterly Review* for August, 1848, found Frank to be a combined iconoclast and Chartist, a destructive rationalist in the school of Strauss. It was, after all, a pioneering effort in England, described by J. E. Carpenter (*The Bible in the Nineteenth Century*) as 'a strenuous voice', lifted up against the current stupor, 'far in advance of its time', though inevitably superseded by later and more exact scholarship.

John's use of Church documents and patristic writings is of course different even in kind. He is concerned not to disentangle fable from history, but to recount the triumph of the Trinitarian doctrine, as it emerged in the Nicene creed, over the Arian heresy which denied the consubstantiality of the Son with the Father. There was, he says, a *need* at the time, a need to settle a metaphysical doctrine for the safety of the Church, by transcending the 'unintentional systematizing' of the Ante-Nicene Fathers. This systematizing being 'conventional and individual, was ambiguous', and so gave rise to heresies and produced schisms. In this context, John's way of arriving at truth is more subtle and sophisticated

---

[1] *A History of the Hebrew Monarchy*, London, 1847, p. 180. Free critical inquiry was not Frank's only weapon against authoritative interpretation. Sex and science apparently harmonized on the Song of Solomon. 'I had been accustomed to receive this as a sacred representation of the loves of Christ and the Church; but, after I was experimentally acquainted with the playful and extravagant genius of man's love for woman, I saw the Song of Solomon with new eyes, and became entirely convinced that it consists of fragments of love-songs, some of them rather voluptuous.' (*Phases of Faith*, p. 140.)

than Frank's. It takes account of the difficulties of translation from Greek into Latin, the prevalent use of allegory and figure (sanctioned by Scriptural practice), and the 'economical' teaching, whereby the secrets of Scripture are judiciously communicated to the unenlightened. For although much of ecclesiastical doctrine 'was derived from direct Apostolical tradition', much also 'was the result of intuitive moral perception in Scripturally informed and deeply religious minds'.[1] This 'economy' in conveying truth is for John a reverential safeguarding of the sacred mysteries of revealed religion; he earnestly apologizes in his book for 'venturing to exhibit publicly the great evangelical doctrine, not indeed in the medium of controversy or proof (which would be a still more humiliating office), but in an historical and explanatory form' (p. 137). But 'economy', or reserve, could strike a man of Frank's temper, as it later struck Kingsley, as an unfortunate term, suggesting simply a lack of candour in the interests of priestly power. Even John's friend Rogers, later Lord Blachford, was unhappy about it. If a new edition of the *Arians* is planned, he wrote in August, 1836, let Economy be made a 'little more palatable. . . . Sir W. Heathcote, who people say is a clever man, and I suppose a well-principled, has need of all his respect for you and apostolicity to help him to stomach it at all.'[2]

It is true John warns against the 'abuse of the Economy in the hands of unscrupulous reasoners', as he warns against the abuse of allegorizing, and urges that 'the obvious rule to guide our practice is, to be careful ever to maintain substantial truth in our use of the economical method'. He has many defences for the *Disciplina Arcani* (besides the blunt text, 'Cast not your pearls before swine'), and offers as examples the teaching of children, or the heathen, or the

---

[1] *Arians of the Fourth Century*, 5th ed., London, 1883, p. 179.
[2] *Letters of Frederic Lord Blachford*, ed. G. E. Marindin, London, 1896. Whately wrote to Hawkins in 1843, on the 'doctrine of reserve', that many well-meaning but not clear-headed men 'have confused together the necessity of teaching beginners the first page before they come to the second with the keeping back of Gospel truths from those able and willing to learn them'. Waxing warm over the 'Tractites', and Newman's *Elucidations* of Hampden's position as a 'tissue of deliberate and artful misrepresentations', Whately declares that reserve can be impiety in the garb of piety, imitating God and the apostles and prophets in judging who are worthy to receive and from whom shall we keep back 'the counsel of God'. (E. Jane Whately, *Life and Correspondence of Richard Whately, D.D.*, 2 vols., London, 1866.)

ignorant. 'It is surely no extravagance to assert that there are minds so gifted and disciplined as to approach the position occupied by the inspired writers, and therefore able to apply their words with a fitness, and entitled to do so with a freedom, which is unintelligible to the dull or heartless criticism of inferior understandings' (p. 63).

His fundamental defence, however, is the inadequacy of private judgment, of the erring human reason. For 'the sacred Volume was never intended, and is not adapted, to teach us our creed; however certain it is that we can prove our creed from it'. From the very first, the 'rule has been, as a matter of fact, that the Church should teach the truth, and then should appeal to Scripture in vindication of its own teaching' (p. 50). When we add to this principle the re-marks on prophecy—that 'the secondary and distinct meaning' is hidden, that from 'recesses of sacred language . . . the further truths deposited in them' are given up only when the literal text is fulfilled, that 'no prophet ends his subject: his brethren after him renew, enlarge, transfigure, or reconstruct it'—when we add further the frequent use of the word 'unfold'—we have the germ of the idea of development of doctrine, to which end 'creeds and teachers have ever been divinely provided'. Through the sermons and essays and letters of the succeeding twelve years the idea recurs increasingly. It emerges in 1845 fully treated, and with liberal reference to his own earlier writings, in *An Essay on the Development of Christian Doctrine.*

If this essay grows in part out of the principle of economy as ex-pounded in the *History of the Arians*, it also describes the method of reasoning by cumulative probabilities more fully treated twenty-five years later in the *Essay in Aid of a Grammar of Assent. The De-velopment of Christian Doctrine* is Newman's main philosophical and theological work, central to his career and thought, the formal presentation of his matured views on the Catholic religion and the Christian faith. It may also be considered an elaborate piece of rationalizing, on the part of a man to whom religion without dogma was no religion at all, and who deliberately wrote the essay to justify to himself and to others his imminent conversion. Actually, it is both. From wide reading and long and anxious thought, he was replying to the 'assailants of dogmatic truth', in an age when 'philosophy is completing what criticism has begun', with a theory to account for 'the facts of revealed religion' as presented in Roman

Catholic teaching. For himself, he was removing by formal argument the obstacles of Romish corruption and Papal supremacy which had kept him in the Anglican Church, obstacles which his mind and feelings had for some time found unreal. It was simultaneously a home-stretch tract for the times and a dry run at the *Apologia*. He needed, he explains later in the *Apologia*, to convince himself that he would not change again. 'So, I determined to write an essay of Doctrinal Development; and then, if, at the end of it, my convictions in favour of the Roman Church were not weaker, to make up my mind to seek admission into her fold.' Written steadily over the best part of a year, the essay brought no fresh grounds for hesitation. 'As I advanced, my view so cleared that, instead of speaking any more of "the Roman Catholics", I boldly called them Catholics. Before I got to the end I resolved to be received, and the book remains in the state in which it was then, unfinished.'

The essay, generally regarded as a classic in its field, is perhaps the most readable of Newman's longer scholarly works. The well-ordered argument never becomes mechanical in progression, the quotations from authorities are interesting in themselves and support the argument without taking over, the wealth of analogy and illustration makes for colour and concreteness. The tone is reasonable, from the opening sentence of the Introduction ('Christianity has been long enough in the world to justify us in dealing with it as a fact in the world's history')—to the cool comment (p. 236) on Locke's demand that individual assent to doctrine be made only on the grounds of logical proof ('It does not seem to have struck him that such a philosophy as his cut off from the possibility and the privilege of faith all but the educated few, all but the learned, the clear-headed, the men of practised intellects and balanced minds, men who had leisure, who had opportunities of consulting others, and kind and wise friends to whom they deferred')—to the realistic admission in the chapter on monasticism ('Yet it may fairly be questioned, whether, in an intellectual age, when freedom both of thought and of action is so dearly prized, a greater penance can be devised for the soldier of Christ than the absolute surrender of judgment and will to the command of another.')[1] Feeling plays its part in the eloquence, but the devices of rhetoric (and nowhere

[1] *Essay on the Development of Christian Doctrine*, London, Sheed and Ward, 1960, p. 286.

is his mastery of rhetoric better shown) control and forward the thought.

> We know that no temper of mind is acceptable in the Divine Presence without love: it is love which makes Christian fear differ from servile dread, and true faith differ from the faith of devils; yet in the beginning of the religious life, fear is the prominent evangelical grace, and love is but latent in fear, and has in course of time to be developed out of what seems its contradictory. Then, when it is developed, it takes that prominent place which fear held before, yet protecting not superseding it. Love is added, not fear removed, and the mind is but perfected in grace by what seems a revolution. "They that sow in tears, reap in joy"; yet afterwards still they are "sorrowful", though "always rejoicing" (p. 302).

So it goes to the end, when an emotional farewell to the reader concludes on a note of, for some readers, unconscious irony. 'Wrap not yourself round in the associations of years past; nor determine that to be truth which you wish to be so, nor make an idol of cherished anticipations.'

The essay falls into two main parts. In the first Newman examines Catholic dogma and doctrine as developed, culminating in Papal Supremacy, and analyses the thinking process by which we may accept them. In the second, he sets down seven 'Notes' of true development as found in the Roman Catholic Church. They are Preservation of Type, Continuity of Principles, Power of Assimilation, Logical Sequence, Anticipation of the Future, Conservative Action upon the Past, Chronic Vigour (i.e. Life, the last Note he had tried to claim for the Anglican Church before giving up). Having already established the infallibility of the Church, he has little difficulty in applying these 'Notes' to the development of doctrine over the centuries, and so proving to his own satisfaction that the Roman Church stands where she did in earliest times. There is no corruption, for corruption implies decay, and after each dormant or disorganized period in her history the Church has renewed her life.

> Doctrine is where it was, and usage, and precedence, and principle, and policy; there may be changes, but they are consolidations or adaptations; all is unequivocal and determinate, with an identity which there is no disputing. Indeed it is one of the most popular charges against the Catholic Church at this very time, that she is "incorrigible";—change she cannot, if we listen to St Athanasius or

St Leo; change she never will, if we believe the controversialist or
alarmist of the present day (p. 319).

The first half of the book carries the more sustained argument.
What Newman has to meet are (mainly Protestant) objections that
the later Church differs from the early in doctrine and practice,
and that these lack warrant in Scripture. The latter objection he
had already met in the *History of the Arians* by the principle of
Economy, practised by inspired revealers of the (often figurative)
Revealed Word. He now gives himself more leeway by saying, 'Of
no doctrine whatever, which does not actually contradict what has
been delivered, can it be peremptorily asserted that it is not in
Scripture.' Meeting the former objection, to those 'corruptions'
which he had himself held against Rome while an Anglican, is of
course the reason for his theory, summed up near the end of the
Introduction.

> . . . from the nature of the human mind, time is necessary for the full
> comprehension and perfection of great ideas; and that the highest
> and most wonderful truths, though communicated to the world once
> for all by inspired teachers, could not be comprehended all at once
> by the recipients, but, as being received and transmitted by minds
> not inspired and through media which were human, have required
> only the longer time and deeper thought for their full elucidation.
> This may be called the *Theory of Development of Doctrine*.

This is, he admits, 'an hypothesis to account for a difficulty'. But
so, he adds, are the explanations of astronomers for the motions of
the heavenly bodies; the theory may be an expedient, but so are the
art of grammar and the use of the quadrant. One may well ask
whether this is a fair use of analogy, whether the 'facts of revealed
religion' are subject to inquiry, testimony, and proof in the same
way as the facts of physical science, whether one can, in short,
reason back in the same way from creed and meteorite to a probable source outside historical (human) experience. Even granting
an 'act of faith' in both cases, the initial assumptions and the kind
of authority invoked differ as much as the objects of faith.

There is little point, however, in pursuing the many analogies,
interesting as they are. Whether or not one is convinced by its
application, one may agree that a theory of evolutionary development, in arguing that what is explicit in later doctrine was implicit
in Apostolic times or in the Revealed Word, is both modern and

expedient. Applying concepts of organic growth or logical process, or both, is effective in proving that 'large accretions' are the 'very developments contemplated in the Divine Scheme'. But the further one goes in the book the more apparent it is that what really matters are the metaphysical assumption anterior to the theory and contained in the phrase 'Divine Scheme' ('Christianity being from heaven'), and the psychological assumption underlying it ('The absolute need of a spiritual supremacy is at present the strongest of arguments in favour of the fact of its supply'). These blend into the religious attitude of worshipful acceptance of Supreme Mysteries as embodied in dogma, and make inescapable the logic of the inference: 'If Christianity is both social and dogmatic, and intended for all ages, it must humanly speaking have an infallible expounder.' The main assumption behind the theory of development is apparent in the words, 'whereas Revelation is a heavenly gift, He who gave it virtually has not given it, unless He has also secured it from perversion and corruption' (p. 67); the assumed *need* for dogmatic authority, and the thinking which accepts it, are clear in a later passage. 'Our dearest interests, our personal welfare, our property, our health, our reputation, we freely hazard, not on proof, but on a simple probability, which is sufficient for our conviction, because prudence dictates to us so to take it. We must be content to follow the law of our being in religious matters as well as in secular' (p. 84). The phrase, 'the law of our being', is Spinozist, but hardly the application.

There are passages in Part Two which elaborate the need for inspired and even infallible interpretation: ('. . . it may be granted that the spontaneous process which goes on within the mind itself is higher and choicer than that which is logical; for the latter, being scientific, is common property . . .'); the Church's 'most subtle and powerful method of proof, whether in ancient or modern times, is the mystical sense', especially in dealing with dogma ('supernatural truths irrevocably committed to human language'). But a slightly longer passage, on the supremacy of faith, may do to conclude with. It sums up the reasons for believing, and the need to believe, in a way that suggests Browning may have read these words before writing *Bishop Blougram's Apology*.

The principle . . . is of the following kind:—That belief in Christianity is in itself better than unbelief; that faith, though an intellectual action, is ethical in its origin; that it is safer to believe; that we must begin with believing; that as for the reasons of believing, they are for the most part implicit, and need be but slightly recognized by the mind that is under their influence; that they consist moreover rather of presumptions and ventures after the truth than of accurate and complete proofs; and that probable arguments, under the scrutiny and sanction of a prudent judgment, are sufficient for conclusions which we even embrace as most certain, and turn to the most important uses (p. 236).

Frank's book *The Soul* (1849) has been described as a study in religious psychology. Martineau called it 'a milestone in my spiritual life'. It too is a search for safeguards to spiritual truth, but with church and dogma and doctrine discarded, the search carries inward, and the individual is on his own. That it is the opposite of John's book is evident in the full title, *The Soul, Its Sorrows and Aspirations: An Essay Towards the Natural History of the Soul as the True Basis of Theology*. The contrast is even clearer in a sentence from the preface. Frank declares that the idea of an arbitrary 'external authority' in morals has faded away, because 'in the later stages of mental culture it is clearly discerned that Ethics, as a science, is as unchangeable as the ethical nature of man'. He then adds: 'So also, that in spiritual things each worshipper sees by a light within him, and is directly dependent on God, not on his fellow-men, is an axiom pervading the thought of every New Testament writer.' Ironically, his object in writing is set forth partly in words that could have been used by John. It is to 'show those who know not on what to rest their faith, to what quarter they must look for solid ground', and so save them 'from the desolating negations which are abroad'. But he will be even more rewarded, Frank continues, if he has 'stimulated independent thought in men of holy feeling and devout practice', and has 'made them meditate solemnly on the insufficiency of our present Theology to evangelize any portion of the professedly unbelieving world'.[1] For 'our misery has been, that the men of thought have no religious enthusiasm, and the enthusiastically religious shrink from continuous and searching thought, and this must go on until our Theology is shifted away from its present basis' (p. 244).

The *Zeitgeist* speaks clearly through Frank in his avowal that his aim is scientific—a study of the nature and growth of the soul, and the discovery of a method for ascertaining spiritual truths. He

[1] *The Soul*, London, 1905, p. 40.

adopts as his first principle, that 'no higher arbiter of truth is accessible to man, than the mind of man'. It speaks too, in firm Victorian accents, in his belief in the universality of moral law, with general propositions operative in collective human nature, even though experience and reasoning help to develop specific moral truths. These are his assumptions, along with the basic assumption that there is a separate and distinct 'side of human nature upon which we are in contact with the Infinite, and with God, the Infinite Personality; in the Soul therefore alone is it possible to know God'.

There are two ways in which Frank's attempt at 'scientific' analysis proceeds. First is a classifying of eight 'elementary phenomena' (one thinks of John's seven Notes), sentiments which mark the development of the soul. These are Awe, Wonder, Admiration, Sense of Order, Sense of Design, Sense of Goodness, Sense of Wisdom, Reverence. The first three are 'affections', with which religion begins. The next four bring in the concept of a personal Deity, but they belong rather to the intellect than to the soul. The old argument from design Frank tries to salvage by limiting it to a general sense of universal mind, impressed on us by fitness to function, and by rejecting such 'fantastical' particularities as shown in the report of a 'well-known engineer, who before a Parliamentary Committee expressed his opinion, that "large rivers were intended to feed navigable canals" '. The old moral difficulty with the belief in Divine Goodness he tries to meet by arguing that evil is transitory, and that 'pain and suffering undoubtedly are among God's most efficacious means for perfecting all His creatures, and, not least, man' (p. 101). The sign of the awakened soul is '*Reverence* towards the mighty inscrutable Being whom we have discerned in the Universe'. The more elevated the standard of human morals, the more elevated will be the ideas of God's moral nature, until the link is forged between the conscience and the soul. A child's love and reverence for a tender and wise parent exhibits 'the principal actions of the religious soul'. So the man's living faith will mean a sense of personal relationship with this Person, this Father, realized in love, joy, peace. 'A man can but adore his own highest Ideal; to forbid this is to forbid all religion to him.' This worship, unlike the old polytheism, and the new Ecclesiolatry and Bibliolatry, runs no risk of idolatry.

It is unlikely that Frank's 'demonstration' will impress anyone as 'scientific', or as more convincing than his fanciful speculations about the masculine-feminine principle, with the soul becoming a woman (the feminine type being higher) in order to enter into the 'highest spiritual blessedness'. It is when he analyses the sense of sin, of spiritual progress, of personal relations with something higher and more inclusive than oneself (to use Reinhold Niebuhr's phrase), as facts of individual religious experience, that we recognize a genuine and often moving witness, recording and revealing states of mind and feeling. 'To despise wide-spread enduring facts', says Frank, 'is not philosophic; and when they conduce to power of goodness and inward happiness, it might be wise to learn the phenomena by personal experience, *before* theorizing about them' (p. 196). William James accepted the force of this as argument, if not as demonstration, and took over Frank's distinction between 'once born' and 'twice born' in *The Varieties of Religious Experience*. (Modern Library edition, p. 79.)

The reader can follow Frank when he says, 'We need to see and know something for ourselves, and to learn to feed ourselves spiritually,' not to become little Christs or Pauls, or even little Homers, but to achieve 'the expansion of individual life'. Or when he says: 'There is no war between the parts of the human mind: and (other things being equal) he who best loves God will with most untiring energy and singleness of purpose pursue whatever good work his genius has fitted him for' (p. 262). Or when he says that 'God has myriads of forms, but one essence', to the end that 'in all higher types of spiritual life each must at length shape to himself *his own Ideal*, and know what is his service' (p. 248). Or when he gives a humanistic breadth to his spirituality, and says:

> *He* works the work of God (even if he knows not God), who works unselfishly for a good end: thus also Faith in God is justly said to 'overcome the *world*,' or, to mortify all the selfish principles which are collectively so denoted. Now nothing is more unworldly than enthusiasm in every form: in Art, in Science, in Politics, in Trade, it is an inveterate antagonist of selfishness: nor is there any character for whom the worldly (or selfish) man feels so much contemptuous pity, as for an enthusiast, until some undeniably great result forces him to confess that enthusiasm is a powerful reality (p. 248).

The reader can follow all this, though he may not find it 'scientific' or even entirely consistent.

'There is no book,' Frank tells us, 'in all the world which I love and esteem as much as the New Testament, with the devotional parts of the Old.' But to take the Scriptures as 'inspired', and to draw from them a fixed body of dogma for an infallible Church, has done only harm. The philosophical ideas, even the specific virtues, of a modern age, must govern the interpretation of ancient documents and question the doctrines extracted from them. Frank is as intense as John about the two supreme and self-evident entities, God and the soul, and declares that 'Religion can never resume her pristine vigour until she becomes purely spiritual and, as in Apostolic days, appeals to the Soul.' He not only has learned, like John, that in morality there is no simple black and white; he also agrees that spirituality transcends and energizes morality. But he turns both the intellect and the moral sense to a destructive criticism of the old religious forms, for we cannot subject 'progressive knowledge to some fixed standard in the past', and 'he who knowingly sets Religion into contest with Science, is digging a pit for the souls of his fellow-men'. His evangelical fervour and piety, undiminished but transformed, emerge in the most individual of faiths, in effect putting the mystical in the place of the historical and miraculous. 'The upright and faithful soul knows and feels what things do, and what do not, impair communion with God; this is its great clue to its wrong and right; so it is alternately scrupulous where a moralist would be bold, and bold where a moralizer might be prudish' (p. 244).

Frank admits that, being in sympathy with 'the real Paul of the spiritual life', he will displease both sides, and will be criticized both for treating 'certain Christian experiences as a matter of fact', and for treating 'as unimportant those things which are indifferent to the life of the soul'. Yet the book made a deep impression and was widely read. Partly the response was due to a rare note of poetic imagery, as in speaking of conversion to belief in God ('the soul, weak and wandering like a storm-driven bird, learns to nestle in the bosom of the Infinite One, seeking peace and strength, until at length love towards Him is born within it'); partly it was due to a recurring eloquence clothing the personal avowal. 'The kingdom of God is not meat and drink, nor sermons and sabbaths, nor a belief in the infallibility of any book, nor in the supernatural memory of any man; but it is, as Paul says, righteousness and peace and joy in the Holy Spirit' (p. 340). No doubt the evangelical tone disarmed some critics, as the rational-istic criteria disarmed others.

In a review of the book, Arthur Clough admired both the knowledge and critical acumen, on the one hand, and the power-ful searchings of the spirit on the other. He found too much emphasis on the sense of sin ('Is it that in our time the conscience has been over-irritated?'), and was dubious about finding in phenomena of the human soul reasons for believing in super-human existences. In all, he was not sure whether the book would be a novelty, or mark an epoch. Martineau, deploring the absence of a sound metaphysical basis for the morality, was responsible for Frank's writing an enlarged preface to the third edition in 1852. He made other criticisms as well. Yet nothing he had read, 'unless some scattered thoughts of Pascal's, has come so close to me, and so strengthened a deep but too shrinking faith'. To R. H. Hutton, on August 11,1849, he expressed surprise that J. J. Taylor, a pro-fessor at Manchester New College, showed such enthusiasm for the book, and wondered whether Taylor 'rightly apprehended Mr Newman's scheme of religious thought. But I never met with such discrepant criticism as this book seems to have elicited, whence I infer that, at least, it is a *real* and *living* book.'[1] John, without the pain of reading it, had no doubt as to the nature of *The Soul*. He wrote to Miss Giberne on February 7, 1850: 'My dear brother Frank has published a dreadful work, as I am told it is—denying Scripture *as a whole* to be true, denying dogmatic truth in toto, railing at some doctrines etc. etc. I can't be surprised—he must, with his independent mind, work out his principles, and they tend to atheism. God grant he may be arrested in his course.' (Dessain, v. 13, p. 415.)

Clough had declared of *The Soul* that the public, or 'many thousand quiet souls in private . . . are ready for all this, and

---

[1] J. Martineau, *Life and Letters*, London, 1902. Martineau, after defending the course of the liberal and rationalist, was to find that sectarianism is not confined to religion. In 1866, applying for a vacant professorship at University College, he was supported warmly by Frank and received a most appreciative letter from J. S. Mill, whose support would have been decisive. But Mill had to give his support to 'a disciple of his own school'. The Archbishop of York, also applied to, did not reply for twelve months, held back by scruples against supporting a non-Trinitarian. 'In this spectacle,' Martineau observes, 'of Mr Mill and the Archbishop moving hand in hand, under the common guidance of a sectarian motive, there is a curious irony.'

perhaps for more than this'. They got more the next year. If *The Soul* was subjected to 'discrepant criticism', *Phases of Faith* provoked critics, especially Evangelicals, to verbal violence. Such books, declared one reviewer, are 'symptoms of a spirit of speculation which may issue in a wide-spread infidelity'. The fundamentalist Darby issued a 354-page volume, *The Irrationalism of Infidelity*, with a preface to Frank recalling with sorrow the memory of earlier times, but stating that he must not spare this book, 'a mass of nature's ruins and filth'. A 55-page article in the *British Quarterly Review* for August, 1850, doubted that Frank ever was a Christian, and accused him of writing one of the 'most dishonest books in the English language'. An attack in book form by Henry Rogers, *The Eclipse of Faith* (mainly on *The Soul*), ran to ten editions by 1861; a second book by him, *A Defence of 'The Eclipse of Faith'*, called forth by Newman's indignant rejoinder, also reached ten editions by 1861. Martineau came to Newman's defence, but a 50-page article in the *Westminster Review* for October, 1858, entitled, "F. W. Newman and his Evangelical Critics", was the most impressive piece on his behalf. Though critical in part, it was highly laudatory of both the man and his works. With specific reference to Rogers's *Eclipse of Faith*, the writer proved by parallel passages his charges that Frank had been misrepresented by omission of words and by garbled quotations. He then passed to two articles in the *North British Review*, written under 'archiepiscopal influence', one of which had actually falsified extracts. In short, he said, Newman's critics had been guilty of arrogance, incapacity, and downright falsehood. *Odium theologicum in excelsis.*

Though the names of the periodicals suggest a prompt lining up of forces, the rationalist historian A. W. Benn seems justified in saying, 'For years to come the great issue between reason and faith almost resolved itself into a personal controversy between Francis Newman and the Evangelical party.' The judgment Benn offers in a foreword to the 1907 reprint of *Phases of Faith*, on this 'charter of freedom', gives the reason for the storm. In spite of his sincere moral theism, Newman's book was 'from beginning to end . . . destructive criticism'. As the first full-dress rationalistic manifesto by an English 'scholar and gentleman' in line with modern thinking, it helped release science from the prevalent obscurantism, and encouraged publication by such other rationalists as

W. R. Greg, whose *The Creed of Christendom* had been ready for two years. We are reminded of John's prophecy, that once started, 'a clear-headed man like you' will go all the way, and 'unravel the web of self-sufficient inquiry'. In going all the way, Frank had attacked Evangelical anti-intellectualism as vigorously as Catholic sacerdotal authority, and had added to his offence in his auto-biography by pointing to if not naming his early Evangelical friends.

Many of the 'phases' in this, Frank's *Apologia*, have already been referred to. In brief, his moral sense and critical intellect together carried him from the rejection of the Old Testament to the rejection of the New, including the gospel of John (thought of by Dr Arnold as impregnable), and finally even to a severe stricture on Paul, whose 'moral sobriety was no guarantee against his mistaking extravagances for miracles'. The Bible was found unsatisfactory for morality, though still a useful 'quarry', because it supports superstition, slavery, and the subordination of women. The idea of universal brotherhood is strong and noble, but what is love without justice? As belief in revelation and infallibility faded, so Christ and the Devil faded 'out of my spiritual vision; there were left the more vividly, God and Man'. Hence the rationalistic approach came to blend with spiritualistic fervour. 'Religion was created by the inward instincts of the soul: it had afterwards to be pruned and chastened by the sceptical understanding. For its perfection, the co-operation of these two parts of man is essential. While religious persons dread critical and searching thought, and critics despise instinctive religion, each side remains imperfect and curtailed.' (*Phases of Faith*, p. 232.) The elements of a 'modern' religion follow. 'Surely the age is ripe for something better;—for a religion which shall combine the tenderness, humility and disinterestedness, that are the glory of the purest Christianity, with that activity of intellect, untiring pursuit of truth, and strict adherence to impartial principle, which the schools of modern science embody' (p. 233).

It was typical of Frank not to stop there, but to take the next logical step. Having rejected the divinity of the Son, he was impelled to submit all the utterances of Christ to examination as those of a merely human being. In a chapter added to the edition of 1853, called "On the Moral Perfection of Jesus", he finds Jesus to be much less than the perfect man exalted by most of his

Unitarian friends. He finds vain conceit and blundering self-sufficiency in the retort, 'Render unto Caesar'; arrogance in the parabolic way of speaking, making a little wisdom go a long way with the many; a dislike of being put to the proof; a pretentious omniscience; a lack of good sense, in the advice to the young man to sell all he had and give to the poor; and finally, a wilfulness in exasperating the authorities to the point of putting him to death. He concludes that far from being perfect, 'in *consistency* of goodness, Jesus fell far below vast numbers of his unhonoured disciples'.

This was too much for Martineau, though he defended Frank warmly. He criticized Frank for analysing with such a 'curious literalness', especially the case of the rich young man. He also accused Frank of judging Jesus as a spiritual guide with criteria 'more severe than the highest standard compatible with the conditions of historical existence would require'. These are shrewd criticisms, and put a finger squarely on the inconsistency that runs through much of Frank's Biblical criticism. Martineau points out that Frank stresses the unreliability of Scripture, and other accounts and documents, as 'an assemblage of popular traditions —messianic ideas—beliefs of attendants and disciples', yet he scrutinizes them for credibility as rigorously as if they were authentic eye and ear reports. Did Jesus really claim Messiahship, asks Martineau? These statements are the 'retrospective imaginations and interpretations of the disciples'. To Martineau, Jesus appears 'the highest of realities', and 'every departure from him as the essential Type of spiritual perfection seems to me a declension to something lower'. The main point is that God may speak through 'our moral perceptions and affections,—according to the manner of Art, by creation of spiritual Beauty, rather than after the type of Science, by logical delivery of truth'.[1] In short Martineau was accusing Frank of a lack of imagination, leading him to over-emphasize the role of the logical intellect in attaining to truth.

This could not be said of his brother's spiritual autobiography, the *Apologia Pro Vita Suâ*, where in looser form is evident the process described in *The Development of Christian Doctrine*, one proposition leading to another by 'fresh evolutions from the original idea' until 'what was an impression on the Imagination has become a system or creed in the Reason'. The primacy and

[1] Review of *Phases of Faith* in the *Prospective Review*, August, 1850.

supremacy of the imagination is attested in the *Apologia* from the early years when 'my imagination ran on unknown influences, on magical powers, and talismans', and when 'childish imaginations' made 'me rest in the thought of two, and two only, supreme and luminously self-evident beings, myself and my Creator'. At the time of his conversion John accepted the idea that the Pope was Antichrist. 'My imagination was stained by the effects of this doctrine up to the year 1843; it had been obliterated from my reason and judgment at an earlier date, but the thought remained upon me as a sort of false conscience.' The propositions that clothed these imaginations are set down as the inspiration behind John's drive to restore full Anglo-Catholicism. These are, (1) the dogmatic principle, proceeding from the fact of a Supreme Being; (2) the sacramental channels for 'invisible grace', and the episcopal system; (3) the anti-Roman prejudice, which led to a 'conflict between reason and affection'. Reason lost, as it laboured through scholarship and argument to reconstruct an Anglican home for the first two principles, and recovered itself in the service of the imagination. 'As in 1840 I listened to the rising doubt in favour of Rome, now I listened to the waning doubt in favour of the English Church.' The first two propositions, following upon this one major adjustment, were elaborated in the *Essay on the Development of Christian Doctrine*, and the 'system or creed' was complete.

Bringing in the *Apologia* at this stage has been justified on the grounds of the years and events it narrates; as with *Phases of Faith*, frequent reference to it has already been made. 'Detached from the context in which it originally stood' (the controversy with Kingsley), as Newman's preface to the second edition puts it, the book invites comparison with his brother's. Even without the dramatic setting of the clash of personalities and the triumph over a clumsy adversary, its superiority as a literary composition is evident. The organized continuity of development, the wealth of local and personal detail, the lucid yet allusive and varied style, all maintain a narrative interest, and, in the case of a sympathetic reader, a degree of emotional involvement. Frank tends to overlap and digress, and to get stalled at times in the minutiae of textual or doctrinal comment. Yet the thought is clear and the style has vigour, and the spectacle of a questioning mind working its painful way to a position of lonely integrity can hold the reader. To some extent, *Phases of Faith* has faded because of the very strenuousness of its battling for opinions long since conceded or transformed or forgotten. The *Apologia*, in an increasingly sceptical and secular age, continues to have the novelty of a challenge to modern beliefs and assumptions, to remind those who need answers that answers are available, and to yield a romantic-antiquarian interest to students in Victorian prose courses.

PART THREE

TO THE 1890's

CHAPTER 7

The Highway

IN NOVEMBER of 1844, John Henry Newman wrote to Henry Edward Manning, another future convert and Cardinal. Though he would not move for 'a long time yet', he would do so when he reached a firm conviction that the Church of England was in a state of schism, and that salvation lay with Rome. 'And this most serious feeling is growing on me, viz., that the reasons for which I believe *as much* as our system teaches, must lead me to believe more, and not to believe more, is to fall back into scepticism.' The compulsive drive to religious certainty is here, and the distrust of mere reason as offering dusty answers, attitudes which explain an impatient remark by Connop Thirlwall in 1867. 'I believe him to be at bottom far more sceptical than his brother Francis; and the extravagant credulity with which he accepts the wildest Popish legends is, as it appears to me, only another side of his bottomless unbelief.' (*Letters Literary and Theological*, p. 260.) Also evident in Newman's statement is the instinctive need for authority, which took him, with the payment of a few tolls, from the Anglican way into the Roman road. Yet his relief at getting into the high road was premature; there were still tolls to pay.

Newman could hardly be blamed if he entered the Roman Catholic Church with great expectations. His reputation and scholarship and influence were such that his conversion, preceded and accompanied by the conversion of friends and disciples, raised eager hopes in Bishop Wiseman and at Rome that a wave of Anglicans would follow, even extravagant hopes that a return of England to the true Church was imminent. Newman himself did not encourage such visions, nor did he wish his value to Catholicism to be measured by the number of conversions. His letters tell of the sense of peace and fulfilment that had come to him personally; they tell also of coldness and suspicion, and of attacks upon his ideas, especially upon the doctrine of development. His example and powers of persuasion would, he knew, be influential in making converts. But he conceived his active role to be that of teacher and preacher and writer, making an intellectual and spiritual impact by talents already matured and proven. 'To me,' he wrote in his *Journals* for 1859–79, 'conversions were not the first thing, but the edification of Catholics.' He admitted to a sympathetic Wiseman that he was 'rash and ambitious in thinking of a theological college', or of an offshoot of the Roman College of Propaganda, as his future work on returning to England. Yet the letters from Rome show that some of his enthusiasm for the Oratorian Rule lay in the simplicity and freedom that seemed to promise a diversified scope and influence. The members, he says, will have time to be learned men, time for reading and writing, for lecturing and disputation, even for 'the discussion which would be found in a mechanics' institute', so conducted that 'confession and *direction* would come in'.

It was characteristic of Newman to deprecate, in a letter to Cardinal Acton on November 25, 1845, the excitement about his move and the anticipations of zealous proselytizing, '. . . earnestly as I might labour (as is my duty) to minister in a humble way to the Catholic Church'. It was equally characteristic to have said a fortnight earlier, '. . . my line has hitherto lain with educated persons, I have always had a fancy that I might be of use to a set of persons like the lawyers—or again I might be of use to the upper classes; now London is the only place for doing this in. London is a centre—Oxford is a centre—Brummagem is not a centre.' Humility and patience were in him cultivated virtues. As the pages of the *Journals* show, they often fought a losing battle with the consciousness of unusual powers too often frustrated. It is this psychological conflict, in its various forms, that makes Newman so humanly interesting; it also explains his skill, shown in essay and letter and sermon, at laying bare the temptations and rationalizings of reader or listener.

There were many reasons for the suspicion and misunderstanding that seemed to Newman to block him at every turn, and led him to confide to his *Journal* in 1861, '. . . since I have been a Catholic, I seem to myself to have had nothing but failure, personally'. One reason was the reserve or fastidiousness that had once found Frank's Evangelical fervour distasteful, and now found equally distasteful the 'Italianate' piety, demonstrative and

JOHN HENRY NEWMAN IN 1863

FRANCIS NEWMAN IN MIDDLE AGE

colourful, of Catholics like Faber and his London Oratorians. A
funeral sermon preached in Rome for a young relative of Lord
Shrewsbury, 'in my own way, which was quite a novelty and not
a pleasing one', repelled Protestants by its matter and Catholics
by its manner. This response drew from the Pope the dry remark
that Newman was, he supposed, 'more of a philosopher than an
orator'. One recalls that not everyone at Oxford had been enthralled by the subtle and searching sermons, carefully written and
delivered without flourishes. There were some who used words
like 'awkward' and 'constrained', and criticized both manner and
voice. Added to his own feeling for tone and style was a conviction
that extravagance and emotionalism were to be avoided, as a way
of approach to educated Englishmen, especially by a religious
body slowly emerging from the persecution of centuries. 'I am
very averse', he said at the end of 1848, 'to the publication of F.
Wilfrid's sermon. There is row enough in the Catholic world just
now.' It is clear enough what disturbed him. The sermon
exhorts hearers to 'beware of representing [the Church] as abating
one jot or tittle of the greatest of those pretensions which seemed
most arrogant and most preposterous even in the Middle Ages. . . .
And again, beware of another evil, that of trying to throw aside or
to pare down what seems most faithful and warm in the devotions
of foreign lands.'[1]

Another reason for Newman's difficulties was the almost fierce
independence of mind towards living human authority, one source
of the manifold inner struggles recorded in his *Journals*. The
Father on earth, an image of that other 'self-evident being', was
a desperate need of his nature, to counter wilfulness and the
dangers of scepticism and to give the peace he sought. He could be
submissive, if sometimes at the cost of rationalizing his intellectual
position, and not without critical reservations, towards pronouncements of the Church conveyed through Council decision and
Papal decree. He could also be firm or prickly, as mood or occasion dictated, towards any lesser authority, even at times that of
Bishops. When Ullathorne, Vicar Apostolic of the Western District and later Bishop of Birmingham, tentatively broached the
question of his responsibility as 'visitor' to the newly-founded
Oratory, Newman was quick to assert his rights and privileges.
Supporting himself by Papal brief and Oratorian Rule (and

[1] Dessain, v. 12, p. 386.

characteristically reasoning from authority to reject authority),
Newman summed up his case in a letter of December 18, 1848.

> I assure your Lordship we have no wish whatever to stretch our own
> privileges; but as to the question of Visitation, we were told dis-
> tinctly by our Father Director of the Chiesa Nuova at Rome that the
> Congregations of the Oratory, *because* they are separate bodies, had
> no visitor short of the Holy See. He made a very great deal of this
> point, and wrote a paper for our guidance upon it. And this opinion
> has been confirmed to us by the independent judgment of a Canonist.
> And we have a Brief of Benedict XIV's, copied from the Archives of
> the Chiesa Nuova, proving it at length.

The language is diplomatic, if firm, in this exchange with
Bishop Ullathorne, but a cutting edge develops over the years,
especially as applied to the feud with Manning, the relations with
Archbishop Cullen in the matter of the Irish University, the
hostility of the egregious Monsignor Talbot, the disappointing
behaviour of Cardinal Wiseman. Even after the triumph of the
Apologia, Newman broods over the 'twenty years' of misunderstandings, frustrations, and misrepresentations to Rome. He compares himself to Job, and writes in the *Journals* for 1867, 'And now,
alas, I fear that in one sense the iron has entered into my soul. I
mean that confidence in any superiors whatever never can
blossom again within me. I never shall feel easy with them.'

In all this we are reminded of Newman's attitude to bishops
while yet an Anglican. He tells us in the *Apologia* that his own
Bishop was in those days his Pope, the Vicar of Christ, whose
'lightest word *ex cathedra* is heavy'. Before his Bishop he 'loved to
act, as it were, in the sight of God'. After the charges against
Tract 90, and the affair of the Jerusalem Bishopric, the attitude is
very different. 'The more implicit the reverence one pays to a
bishop, the more keen will be one's perception of heresy in him.
The cord is binding and compelling, till it breaks.' Where Frank
had passed a moral judgment on bishops as hypocrites, John had
passed a theological judgment on bishops as heretics. Each exercised his own judgment, but whereas Frank's kind of reasoning
took him inexorably out of the Christian Church towards the clear
light of free thought, John's kind of reasoning led him deeper into
the Christian Church towards the warm glow of infallibility. Each
followed a gleam—or a will o' the wisp?

A third source of Newman's frustrations, and by far the most important, was the meaning he gave to 'the edification of Catholics' that he saw as his proper role in the Church. Such activity, on Newman's terms, was viewed with alarm as at least presumptuous, at most subversive. It was a situation replete with irony. Driven by religious zeal to seek ancient authorities and become a reactionary in the Anglican Church, he was now compelled by his critical intellect to espouse certain trends in modern thought, and so to become a liberal reformer in the Roman Catholic Church. The one thing needful for Catholicism, he believed, was to be brought into the nineteenth century, to become intellectually alive to modern developments in science and scholarship, without of course sacrificing any claims to the exclusive possession of spiritual truth. Vis-à-vis the goatish Protestants, the sheep were still to be the sheep, only less sheepish. 'I have seen great wants which had to be supplied among Catholics,' he wrote in the *Journals* for 1860, 'especially as regards education.' To be called 'restless' or 'crotchety' for trying to improve matters was indeed hard. What did they know at Rome 'of the state of English Catholics, or the minds of English Protestants'? Affirming that 'from first to last, education, in this large sense of the word, has been my line', Newman sums up in the *Journals* his original purposes and his bitter sense of jealous opposition. 'To aim then at improving the condition, the status, of the Catholic body, by a careful survey of their argumentative basis, of their position relatively to the philosophy and the character of the day, by giving them juster views, by enlarging & refining their minds, in one word, by education, is (in their view) more than a superfluity or a hobby, it is an insult.'

Newman's efforts on behalf of Catholicism do indeed suggest a cross to bear as well as to hold aloft. As an Anglican he had invoked bigotry against liberalism; as a Catholic he found himself the object of bigotry. Even the popular and successful *Lectures on the Present Position of Catholics*, given at the Birmingham Corn Exchange by the recently made Doctor of Divinity in 1851, had an unhappy sequel. Appealing for fair play and exposing the roots of Protestant prejudice, he felt obliged to attack in the severest terms the renegade priest Dr Achilli, whose scandalous 'disclosures' about the Roman Church were delighting Protestants at a time when 'Papal aggression', in the form of the newly established hierarchy in England, had enraged them. Using evidence supplied by an article of Cardinal Wiseman's in the *Dublin Review*, Newman exposed the scandalous life of Achilli himself, for which he had been condemned and degraded by the Inquisition. The list of his seductions of women, married and unmarried, was impressive; he had even chosen 'the sacristy of the Church for one of these crimes and Good Friday for another'. The only scandal to Rome, said Newman, was 'that our Holy Mother could have had a priest like him'.

Achilli sued for libel within a month of the lecture, and the plea of 'not guilty' was entered. Wiseman's delay in searching out and forwarding, too late, the documents on which the charges against Achilli were based, meant expensive and time-consuming exertions to bring (naturally reluctant) witnesses from Italy. A biased judge and jury found against Newman, admitting only one of twenty-three charges, namely that Achilli 'had been deprived of his professorship and forbidden to preach'. The upshot of the whole sordid business was a triumph for Newman and a gain for Catholicism. There was no imprisonment, which Newman had feared, but a small fine of £100. The huge expenses of over £10,000 were paid by subscription raised among fellow-Catholics everywhere. Achilli was thoroughly discredited, and the revulsion among Englishmen, to whose sense of fair play Newman had not appealed in vain, is suggested by a leading article in the *Times*. It described the proceedings as 'indecorous in their nature, unsatisfactory in their result, and little calculated to increase the respect of the people for the administration of justice or the estimation by foreign nations of the English name and character'. The main impression left was 'that where religious differences come into play, a jury is the echo of popular feeling, instead of being the expositor of its own'. (Ward, v. i, p. 292.)

Newman had lost the verdict and won the battle. In this case, it is true, the bigotry was Protestant, but Newman felt keenly what he saw as hierarchical indifference. Ten years later, listing his many frustrations in his *Journals*, he does not actually include 'the Achilli matter' among them, but he refers to it as 'abnormal (except as regards Wiseman's conduct) in any life'.

The Corn Exchange lectures, combining the satirical and the serious, effectively appealed to the sense of justice and the sense of humour in Protestants. Catholics were delighted with their witty and powerful champion. But it was a different story with his efforts to act as an intellectual leaven, an educational force in Catholicism itself. Even the project to edit a new version of the Scriptures for Catholic use, put forward by Wiseman in 1857, came to nothing. Newman felt the honour deeply. He obtained translators, and set himself to write a *Prolegomena*, apologetic and philosophic in nature, which would apply developmental principles to the growth of religious belief, defend revealed religion, and confront the scepticism and agnosticism of the day. But a competitive American project, financial difficulties, and, Wilfrid Ward adds, pressure from a bookseller overstocked with the old Douai version, led to abandonment of the venture in an unfinished state. No explanation was forthcoming for the lack of support, and Newman assumed that in his case officialdom was only too willing to let an important project die of apathy and neglect.

There were three major matters in which Newman, attempting to be a moderately liberalizing influence on the Catholic mind, felt that he had not only been opposed but had also been 'misrepresented, backbitten, and scorned'. The first was his rectorship of the Catholic university in Ireland; the second was his association with the *Rambler*; the third was the attempt to establish a Mission or Oratory at Oxford. He reminds himself that God had permitted him to do much—to found the Birmingham Oratory, the first of its kind in England, to found the London Oratory, to found a Catholic university in Ireland. But these pioneering achievements did not compensate for carpings and suspicions. 'They are works of my *name*; what I am speaking of is what belongs to my own person;—things, which I ought to have been especially suited to do, & have not done, not done any one of them.' (*Journals*, p. 257.)

Newman was Rector of the Catholic University in Ireland for seven years, from November, 1851, to November, 1858, though he did not 'commence the University till November, 1854'. During this period he 'crossed St George's Channel 56 times in the service of the University'. The allegiance (and residence) divided between Dublin and Birmingham, the strangeness of the country, the local jealousies and hostilities, episcopal delays and procrastinations, a failure to consult him properly in the matter of staff and committees, a reluctance to give him formal public recognition as the new Rector—all these perplexities and difficulties led Newman at one point to think of resigning. He wrote with some asperity in a Memorandum for December 29, 1853 (*Autobiographical Writings*, p. 305): 'If I am intrusted with the commencement of the University, *I* am to be the judge what is necessary or not for that object.'

It took a Pontifical Brief to get the university under way, with Archbishop Cullen as Chancellor and Newman as Rector, accompanied by a false report that he was to be made a bishop. On this disappointment Newman comments as a narrow escape, 'I might have been in Ireland till now. I am ever thankful to St Philip for having saved me from this.' Another comment, on Roman persistence in the face of Irish disunity, is to the effect that his belief in Papal sagacity 'has been considerably weakened as far as the present Pope is concerned'. At the other extreme from such matters of high policy were duties hardly of a stimulating kind, if we are to believe Aubrey de Vere, reminiscing in 1896. 'I confess I was pained by the very humble labours to which Newman seemed so willingly to subject himself. It appeared strange that he should carve for thirty hungry youths, or sit listening for hours in succession to the eloquent visitors who came to recommend a new organist and would accept no refusal from him.' ("Recollections of Cardinal Newman", *Nineteenth Century*, v. 40, p. 401.)

There were other reasons than lack of timely co-operation for Newman's decision to resign. For one thing, the Irish gentry and professional people were as divided in their support and as pessimistic about the outcome of the scheme as certain of the bishops. For another, the English Catholics were not interested, and Newman had no desire to preside over a completely Irish university. But what seems to have tried him most was the attitude of Archbishop Cullen, compounded of the dilatory and the obstructionist. He objected to Newman's wish to bring the laity into the governing of the university, especially on the finance committee; he was alarmed at Newman's willingness to use able men of dangerous (i.e. nationalist) political leanings on the staff; he would not agree that Newman should retain partial residence at Birmingham. 'This was the main cause of my leaving, then,' we are told in the *Journals*, 'that I could not give to the University that continuous preference that Dr Cullen wished.' The 'main cause' can be otherwise stated. Wilfrid Ward sums it up as a clash of ideals, Cullen wishing for the University to be 'a new centre for enforcing ecclesiastical rule in Ireland' by a staff of 'Irish priest-professors', Newman wishing for 'a Catholic intellectual republic, in which literature and science should have independent status and be taught by lay professors'.

If the high purpose of establishing a flourishing university for enlightened Catholic education met with frustrating difficulties, the association with liberal Catholic periodicals made Newman virtually a storm centre. The extremist Ultramontane party was convinced that the apostasy of the age could only be countered by an uncompromising stand on dogma and tradition, W. G. Ward declaring with zest that he would like a new Papal Bull every morning with his *Times* at breakfast. Ward was consistent in his extremism, having helped wreck the Oxford Movement before his conversion by his authoritarian *Ideal of a Christian Church*. It was natural that great things should be hoped of Newman, the leader who had left the Anglican Church because it had failed in doctrinal and ecclesiastical purity. But here Newman's sense of history and of strategy compelled him to a different course. In his view it was a time for alert, if defensive, response to the ideas and intellectual methods increasingly commanding adherence in the nineteenth century, a time to foster a liberal Catholicism. Accordingly, he undertook in March, 1859, the editorship of the *Rambler*, a lively though scholarly review whose editor Simpson had resigned under threat of episcopal censure to Rome.

Newman hoped to moderate the tone of the review and so gain hierarchical sympathy, or at least tolerance, for free discussion in the cause of ultimate Catholic truth. But he was not given time to bring about such a change. In four months he was asked by Bishop Ullathorne to resign, and though he continued to contribute for a time, the connection was hardly a happy one. An article of his own, "On Consulting the Faithful in Matters of Doctrine", was delated to Rome for heresy, a move which for years kept him under something of a cloud. At the same time the temper of those in control of the paper with respect to interference by bishops, and the tendency to take a line critical of ecclesiastical or even papal decision, made approval impossible. Another *via media* had failed, and Newman could only agree that the periodical should cease publication.

It did not die at once, but took on a new lease of life until April, 1864, as a quarterly entitled *The Home and Foreign Review*.

With no active connection this time, Newman found himself again in a dilemma. He sympathized with the aims of a review which commanded wide respect for its range of knowledge and quality of thought. Yet it continued to give offence to Catholic authority, and distress to himself in the tone of some of its articles. Formal censure was at last laid upon both periodicals by name, and Newman wrote a letter of submission to his Bishop. When it came to a choice between rebellion and acquiescence, he acquiesced. All that came to him from the association, he complained, was a full share of odium for the faults of the *Rambler*, and for his sympathy with its intellectual aims, 'to raise the status of Catholics, first by education, secondly, by a philosophical basis of argument'.

Even after the success of the *Apologia* the opposition to Newman's attempts at practical innovation continued (on any higher level than the establishment of the Edgbaston School in connection with the Oratory). The abortive Oxford scheme was conceived with high hopes by the man who was now, in Wilfrid Ward's words, recognized as 'the great and successful apologist for the Catholic religion'. Religious tests having been abolished, Catholic students could at last enter Oxford and Cambridge. Short of his ideal, an English Catholic university, this was to Newman the golden opportunity for intellectual training. What was needed, however, was a Hall or Mission, or an Oxford Oratory, where the spiritual welfare of Catholic students could be safeguarded. Lay opinion was favourable, land was purchased and an architect engaged, and for a short time Newman had the exciting prospect of returning to Oxford, still to him the centre of intellectual influence in England. But the fears of mixed education proved too strong. The Ultramontane Party easily prevailed with Propaganda, and the view that Catholic youth must be protected against modern free thought won out over the view that they had better be immunized by early exposure.

Robbed of his dream of Oxford, Newman wrote his poem *The Dream of Gerontius*, and showed once more that he could gain the admiring attention of the English-speaking world by his literary talents when he had antagonized powerful co-religionists by his ideas and actions. He had spoken against 'the hydra-headed prejudice' of Protestants; his experience of Catholic prejudice found gloomy expression in his *Journals* on February 22, 1865. Cardinal Wiseman and Father Faber had died, 'the two persons

whom I felt to be unjust to me', but 'their place has been taken
by Manning and Ward'. This combination, with Manning made
Archbishop in 1865, was strong enough to defeat a second and
more protracted effort to realize the Oxford dream in 1866–7,
after Newman had again demonstrated his powers by his published letter to Pusey. The tone of the *Journals* shows more of
resignation by then. If Manning and Ward have kept him out of
Oxford, 'the only place where I could be of service to the Catholic
cause', at least he has gained tranquillity and private comfort.
In lighter vein he once said that he had been in hot water so long
that he was in some sort boiled, and could justly claim to have
passed through Purgatory while on earth. He even criticizes the
Journals in 1870 as being one long complaint, as 'affected, unreal,
egotistical, petty, fussy'. Yet this self-criticism does not mean a
surrender of fundamental positions or of cherished grievances.
Anglicans think more of what he has written than do Catholics,
he confides on August 30, 1874. Catholics, especially Jesuits,
'think my line too free and sceptical'. Yet 'I *cannot* at all go along
with them—and, since they have such enormous influence just
now, and are so intolerant in their views, this is pretty much the
same as saying that I have not taken, and do not take, what would
popularly be called the Catholic line.'

Newman by no means exaggerated the attitudes of those who
opposed him. To absolutists, even friendly ones like W. G. Ward,
he was a 'minimizer', an 'inopportunist' (a later absolutism uses
'deviationist' and 'revisionist'); to the rather hysterical Talbot he
was 'the most dangerous man in England'. There were even
rumours that he contemplated a return to the Church of England. Manning, it is true, defended Newman against Talbot's
zealous attacks, but it was a somewhat cynical defence that could
say, when Newman supported an article that criticized Ward's
undiscriminating zest for Papal Encyclicals, 'This is opportune,
but very sad.' Newman opposed the move to define and pronounce
the dogma of Papal Infallibility, as inexpedient, ill-advised, and
a throwing down of the gauntlet to modern science. He also, when
the dogma was formally defined and proclaimed in 1870, made
full submission to authority. The opposition, of course, was what
his critics seized upon.

Newman's Catholic career almost invites the paradoxical summary that finding the shelter of absolute authority freed the critical

and relativist tendencies of his mind. When the enthusiastic convert T. W. Allies wrote *The Formation of Christendom*, Newman
startled and distressed him by coolly denying, in a letter of
November 22, 1860, that a Catholic civilization is superior *per se*.
Times differ, and the world is evil anyhow. 'A medieval system
would now but foster the worst hypocrisy,—not because this age
is worse than that, but because imagination acts more powerfully
upon barbarians, and reason on traders, *savants*, and newspaper
readers.'[1] The Church is for saving souls, and any system, medieval
or other, is only accidentally best at a given time or place to assist
in this purpose. Here Newman is merely urging a naïve friend, in
the privacy of correspondence, not to let his zeal cloud his judgment. But when this historical-relativist view achieved public expression it is not hard to see why Manning, while regretting the
gulf between the two most important figures in English Catholicism, was moved to say in 1887, 'If I have been opposed to him, it
has only been that I must oppose him or the Holy See.'[2]

If Newman's attempts to give practical expression to some of his
ideas alarmed conservative Catholics, his writings—philosophical,
imaginative, controversial—were of such service to his adopted
Church that even his opponents recognized his stature. Indeed,
much of the opposition to him was the expression of disappointment that such powers were not dedicated to the cause of the
Ultramontane party. For his writing reached a steadily-widening
audience, either as skilful Catholic apologetics or as intellectual
and imaginative contributions to the body of English literature.
He may have been a prophet without honour in his own Church,
but he exacted full tribute even there by becoming the major religious figure in his country.

Newman's most influential pieces of controversial writing in his

[1] Mary H. Allies, *Thomas William Allies*, London, 1907.

[2] E. Purcell, *Life of Cardinal Manning*, London, 1896, v. 2, p. 351. That
Newman had to defend himself from misunderstanding on two fronts is evident
from a letter to Mark Pattison on May 7, 1861, thanking him for 'a kind and
touching' inquiry about his health. He continues: 'You must not for an instant
so interpret what I said to you about myself, as if I could be led to think "the
Catholic theory," as you express it, "hard and stiff in texture," except in the
sense that what God has given is unchangeable and immovable. What I should
be concerned with is not the revealed doctrine itself, but its philosophy, that is,
its relations to other things. You must not think me over-particular in thus
writing—but so many groundless reports are circulated about me, that I feel
obliged to write this, as a matter of conscience.' (*Bod. Lett.*)

later years were *A Letter to the Rev. E. B. Pusey, D.D., on his Recent Eirenicon* (1866), and *A Letter Addressed to His Grace the Duke of Norfolk* (1875). His old friend, and successor as the leader of Anglo-Catholicism, had, Newman declared, deprived his "Eirenicon" of any value as a basis for Catholic union by his hostile tone, and by his tactic of treating extremist positions on Virgin worship and Papal Infallibility as characteristic of the Roman Catholic Church. He had discharged his 'olive branch as from a catapult'. Concentrating on the charge of Mariolatry, Newman accused Pusey of making a catalogue of fanatical utterances instead of referring to judicious statements by authority, of ignoring the circumstances of time and place, of making no allowances for the language of love in saintly characters. 'Good sense and a larger view of truth' can not only correct logic, they can also recognize the superstition that comes in when the burning words of holy and refined souls have stirred the vulgar. 'A people's religion is ever a corrupt religion.' Here enters a distinction that we have seen before. To say that no one can be saved without devotion to the Blessed Virgin is an untrue proposition dogmatically, yet 'if an Italian preacher made it, I should feel no disposition to doubt him, at least as regards Italian youths and Italian maidens'. The whole approach in the letter is typical of Newman strategy. Attacking Protestant prejudice for equating intellectual and emotional extravagances with Catholic doctrine, he was able at the same time to make an oblique attack on what he regarded as the unfortunate extremism of men like Ward and Faber.

In 1874 Gladstone, angered and alarmed by the aggressive attitude of Manning and others, attacked the dogmas of the Immaculate Conception and Papal Infallibility as a repudiation of history and modern science. He showed the special object of his concern in a political expostulation entitled, "The Vatican Decrees in their Bearing on Civil Allegiance". With his own doubts on the score of expediency resolved by submission to the fact, Newman could return to the subject of infallibility that was too difficult and dangerous to treat at the time of the Pusey letter. Again he was able to rebuke extremists while replying to a Protestant attack as misrepresentation. He skilfully makes Gladstone appear the rigid absolutist and himself the relativist, Gladstone having translated the decree as calling for absolute obedience, whereas his own translation is 'true obedience'. Neither Pope nor Queen, says Newman, can demand an absolute obedience that goes against conscience—conscience, that is, recognized by both Catholic and Protestant as a rule of ethical law implanted in the mind by God, and not, as modern thought will have it, 'a twist in the mind of primitive man', a guilt notion, an imagination, an irresponsible element in a network of cause and effect. It is the latter the Pope means when he speaks against 'liberty of conscience'. With true conscience no deadlock is possible, even on those extraordinary occasions when conflict may arise. 'Infallibility alone could block the exercise of conscience, and the Pope is not infallible in the subject-matter in which conscience is of supreme authority.' The prospect of such conflict is 'hypothetical and unreal'.

Here Newman uses relativist and developmental argument for Catholic ends, explaining that loyalty to the latest dogma is a necessary religious growth. Centuries hence a way may be found 'of uniting what is free in the new structure of society with what is authoritative in the old'. But now the revolutions in thought and politics ('No one can hate the democratic principle more than I do') make necessary the growth of doctrine into dogma, to be handled 'with a wise and gentle *minimism*'. There is no perversion of history, he tells Gladstone. It might appear (antecedently) that there were insufficient grounds to convert a doctrine into a dogma. Not so, however. 'This adverse anticipation was proved to be a mistake by the fact of the definition being made.' The reasoning that here clinches his argument may have baffled obtuse Protestants and agnostics, but it should certainly have removed any doubts about Newman that lingered at Rome.

Of less direct service to Catholicism than controversial pamphlets, but of much wider appeal, were the *Discourses on the Scope and Nature of a University Education* (1852), which introduced the Dublin experiment and which, under the later title of *The Idea of a University*, is the work of Newman most familiar to the English-speaking world of today. Anthologies of nineteenth-century prose, or of prose and verse, sometimes have a section of the *Apologia*; they almost always have one of the 'Discourses', usually that on 'Liberal Knowledge Its Own End'. For in *The Idea of a University* appear questions of perennial interest and importance in the philosophy of education as well as a consideration of the role of religion. The modern mind, conditioned to the monopoly of the word 'science' by investigators into physical nature, may not accept Newman's definition of Theology as 'the truths we know about God put into a system; just as we have a science of the stars, and call it astronomy, or of the crust of the earth, and call it geology'. It may find confusing the treatment of Theology both as a science to be studied in itself and as the Queen of the Sciences, the apex *and* the foundation of all knowledge. It may dislike the note of aristocratic condescension to merely useful knowledge, whether of manual operation or of business or of the professions. But it may listen, perhaps with increasing attention through the discordant clatter of specializations, to reminders that a liberal education is its own reward, that intellectual culture is an end in itself and has its *use* in that end, that unity as well as universality of knowledge is a human need, whether or not Theology is to be the unifying power. The largeness of theme, breadth of illustration, and rhetorical mastery have made the book a classic of educational theory. It has even been described, by Dwight Culler in *The Imperial Intellect*, as an attempt to absorb the Baconian sciences into a new and fruitful and reverent synthesis, much as the twelfth-century absorption of Aristotelian science prepared the way for Aquinas in the thirteenth century.

The *Apologia Pro Vita Suâ* has already been treated as autobiography, and its history is too well known to repeat. Enough to say that Kingsley's attack on the Catholic priesthood for advocating that truth need not be practised for its own sake, and on Newman as their representative, was a (presumably) Heaven-sent opportunity, and a restoration of sunshine to Newman's life. The boxing gloves of the muscular Christian were no match for the rapier of the Catholic apologist. It was, we read in the *Journals*, 'a wonderful deliverance' and 'marvellously blest, for, while I have regained, or rather gained, the favour of Protestants, I have received the approbation, in formal addresses, of good part of the English clerical body. They have been highly pleased with me, as doing them a service, and I stand with them, as I never did before.' The previous two decades, and especially the five years from 1859 to 1864, called the 'Sad Days' by Wilfrid Ward (Arthur Stanley after a visit in 1864 had the impression of a wasted life in a backwater), were now compensated for by one tremendous success. 'It was my lowest point, yet my turning point.' Though the opposition of Manning and Ward continued, Newman could feel that he was '*indirectly* doing a work', the success of which 'has put me in spirits

to look about for other means of doing good'. He had almost over-
night restored and enhanced his reputation in the Protestant
world, and rendered a signal service to Catholicism. True, there
were dissentient voices in both camps. Manning declared that to
many Anglicans the *Apologia* was a plea to stay where they were.
Rather different from George Eliot's indignation with the mixture
of 'coarse impertinence' and 'intellectual incompetence' in Kingsley, and her rapture over the 'beautiful passage' of 'sweet brotherly
love' in which Newman thanks his friend Ambrose St John, is a
cool comment by that cynical man of the world Monckton Milnes.
A decade later he wrote to H. A. Bright, 'I quite agree with you
about Kingsley. He literally rowed himself to death, and every-
body about him. How preferable was Newman's gentlemanlike
falsehood to his strepitose fidgety truth.'[1]

The major work of Newman's later years, *An Essay in Aid of a
Grammar of Assent* (1870), was the culmination of his thought, the
one piece written without an immediate stimulus. 'What I have
written has been for the most part what may be called official,
works done in some office I held or engagement I had made—all
my Sermons are such, my Lectures on the Prophetical Office, on
Justification, my Essays in the British Critic and translation of
St Athanasius—or has been from some especial call, or invitation,
or necessity, or emergency, as my Arians, Anglican difficulties,
Apologia or Tales. The Essay on Assent is nearly the only exception.' (*Autobiographical Writings*, p. 272.) The main themes in
Newman's writing, like the main moves in his life, themselves
illustrate his central doctrine of continuity by development. Just as
his discovery of spiritual certainty in his earliest conversion had to
be safeguarded by a search for infallible authority, so in his intellectual restlessness he could not be content with a philosophical
theory of how religious truth had developed, but had to press on
to a psychological theory of how we assent to such truth. Through
his sermons and essays run the questions and affirmations about
kinds of reasoning, about reason and faith, about degrees of faith,
until, holding to probability as his clue, he arrives at this late essay
with its tentative-sounding title. Judging by the addition of a
passage from it to the 1878 reprint of the *Essay on Development of
Christian Doctrine* (Chapter 2, Section 2, Part 8), Newman had

[1] T. Wemyss Reid, *The Life, Letters and Friendships of Richard Monckton Milnes*,
London, v. 2, p. 354.

never been quite satisfied with the semantics or logic of the earlier essay. Here now was his final attempt to rationalize the grounds of religious belief, a gesture to the century whose spiritual bankruptcy he castigated, and whose intellectual scepticism he detected, and had to sublimate, in himself.

Newman admits, and as usual he quotes liberally from himself, that most of what he has to say he said long before, especially in "The Tamworth Reading Room" in 1841. Life, he had said, is not long enough for a religion of inferences. 'To act you must assume, and that assumption is faith.' Neither letters nor science will suffice, for knowledge does not create moral life. Only faith does, and hence religion is a matter of revelation. 'It has never been a deduction from what we know; it has ever been an assertion of what we are to believe. It has never lived in a conclusion; it has ever been a message, a history, a vision. No legislator or priest ever dreamed of educating our moral nature by science or argument.' For 'man is *not* a reasoning animal; he is a seeing, feeling, contemplating, acting animal'. Life is for action, then, and to act one must give assent to the kind of belief or assumption that, from historical witness and pragmatic test, has in its favour the overwhelming probability that a (morally) fruitful life will result. The passage quoted earlier from the *Essay on Development of Christian Doctrine* also comes to mind here, with its slightly Blougramesque flavour of 'Come, come, it's best believing, if we may.'

One may wonder why Newman felt he had to make his position clearer, and whether he gains more than verbal refinement when he replaces 'inference' by 'notional assent', and his old term 'certitude' by 'real assent', and coins the phrase 'the illative sense' to describe the reasoning from cumulative probabilities by which the mind is led to positive and fruitful belief. Two answers are possible. For one thing, he wished to show that it *is* by a kind of reasoning process, not by mere passive asquiescence, that religious truths are gained. For another, he had to elucidate the nature of this process more fully as a power 'seated in the mind of the individual'. In a letter of February 5, 1871, he said: 'My book is to show that a right moral state of mind germinates or even generates good intellectual principles.' The priority, then, is given to conscience, which supplies premises of which the illative sense makes use even while it may be unconscious of their existence. And what in turn supports the conscience, or moral state of mind?

In a famous letter of April 13, 1870, where Newman said, 'I believe in design because I believe in God, not in a God because I see design,' he adds: 'Something I must assume, and in assuming conscience I assume what is least to assume, and what most will admit.' But of course he assumes a good deal more in *The Grammar of Assent*, viz., 'the providence and intention of God', a 'momentous doctrine or principle which enters into my own reasoning, and which another ignores'.

The book has witty writing, as in the chapter on 'Simple Assent', and it has an eloquence reminiscent of the best sermons, as in the chapter on 'The Sanction of the Illative Sense'. It is also unconvincing, as in the chapter on 'Belief in the Holy Trinity', where not all Newman's rhetorical questions, exposition of dogma, and arguments from analogy can disguise the fact that 'real assent' to a mystery, in spite of his denial, is required. But the moment this is said, one comes back, as in the case of the *Essay on Development of Christian Doctrine*, to such assumptions as that concluding the above paragraph, and that which ends the chapter on 'Belief in Dogmatic Theology'. The following sentence hardly seems to offer ground for meaningful debate. 'That the Church is the infallible oracle of truth is the fundamental dogma of the Catholic religion; and "I believe what the Church proposes to be believed" is an act of real assent, including all particular assents, notional and real; and, while it is possible for unlearned as well as learned, it is imperative on learned as well as unlearned.' On the analysis of thought processes, especially the extent to which emotional and intuitive elements influence 'reasoning', the *Grammar of Assent* is fascinating reading for anyone. On the question of assumptions and objects of belief, as Newman was well aware, and as his dialogue with William Froude a quarter century before had brought out, it is a matter of different kinds of mental constitution. On the two-way road of probability, never the twain shall meet, though they may avoid collision and learn to respect each other's right of way.[1]

[1] Writing to J. R. Mozley in January of 1891, Henry Sidgwick commented on Newman's thinking processes. 'The Cardinal interests me—always has interested me—as a man and a writer rather than a reasoner. I delight in the perfect fit of his thought to its expression, and the rare unforced *individuality* of both; but as a *reasoner* I have never been disposed to take him seriously, by which I do not of course mean that I treat his views with levity, but that regarding him as a man whose conclusions have always been influenced,

A year before the *Grammar of Assent* appeared, Frank had drawn, as against the argument for belief from cumulative probabilities, an argument for *disbelief* from cumulative *improbabilities*. The modern tendency, he said, is to disbelieve miracles *à priori* because of the results of *à posteriori* investigations, to display an earned incredulity based on 'countless disproofs in the past'. This attitude does not, however, justify a harsh dogmatism on the part of the physical scientist in saying that 'no *imaginable* testimony could prove that for moral or religious causes God might alter or suspend physical laws', a dogmatism not needed to confute religious pretensions. (*The Bigot and the Sceptic*, 1869.) John's reasoning does not of course depend upon miracle and dogma, but upon psychological and moral arguments. Yet it leads finally to the acceptance of a system whose authority rest on dogmatic pronouncements on matters of mystery and miracle. The sceptic's attitude to such systems was summed up by Hume in his *Dialogues Concerning Natural Religion*: 'A total suspense of judgment is here our only reasonable resource.' This was further than Frank cared to go. Though he told the 'bigot' that religious truth is achieved by that co-operation of mind with mind 'normal to cultivated nations, as already is the case with Science', he also warned the sceptic that truth is eminently precious, especially in religion.

The rather diffident full title of Newman's book supports his own view of it as opening up a line of inquiry for others by drawing together his cumulative experience of how far intellectual processes affect the grounds for belief. It was his last sustained effort. It gained the approval even of W. G. Ward, and together with the spirited counter-attack on Gladstone, set the crown on his public services to the Catholic Church. Honours came to him from both sides. His old college of undergraduate days, Trinity, made him an Honorary Fellow in 1877, and the new Pope Leo XIII finally dissipated the cloud which had obscured him in the days of Pius IX by making him a Cardinal in 1879. A letter of his in 1882 may, in Wilfrid Ward's view, have influenced the Pope to reconsider the question of Catholic attendance at the English universities, a

---

primarily by his emotions, and only secondarily by the workings of his subtle and ingenious intellect, I have never felt that my own intellect need be strained to its full energies to deal with his arguments; they always seemed to me to admit of being referred without much difficulty to certain well-known heads, to which the *generic* answers were known.' (*Memoir*, p. 507.)

disability finally removed in 1893. The return from Rome as
Cardinal was an English triumph, a comment on the change,
much of it due to Newman, over the thirty years since the outcry
at the establishment of the Catholic hierarchy under Cardinal
Wiseman. The last decade saw him, rich in friendships and in
public esteem, still active in correspondence and in guiding the
work of the Oratory. Physical decline was gentle and gradual,
until at the last, Father Tristram tells us, failing sight and insensi-
tive fingers made it difficult to say the Rosary, 'although he perse-
vered with larger and larger beads'. Even Cardinal Manning
called him 'our greatest witness to the faith', though he could also
tell a young friend in 1890 of 'ten distinct heresies to be found in
the most widely-read works of Dr Newman'.[1] The recollected
heresies did not prevent his preaching at Newman's funeral in
that year; the detested Catholicism did prevent brother Frank
from attending it.

[1] E. E. Reynolds, *Three Cardinals*, London, 1958, p. 245.

CHAPTER 8

The Byways

IF JOHN's early career suggests a camouflaged half-track inching towards the old Roman road, Frank's later career reminds one of Leacock's horseman, who mounted his steed and rode off in all directions. A constant stream of tracts and sermons, articles and essays, appeared in the second half-century on topics timely and timeless, fittingly represented in five volumes of *Miscellanies*. Volume 1 appeared in 1869, a selection of earlier pieces, mainly lectures, on Logic and Poetry and History, on Mathematics and Elocution and National Loans. Of the other volumes, extending the selections up to 1889, two show uniformity, the second being devoted to articles on Religion and Morals, and the fourth to Political Economy. The third volume, mainly social and political, ranges over war, India, imperialism, civil government, and the 'woman question'. The fifth, with fine impartiality, is a mixture of nearly everything in the Newman catalogue.[1]

One full length book on the subject of religion and morals requires special notice, revealing as it does the plight of the thinker who distrusts systematic theology or metaphysics and yet would affirm belief in a personal God as something more than a subjective emotion. At the beginning of 1858 appeared a book which Francis Newman thought 'considerably in advance' of his three major productions of 1847-50. Set forth on the page in a loose verse arrangement, and titled *Theism, Doctrinal and Practical, or Didactic Religious Utterances*, its purpose was 'to reinforce Truths Common to Monotheists'. It was enlarged and modified, as *Hebrew Theism*, in 1874. The work is evidence of Frank's earnest life-long effort to preserve the passionate intuition of God derived from Evangelical experience, along with 'the best' of Hebrew and

[1] Titles of items consulted as independent publications will be italicized, as will other collections than the *Miscellanies*. Quoted titles, unless otherwise assigned, are from the *Miscellanies*.

139

248799

Christian moral teaching, without on the one hand making any
concession to orthodoxy, or on the other sliding into secularism.
It reflects the need felt by so many Victorians, while abandoning
religious authority, to adopt progressive ideas and scientific
methods without sacrificing moral absolutes. Unhappily, it reads
at times almost like a parody of such attempts. In part made up
of inspiring utterances—moral, spiritual, prophetic—from all
sources, in part made up of humanistic reflections and humanitarian urgings, the book concludes with four sections entitled
Oaths and Affirmations, Cleanliness, The Rights of Animals, and
Adoration. Moral earnestness, clearly, is not enough.

The book did not lack favourable notice. In the *Revue de
Théologie*, it was described as 'un livre admirable', free of traditional Christianity but animated by 'l'esprit chrétien le plus pur'.
True, it had to be read 'a petites doses', but the reviewer hoped
'les Anglais reconnaitront un jour, qu'ils n'ont pas dans toute leur
littérature religieuse beaucoup de livres plus riches et plus
instructifs que celui-là'. To detect a flavour of French malice in
the last remark is not warranted by the tone of the review as a
whole. But one must, in the main, agree with Martineau, who
wrote to a friend on January 30, 1858: 'Have you seen F. W.
Newman's curious new book—"Theism"? If not, you must get it
and read it, though its form, I suspect, will annoy you not less
than it does me. I tried hard to persuade him out of it, and speak
to us in his beautiful prose; but nothing can move him from these
eccentric fancies.' Martineau goes on to a larger estimate of
Frank's religious writing to date which is both shrewd and generous. 'To the one half of the great religious problem of our age—
the *historical* revelation of God—he turns still a blind side. The
other half—the carrying of our cardinal faiths home to their seats
in human nature and finding their justification and meaning
there—he appears to me often to touch with a hand of masterly
experience. . . . The curious intertwining, as it were, of logical
intellect with tender affections and fine conscience, mediated and
harmonized by no ideality to blend the whole into one pattern, is
more apparent in this book than in any of his former ones.
Frankly he seems to me to be purer and more winning every year.'
In spite of his almost total lack of humour, even Newman might
have appreciated the pun.

A letter to John on December 31, 1857, shows us the inevitable outcome, fragmented if often fruitful, of the direction of Frank's thinking, best expressed in a title of 1886 as *The New Crusades, or The Duty of the Church to the World*. They still find it hard to communicate on 'deepest & highest thoughts', but he will send, unless discouraged, a copy of *Theism*, 'a book which is in some sense the work of my life'. Though passages may be antagonistic to John in 'the general idea', as much so as Paley's *Natural Theology*, the book 'might have been written to *underprop* Christianity in general, without entering on questions which divide Churches. I cannot call Atheism my *chief* antagonist, for the combat with Atheism is begun & ended too quick. My real antagonists are Pantheists, Materialists & (a species of the last) Immoral Statesmen.'

An earlier and longer letter on October 13 shows more fully the range of Frank's crusading zeal, the moral fervour which he brought to diverse social and political questions. Humanity, philanthropy, and honour may abound in private life, but 'the law of Right & Wrong is nowhere dreamed of as the first & vital rule to a Statesman. . . . To establish Justice as the primary law of Policy, would seem to me the most glorious of all moral revolutions, worthy of being bought by thousands of martyrdoms.' Is India in question? Isolated 'atrocities' of the Mutiny must be seen against a background of reasons for the uprising, which Frank gives, and adds, 'to wish our country to prosper in an unjust cause seems to me an impiety and a horror'. Is the Crimean War in question? 'I see that Russian pretences are hypocrisy, her progress subtle & dangerous, & her immediate cause against Turkey unjust: on moral grounds therefore I sided with Turkey.' Is Hungarian freedom in question? On moral grounds Frank sympathizes with Kossuth, and blames English ministers for inaction. 'But they never will ask, What is right? before they choose their course: though they may adorn their course with pretence afterwards.' Not a single government wishes to do the Right: '. . . a far deeper religion is essential in Christendom, before much advance can be made upon our present barbarism'.

The last two questions are yoked together in *Reminiscences of Two Exiles and Two Wars* (1888). Recalling his friendship with Kossuth and Pulszky, in the years from 1851 to 1860 when their search for moral and financial support brought them frequently to London, Frank declares that bungling and duplicity brought the three European powers, who did not want war, into the Crimean adventure.

He agrees with Kossuth that 'we brought it on ourselves, by unrighteously evading our duty of mediating for Hungary'. Austrian perfidy and Russian interference were not to be countered by English double-talk, nor Russian expansionism discouraged. In a sense the war was beneficial. 'If England and France had not fought it, nothing short of an equivalent war must have been fought against Russia by other powers.' But it was an unnecessary war, brought on by panic at the revolutionary movements of 1848–9, by the fear that confronting *any* despotism would encourage the peoples in their struggle for freedom. The lesson Frank drew from the European scene was that the conspiracy of governments against legitimate aspirations for liberty led to treachery and betrayal, and to the barbarism of futile wars. From the bungling of party leaders and cabinets before and during the Crimean War he drew the lesson that England must insist 'on depriving her ministers, and thereby her officers, from making war without previous public debates and judicious approval'.

John too had a fling at the Crimean War, in an essay titled, "Who's to Blame?" To him it was rather a cause for satirical reflections on red tape and jealousies and the elevation of mediocrity, as weaknesses inevitably attached to a constitutional monarchy and to parliamentary rule. Such a government was good for peace and commerce, but the price paid was ineptitude and lack of leadership in time of crisis. A Catholic, of course, must prefer so mild and easy a rule to the tyranny of 'either absolutism or democracy', and could feel that the 'bluster' against Russia was much like that against Catholics. In short, the treatment of the same event is so in contrast that Frank, with reference to other matters, is moved to sum up their differences in a letter of November 9, 1861. As John himself has said, 'on public questions we are sure to be on opposite sides'. Yet not from any fundamental difference—both 'judge of public events from their moral side,'—rather from 'our having seen and been impressed by different sets of facts'.

In the same letter Frank reveals another object of his political passion by championing the cause of the slaves in the American Civil War. He makes a prolonged attack on the South, 'which has *glorified* slavery as an eminently desirable *permanent* state of things', and prophesies victory for the North, unless France and England interfere. It is again evident that the brothers differ. On March 2,

1863, Frank urges John not to believe the *Times* on America, if
that is where he got his facts. On no subject is the force of moral
indignation that shaped Frank's political views more apparent.
He joined the Union and Emancipation Society, of which J. S.
Mill, Leslie Stephen, Tom Hughes, and Goldwin Smith were also
members. In 1863 the Society published a letter of Frank's to a
friend who had joined the opposing Southern Independence
Association. His friend had accused him of intemperate language.
On the question of slavery, he says, 'I frankly confess, though I can
manage to *write* with perfect calmness on these things, I cannot
speak calmly. My heart often becomes like a volcano.' Nor is this
mere emotion. He has gone through the facts for twenty-five years,
even forty years, counting his early interest in West Indian
emancipation. How can he be calm, however, when a Richmond
paper turns our world upside down by saying in print that every
man is an abolitionist and deserves hanging, 'who does not love
slavery for its own sake as a divine institution?' He is not practising
a 'new morality', as his friend suggests. He has applied it with
equal force to the 'baneful and detestable' English treatment of
India. 'Those who yield to explosive pride or crooked expediency
are the mischievous meddlers with state affairs, not those who
"preach morality".'

Frank's disappointment with Gladstone was in proportion to the
high hopes he had entertained, of England having at last a Moral
Statesman who would never sacrifice principle to expediency.
Writing to his old pupil and friend, the pioneering Anna Swan-
wick, he expressed in 1881 his pain at the Coercion Bill imposed on
Ireland.[1]

> I immensely admire *very much* in Mr Gladstone; so do you; of possible
> leaders he is the best—at present! and it is a bitter disappointment to
> find him a reed that pierces the hand when one leans on it. I fear
> you will not like me to say with pain, that only in European affairs
> do I find him commendable. In regard to our unjust wars he has
> simply *betrayed and deluded* the electors who enthusiastically aided him
> to power. . . . He has gone wholly wrong towards Ireland, equally as
> towards Afghanistan, India, and South Africa. . . . He knows as well
> as John Bright that Ireland is not only chronically injured by English
> institutions, but that Ireland has every reason to distrust promises.

[1] Sieveking, pp. 221–3. Translator, philanthropist, and feminist, Anna
Swanwick helped to found Queen's and Bedford Colleges.

Frank had expected 'a *higher morality* than from Palmerston, Wellington, or Peel' in view of Gladstone's 'undoubtedly sincere religion and moral professions'. The remorseless logic of the moral idealist is evident. 'Since Mr Gladstone cannot have *changed his judgment* concerning the Beaconsfield policy in Afghanistan, in India, or in South Africa, the only inference is that (from one reason or other which I may or may not know) *he is not strong enough to carry out his own convictions of right.*' It is possible to offset the rigour of such demands by arguing the necessity of political compromise. It is not easy to evade the truth in the terse summary. 'The attempt to *count votes beforehand* is fatal where great moral issues are concerned.'

On this moral theme Frank kept up a running attack over the years on all wars of imperialism, especially on such face-saving devices as calling a provoked uprising a mutiny (there being no 'possibility that men with skin so black could have a spark of patriotic feeling'), or calling aggression 'hostilities' and revenge 'self-defence'. He offered Bartle Frere's campaign against the Zulus as an example of an action taken contrary to orders and subsequently condoned and supported. He put the whole matter so vigorously in an article of 1860 called "The Ethics of War" that a footnote by the editor of the *Westminster Review* indicates dissent from the opinions of 'our much-esteemed contributor', and gives this as a reason for the article being signed. There has been some attempt to palliate modern war, says Frank, and to observe certain forms among great powers. But not in the case of Burma, Persia, China. 'We forget all our "Christian rules", as though, if these powers be the barbarians we allege, it can be right for us to sink to their level; or, as though we can teach them to observe the international law of Christendom by any other method than by practising that law towards them.' If Frank lacked humour, he could use sarcasm.

The article goes on to consider war in general, and the need for peace through international arbitration. But it is not enough to honour such workers for peace as Cobden and the Quakers, and to be sheep in a world of wolves. If we are to reach a time, 'when men will look back in wonder and pity on our present barbarism', it will be by virtue of an impartial tribunal rising above expediency and special interest. Governments 'will never initiate such institutions unless by public opinion and by the inevitable pressure of circumstances; nor is any nation in the world yet ripe to put forth such pressure; otherwise it would not be difficult to devise a supreme court, or rather jury, which would put a totally new moral aspect on war'. This modern proposal Frank pursues in *Europe of the Near Future* (1871), a pamphlet in which he argues for larger consolidations of power, able to control nations as magistrates control private men, or king's ministers control local grandees. His realism carries him to the next step of a necessary police force. Without this, no combatant will even allow his case to be tried.

For each fears moral damage to his cause from acting against a decree after it has been pronounced. Finally then the problem is not solved unless the arbitration be compulsory; in short, unless the right of private war be forbidden to the separate communities which now possess it, and be vested in far larger federations. These considerations show what development of international institutions is *to be desired*. Unless this question be studied beforehand, one shall not be preferred, if a crisis arise. . . . It is therefore quite wrong to exclude and explode a theoretic organization as utopian and impracticable, merely because as yet we see no mode of introducing it.

This essay is instructive on the difference between a logical (and prophetic) general conclusion, and a wildly erratic particular application. Contemplating the inevitable growth and modernizing of Russia, Frank asks, 'ought it not to be an axiom that a State commensurate with it in Central Europe is become a European necessity?' A strong Germany is needed, he decides, under the leadership of Prussia. This union of 'freedom-loving people' will always resist aggressive war (France having provoked the war of 1870) and England should hope that such a Germany 'may be more and more aggrandized by the willing adhesion of free peoples'. Hindsight, however, is easy. In noting the historic irony of Germanophil enthusiasm, one should recall the Victorians of greater fame who were also bemused by the success of Bismarckian policy.

In *English Institutions and their Most Necessary Reforms* (1865), Frank is concerned with civic as well as imperial government. Various 'immediate reforms' are prescribed, such as holding military and naval men to a sense of 'civilian responsibilities', and opening to natives in India, as promised in 1863, every office except those of Governor-General and Commander-in-Chief.

'Our task there is to rear India into political manhood, train it to English institutions, and rejoice when it can govern itself without our aid.' The larger 'ultimate reforms', mentioned in many letters and articles, are the abolition of hereditary peerages and a planned growth in local government. Frank agrees with Sismondi that 'the essence and energy of aristocracy is corrupted from the day that it becomes formally hereditary'. The answer is to establish the principle of life peers, the candidates being put forward to the Queen in recognition of 'public merit', after a vote upon them in the House of Commons. This reform would bring to the top the true 'aristos', alert to the needs of modern times.

> The inertia of our aristocratic ranks, miscalled Conservatism, has undoubtedly a marvellous resisting force; . . . When all the world beside is in rapid movement, and that world is in intimate relations —industrial, political, social, literary—with England; when more-over our own population is in steady change; organic reforms ought to accommodate themselves easily and quickly,—if possible, spontaneously,—to the changes of society. This would be true Conservatism; for this is vitality. Reform which comes too late, fails to avert political disease. The noblest function of high legislation is to guide and conduct Reform.

Such a reformed House of Lords could only emerge from a reformed House of Commons, not one in which 'Englishmen who come out of practical life and have been deeply immersed in special and very limited occupations are to judge on Private Bills innumerable, and on the affairs of people very unlike to us and quite unknown to us'. Parliament, the representatives of the nation, would be elected from Provincial Councils, which in turn would be elected by a suffrage extending within two generations to every 'ostensibly independent' adult, including women. These Councils, fourteen in all for the whole of Great Britain and Ireland (as elaborated in a lecture called "Re-organization of English Institutions"), would elect delegates to the central Parliament for a three-year term. Ministers would be appointed by the Queen, but with the consent of the House and responsible to it. To Frank the great virtue of such decentralization was not so much the elimination of party politics and hereditary privilege as the relief it would give the central Parliament, e.g. from private bills, Education, Poor Law Courts, and Militia affairs. These 'principalities' would set up other large centres besides London and

check its unhealthy over-growth; they would offer posts of real
distinction, if on a somewhat smaller scene, to meritorious men
of all ranks; they would represent local and territorial group-
ings instead of horizontal strata; they would make for fruitful
emulation.

Frank had no faith in the ballot box as by some magic producing the best of all possible worlds. With respect to democracy,
his moral idealism and his liberalism were often in conflict. But he
felt strongly that 'exceptional privileges' had become 'inde-
fensible', that the vices attributed to democracy 'are almost
always chargeable on the cabals of oligarchs', and that full
political equality for all had become a necessity. A letter of
February 22, 1867, shows the trend of his thinking. If sympathy
with the millions makes a democrat, he tells John, he has been one
all his life. 'Practical democrats' have regarded his theory as
aristocratic, calling as it does for reforms from above by those in
power. He now sees that this will not happen in time to avert
calamity. The *use* of the democratic movement, which John had
queried, is to 'shake down routine, bring new men into power, &
give us a chance & a possibility of reconsidering from the founda-
tions of justice and right vital questions which have never been so
discussed'. Frank too likes 'refinement', but under 'our institutions' the many are brutalized. To George Jacob Holyoake, his
friend of half a century and posthumous editor, he wrote in 1884
in terms recalling his letter to John. 'In my old age I seem to
undergo a transformation very rare. I say, I *seem*; but I do not
believe there is any real change. I have become decidedly Democratic. But it is through utter despair of our now ruling classes.
Those called Liberals disgust and shock me in 9 cases out of 10 as
much as Tories.'[1]

[1] J. McCabe, *Life and Letters of George Jacob Holyoake*, London, v. 2, p. 150.
The groundwork for this growth in political and social philosophy is clear in a
letter of 1855 to Martineau. 'I value *forms* of government in proportion as they
develop moral results in individual man; and if I *now* am democratic for
Europe, it is not from any abstract and exclusive zeal for democracy, all the
weaknesses of which I keenly feel, but because the dynasties, having first
corrupted or destroyed the aristocracies, and next become hateful, hated, and
incurable themselves, have left no government possible which shall have
stability and morality except the democratic. In England my desire is to ward
off this result, to which, I think, our aristocracy are driving fast by uniting their
cause with the perfidious immoralities of the Continent.' (Quoted in Sieveking,
p. 84.)

That there was indeed no 'real change' is evident when we glance back to 1851, to the *Lectures on Political Economy*. In part these are a simplified and conventional exposition (for a ladies' college) of *laisser-faire* capitalist economics, warning that 'philanthropy will only do mischief if it be not guided by a sound understanding of the Economic Forces of society'. Government interference with price or product, wage or choice of work, is deplored. Yet Frank's heart is not in a defence of classical economic theory. It is the political aspect that concerns him, involving questions of political morality and social justice. 'This celebrated maxim, *laisser faire*, must be strictly confined to Political Economy, as contrasted with Politics.' A good example of this distinction is his comment on J. S. Mill, who had dismissed his lectures as puerile. Mill had attacked Adam Smith's equation of foreign trade benefit with the export of surplus produce, saying that a country is not compelled to produce these particular goods. If prevented, and so unable to import equivalents, the displaced labour and capital would find immediate employment in producing those desirable objects which were formerly brought from abroad. Immediate, asks Frank? 'The loss of two or three years may seem as nothing in the life of a nation, but they may be sufficient to starve hundreds of thousands of families, or produce political revolution and demoralization in the convulsive effort to hinder it.'

This ardent humanitarianism disqualified Frank as a theoretical economist or political theorist in the eyes of both liberal and conservative, even though he distrusted 'Procrustean socialism'. He attacked the cant born of Puritan self-righteousness and selfish commercialism. 'Severe affliction may make the good better, but it generally makes the bad worse.' He rejected the view of land as private property, allowing only 'movables', and angrily pointed to the 15,000 persons ejected from the Sunderland estates of the Marchioness of Stafford in 1811–20 because sheep paid better. When landlords are regarded as landowners because of dubiously acquired claims, hereditary or other, 'the rules of mere Economy are no sufficient guide to the conduct of a moral being'.

Deploring the suspicion of workmen for even good employers, and showing an almost Ruskinian feeling for bonds of loyalty, Frank can yet say: 'Kind masters of slaves are apt to flatter themselves that slavery loses its degrading power because *they* are kind. . . . we do not want kind slaveowners, nor kind despots, but loyalty and freedom . . . there is an evident propriety in some public mode of mutual recognition which would make . . . caprice disreputable.' Education is one great need, to lift men into being citizens as we cannot depress them into being slaves (too often they are neither one nor the other); a second need is a sense of security, through participation in local politics by all classes and through partnership of workmen by investment in the employer's business. Only in such ways, he believes, will improved moral and social relations come about. To teach, to unite, to elevate, to give a sense of security—this is 'the true Socialism'. With these views, it is little wonder that by 1884 Frank could tell Holyoake he had become 'decidedly Democratic', or that he could hail with delight in 1872 'the initiative of Joseph Arch' in forming the National Agricultural Labourers' Union.

Frank's attack on 'the rules of mere Economy' takes its place in the wave of social protest steadily gathering momentum at the time, and reflected in such novels as Dickens's *Hard Times*. An article in the *North British Review* for February, 1851, based on a review of Kingsley's *Alton Locke* and Mayhew's *London Labour and the London Poor*, sees the literature of 'Social Reference' as a sign of the times, with 'pure literature' almost superseded. The sterile and degrading maxim, 'to buy in the cheapest market and sell in the dearest', is responsible. 'The economists admit and consecrate it, their adversaries admit and denounce it.' Moral considerations must come into play, says the author. It is silly and heartless of the economists to announce a 'law' and think their political duty is thereby ended. 'The problem of politics is to keep close in the wake of the law with the whole strength of the national intelligence and ingenuity.' The 'Sandy Mackayism' of writers like Kingsley and Maurice, moving towards the organization of labour and of industry on a co-operative basis, is a hopeful sign. But the author, like Frank and other fellow-Victorians, warns that mere external change, the re-organizing of society, is not enough. Balanced against this must be the ideal, the Divine Will, the need for 'an inner process of change in the individual', and this stern truth the literary men are in danger of neglecting.

The multiplicity of crusades which enlisted Frank's moral fervour, like his versatile scholarship, and often esoteric linguistic studies, lessened the influence he might have had. Certainly they prevented a fruitful concentration of his talents and energy. He

F

was anti-liquor, anti-tobacco, anti-vaccination, anti-vivisection. He seemed at times, as he ruefully admitted, to be anti-everything. These activities, together with his eccentricities of dress and behaviour, have given him the names of faddist and crank, names easily repeated by critics who cannot be bothered to look into the body of his work. A case in point is his protracted opposition to the legislative measure of 1864 called with Victorian euphemism the Contagious Diseases Act, a measure requiring periodic medical examination of prostitutes in garrison districts. This realistic acceptance of sex for soldiers outraged Frank's belief in the values of purity and continence, and gave rise to such stuffed owl *obiter dicta* as this: 'We know that a ship-crew of young men, chiefly under the age of twenty-five, and picked for masculine vigour, may go to the Arctic regions for a year or two, and return in splendid condition without seeing a woman's face.'

A closer look, however, shows us that Frank was moved by more than puritanical wrath at worldly acquiescence, at what he sarcastically called the Safe-Harlot-Providing Act. What really roused his indignation was the callous and often brutal treatment of the women by the medical examiners, and the whole matter of sexual exploitation and degradation. The rights of women was one of the causes to which, in common with John Stuart Mill, he gave whole-hearted support. Economic dependence and wage discrimination was no doubt a factor in prostitution (a late nineteenth-century estimate gave the average weekly wage of male workers as 18s., that of female workers as 7s.). But the larger underlying issues were legal disabilities of women, the lack of protection for person or property in public or in the home, and unequal opportunities for education and careers. In his article on "Marriage Laws" (*Fraser's Magazine*, August, 1867), Frank first attacked the moral laxity arising from free love and trial marriage, but he went on to the two reforms most needed in a marriage-centred society. First, the grounds for divorce should be extended to include habitual drunkenness, obstinate desertion, cruelty, and long imprisonment. Second, the husband's powers over his wife's property and person 'are extreme and monstrous. . . . We need a single short, sweeping enactment that, *notwithstanding anything to the contrary in past statutes, no woman henceforth shall by marriage change her legal status or lose any parts of her rights over property.*'

Perhaps no *idée fixe* made Frank seem more of the whimsical faddist than his vegetarianism, as he traded recipes for vegetable soups and nut cutlets, indulged children with gifts of raisins and walnuts from his pockets, and gravely debated whether fish could properly be added to vegetarian diet. Yet again, his anti-flesh meat campaign was the expression of a profound humanitarianism enlarged to take in the animal world. From blood sports to vivisection to simple butchery, Frank's feelings and his reason pushed him as usual to the logical extreme. An article on "Vegetarianism" in *Fraser's Magazine* for February, 1875, is characteristic. The advantages in economy and health of a vegetarian diet take up much space, but optimism at the signs of 'a new religion' which will embrace the rights of animals ushers in a moral peroration that is not without nobility. 'Before man can cease to be the tyrant of the world, and become worthy of being its lord, he must love not only other men, but also all harmless animals. Then they will be his daily delight; and love, gushing through common life, will redound to the joy and perfection of man himself, who cannot harden his heart against birds, sheep, and oxen—all, according to the doctrine of Evolution, his distant kinsfolk—without serious damage to his own higher nature.'[1]

The concern with the 'perfection of man' and with man's 'higher nature', brings us back to Frank's efforts over the latter half of the century to formulate a satisfactory religion. His passion for justice and freedom, his political and social humanitarianism, could not find expression in secularism. His revulsion against Catholic bigotry and Evangelical intolerance, and his rationalistic attacks on Bibliolatry and ecclesiolatry, could not destroy the early experience of conversion that left him with a deep conviction of God's being and God's goodness, and with a yearning to establish a religious sanction for morality. Although attempts at definition led him into inconsistencies and contradictions, his genuine spirituality commanded the life-long respect of the Unitarian

---

[1] The association of ideas here would not seem far-fetched to a later writer on 'animal factories'. Deploring the 'cruelty' in modern methods of raising and slaughtering for maximum profit, Ruth Harrison says: 'The more I studied the subject the deeper became my conviction that other issues are involved. The degradation of the animal in the appalling ways it is now made to eke out its existence must have an impact on human self-respect, and ultimately on man's treatment of man.' ("Inside the Animal Factories", *The Observer*, March 1, 1964. Included with a second article, "Fed to Death", in *Animal Machines*, London, 1964.)

Martineau and the Secularist Holyoake. His rejection of metaphysical reasoning and of Christ's moral perfection did not
estrange the one; his insistent theism was no barrier to friendship
with the other. In *Bygones Worth Remembering*, Holyoake recalls his
great admiration for Frank's moral integrity and intellectual
powers, and declares that if he could have been a theist, Mazzini
and Francis Newman would have influenced him. 'For Theism
never seemed so enchanting in my eyes as it appeared in the lives
of those two distinguished thinkers who were inspired by it.'

The position Frank tried to hold was the one John so often
declared to be impossible, that of a half-way house between
Catholicism and Atheism. Looking back to the split between them,
Frank stated that to John occult powers were First Principles,
whereas 'to deny such occult powers is *now* a reasonable First
Principle'. He added one of his wisest remarks. 'This difference of
mind from mind as to First Principles constantly makes religious
controversy futile.'[1] But Frank was hoist with his own modern
petard. Replying to Holyoake's objection that he had no logical
proof of the first principles for his Moral Theism, he said: 'So: that
the infinite fitness of Animated to Inanimate nature indicates
Mind acting on a vast scale in the universe:—that human intelligence is a result of other intelligence higher than itself—is not a
source, or a result, of what is unintelligent:—this conviction,
which is the foundation of all religion, is in my opinion incapable
of proof, because all proof presupposes earlier principles, and this
is the earliest.' Holyoake answered that to him this assumption of
a higher and prior intelligence was no first principle, and must
itself be proved.[2]

[1] *Contributions Chiefly to the Early History of the Late Cardinal Newman*, London,
1891, p. 49.
[2] McCabe, v. 1, p. 223. An exchange of letters took place between the
brothers on the subject of Holyoake. John will be surprised to hear, Frank
wrote on January 17, 1860, that 'Holyoake, the Atheist Lecturer, is a great
admirer of you—and of me!' An honest man, resolved to learn, he has 'a
gentlemanly honourable mind, pure moral intentions, & great fairness'.
Rival teachers feel he is not enough an atheist; many pupils outgrow him to
become Deists; 'so his opponents have a true instinct of his tendencies'. How
strange, when John's words 'fall flat on an audience of half-educated self-
sufficient gentry or tradesmen here or in Dublin', that he may 'unawares be
giving a sound intellectual impulse to a body which at present has no religious beliefs whatever?' John replied on January 18 that he was not surprised
at such an effect on Holyoake, nor did he undervalue it. 'My creed leads me to

There is no doubt that Frank felt as intensely as John the reality of God, and that his experience too was in essence mystical. 'Spiritual religion', he says, 'is nothing, if it be not mystical.' That God exists, and is the source of truth and goodness, is a revelation given by God himself 'in the universe and in the human heart'. The fatal error is to objectify this revelation in miracle and myth, and to intellectualize it in dogma and creed, inviting the superstitions of priestcraft and the subtleties of metaphysical speculation. How then does one recognize and identify this Power? Rejecting theological dogma and metaphysical system, Frank tried to base his theistic belief in a psychological dualism and a moral idealism. 'The nobler movements of the soul, so far as they are normal to man, may not unreasonably be called the workings of God within us.' ("A Discourse on the Presence of God", in *Sermons*, 1875.)

The attempt to establish an objective correlative for this profound emotional bias in man, this instinct for God, led Frank into all sorts of difficulties. To identify God with laws or forces in the physical universe and so, he hoped, to reconcile religion and science, could lead to an abstract and impersonal Deism or to a diffused Pantheism. Such a God could not satisfy the need of the soul to love and to worship. Frank was fully in sympathy with the piety that could ease its longing only by 'walking with God', and even by supplicating 'the Father'. Yet a personal Theism had its own dangers. In an article of 1870 called "Anthropomorphism" he made a 'theological comment' on some 'elegant poetry' sent him 'with a purpose'. The poet, he says, is right to wish to know something more of God than the surface of Nature shows, even to follow his instinct and address him as Father. 'He evidently attributes to God *a mind that understands us, and a soul that loves us.* To believe this firmly, unchangeably, is the core of religion, in my judgment, and suffices for everything. It gives peace in trouble and

feel less surprise at an Atheist than a Protestant feels. In truth, I think that *logically* there is *no* middle point *between* Catholicism and Atheism.' Of course many men are inconsistent. As Frank and others think, how can John be a Catholic? so John thinks Frank and Holyoake cherish that in their hearts 'of which Catholicism alone is the full account'. It will be a great favour done him by God if he can advance Holyoake and his friends. A note on this letter by Frank says: 'G. J. Holyoake is certainly no longer an Atheist.' (The exchange is interesting; it would be equally interesting to have Holyoake's comments on it.)

even amid a sense of guilt; and not peace only, but joy, if it be intense enough.' The poet wishes further, however, to see 'a *Face* in which my own, beseeching, may read reply'. This is to fall into pernicious superstition, 'to abandon the first principles of manly religion, and go back into ancient puerilities'. Frank is trying simultaneously to agree with Browning's Rabbi Ben Ezra that 'I need now, as then,/Thee, God, who mouldest men'; and to rebuke his David for saying, 'O Saul, it shall be/A Face like my face that receives thee; a Man like to me.'

In a series of essays over the 1870's, including "Moral Theism" and "The Two Theisms" (*Miscellanies*), and "The Relations of Theism to Pantheism" (*Controversial Tracts*), Frank struggled to rationalize his intuition of God, to retain the elements of personality without the concept of Person. Had he contented himself with a simple pragmatism, it might have been easier to maintain a consistent line of argument. In essay and sermon and article we are told that a vivid sense of God's presence stimulates us 'to act up to our highest convictions of right'; that religious feeling energizes moral activity; that religious belief is to be judged by its moral fruits. An essay of 1880, "Errors Concerning Deity", sums it up. To theists who balk at 'divine personality', Frank admits that much of the disagreement is a controversy about words. Let them abandon 'Person' if they wish. All he wishes to retain is a belief in 'rational mind', not in body or form. For if we believe in a Creator, 'We have a right to infer that where Man is God's highest work, man's virtue is the fruit of God's work, in which God most delights; and that His Spirit, which has with us joint consciousness of our inward emotions, is ever in action within us, ready to animate us to every good word and deed. To enter at all into these lofty and purifying thoughts, our religion must be, not a philosophical speculation, but a life of aspiration after higher virtue.' In this view, a careless and unobservant Creator is an unreasonable and unfruitful belief. Virtuous men and women will prefer 'the rich fruit of Hebrew Theism' to the 'dry husks' offered by Greek philosophy.

If this pragmatic line of argument (inadequate to a Martineau, unnecessary to a Holyoake) is consistent in the sense of justifying religious belief on moral grounds, it is hardly consistent as reasoning. Certainly it leaves the hen-and-egg question of priorities hopelessly addled. A Creator, a God of love 'desiring' moral per-

fection in his creatures, suggests that moral values are an out-
growth of religious belief. Yet Frank says firmly, in "On This and
the Other World" (*Controversial Tracts*, 1875): 'In my belief, duty
must stand on its own basis, as a purely human science, to which
religious knowledge contributes absolutely nothing. Upon pre-
existing morals, spiritual judgments are built. Religion cannot tell
us what is moral, though it can give great force to moral aspirations.' The last clause is perhaps the clue, as he continues, 'It can
immensely aid us to self-restraint and sacrifice for the attainment
of virtue, hereby in turn making individuals nobler, and con-
ducing to more delicate moral perception, out of which rises an
advance of moral science itself.' And again: 'In fact it is from the
outer world, reasoned on by us, that the first suggestion of a
World Spirit comes, and from our own spirits we reason out *some*
of the attributes of that Spirit from whom is our origin.'

The inconsistency noted arises at least in part from the use of
older terminology, when God is really a name for the highest
morality evolved by human experience. And the argument is not
so much circular as spiral. The moral judgments of man, resting
on 'universal human reason', criticize and discard false or puerile
notions of the Deity, and with progress in knowledge and refinement conceive more truly of the nature of God. Having reached
this truer conception by the insights possible to his 'higher nature'
(those nobler workings of the soul which are the workings of God
within us) man is in turn stimulated by this religious belief to the
service of God. This service is both self-regarding ('That virtue is
the final object for which man and the whole of human life is
ordained is a main principle of Theism'), and social. 'Now as man
is not a solitary being . . . social life is eminently a part of his
nature, nor can he live according to the laws of Nature and of
God, except by a scrupulous performance of social duty. Thus
right moral conduct becomes a primary precept of advancing and
noble religion. . . . Religion cannot dictate what things are right:
it takes morality for granted . . .: nevertheless it adds energy to
moral precept, urging us to charity and purity, industry and
bravery, as the proper and direct way of pleasing God.' ("Hunger
and Thirst after Righteousness", 1876.)

Considering the variety of assumptions in Frank's theistic
beliefs, and the mixture of traditional terms and modernist views
(he would, for example, keep the word 'sin' but would make it an

offence against morality), it is not surprising that he was attacked by the pantheist and secularist as well as by the orthodox Christian. But while he found theological speculation and controversy irresistible, in spite of condemning it as futile, his own religious feelings found their outlet in the sphere of social morality. As his causes and crusades testify, he was dedicated to the religion of humanity. Speculation on the nature of God, he once admitted, was mere 'reverential conjecture'. Only the love of man gives meaning to the love of God, to realize which we see 'the benefit of this human family as our highest service to the common Father', and discover that 'to purify laws and institutions is a primary mode of establishing the kingdom of God on earth'. To this end religious emotion is useful, but a theist like himself, separated by a moral and spiritual abyss from the religious fanatic, can find common cause with the 'merely good man' of secularist views. 'Religion, whatever its significance as inner illumination, is exhibited mainly in right conduct towards *Man*.'

Though Frank believed in moral truths as intuitional, as 'propositions to which we assent by mere dwelling of the mind upon them', he also believed that the intuition must be 'intensified', that moral wisdom is a product of cultivation. 'Moral judgments are instinctive to every individual; but morality, as a system of rules, grows up with human experience, over the breadth of each society.' Moral law rests on the 'universal reason of mankind', but most people learn morality from the public law, as they have in the past learned their religion from public institutions. There is a certain element of truth in the widespread belief that religion teaches morals. It rests on the fact that when religion, as so often, has been established by law, the moral code laid down has been nationally enforced.

In "Epicureanism, Ancient and Modern" (1871), Frank calls for the State to renew its fundamental purpose, to promote the community welfare, which in turn is dependent upon the moral code. Modern Utilitarianism, though an advance over the old Epicureanism, disappoints him. It lacks the word 'ought'. Yet when Mill makes the ultimate sanctions of morality 'a subjective feeling in our own minds', and 'the conscientious feelings of mankind', he comes near joining the believers in intuitional morals. Furthermore, says Frank, Mill's 'intuition tells him, as mine tells me, that Disinterestedness *is* *better* than Selfishness'. The weakness of any hedonistic calculus is that the 'meaner instincts' have an easy time of it. Cultivating the 'nobler instincts', or 'intensifying the intuition', will certainly not be done 'by exclusive talking about experience, by swamping the most diverse sets of feelings under the word pleasure, or by any preachings about happiness'. To old notions of 'rights' derived from habits of conquering, and still applied to land and property and women, have been added the unrestrained drive for profits by capitalists. Not all the moralists in the world can stem this tide of immorality. The power for good here must be the State, 'the moral heart of the nation, the most potent diffuser of good and evil'.

When Frank adds the sarcastic comment that 'some people, oddly calling themselves Economists, think it a great gain to infuse into a population artificial desires, and name it civilization', and when he says of State-action for the common good that 'collectively we have no higher interest', one expects to find a recantation of his attacks on Socialism. But the solution is typically Victorian. It is still the moralist speaking. The State is, or should be, the embodiment of the 'nobler instincts' of its citizens, a view rather like that of Dr Arnold, that the State should be the Christian conscience of the nation. Individuals cannot much affect other men's conduct; it is the State's function to induce simpler and healthier tastes, and so to exalt public moral standards and depress private cupidity. In his view of the State acting as a super-moral force through wise legislation ('Law would, indeed, be a cold-blooded enormity, if it did not rest on moral right and wrong,') the reformer speaks as a moral idealist. 'A powerful passion can only be countered by a higher passion; and undoubtedly the spiritual passions are the strongest. The moralist's task—whatever name he assume, to whatever school he refers himself—is to strengthen and purify the *intuitions*—the inward choice, the inmost hates: for these are the vital forces of action.' But the language of the social realist is never far off, or the concern with human suffering that led to Frank's adopting democratic principles. In *Religion, Not History* (1877), he puts the matter bluntly. 'Before the general mass of any nation can be elevated morally, it must be delivered from depressing and debasing pauperism.'

That Frank's retention of 'nobler instincts' and 'spiritual passions' was hardly enough to reassure worried fellow-Victorians is suggested by an earlier trenchant review of five books on ethics, in

February of 1851. Agreeing that 'conscience stands apart from necessary reference to God, and may subsist in a great degree unimpaired under a negation of Theism', the reviewer declares that secularized ethics neglects the 'scientific basis' offered in Christianity, namely, the appearance already of the perfect Man that is the ethical ideal, and the moral apparatus for renovation in the view of man as depraved. Let the ignoble systems of Hobbes and Mandeville, 'which have so long hung in chains, without any great benefit to society', be 'taken down and left to rot under the ground instead of above it'. Let the more generous spirits among the ancients, such as Plato and Cicero, be seen as unconscious prophets of Christianity, and let the non-Christian systems of to-day, such as those of Kant and Fichte, be seen as 'the marvellous gropings of the blind to return to the forsaken path'. (*North British Review*, vol. 14.)

The public morality which Frank separates from religious authority, on the grounds that the good of collective humanity is the concern of the State, co-exists with a private morality that reflects one's own beliefs. Here a man 'walks by faith', doing what he sees as right without regard to consequences, even perhaps suffering a degree of that martyrdom without which 'no new and quickening morality will ever rise in a nation'. In a review article titled "Jowett and the Broad Church", Frank makes it clear that to him conscience is something other than doing as other men do in a Christian country. His own precept would be: 'Condemn your own self by the highest law which your conscience discerns, but condemn all others by the current morality of the society to which they fitly belong.' Not only is this a private conscience; Frank's earnest efforts to project a Church of the Future on the broad base of his moral theism cannot alter the fact that his is a private religion. It is apparent here, where the spiritual reinforces the moral. 'We must not call our neighbours to the bar of our private perceptions; but unless we would quench within us the diviner spirit, we must cherish and obey it ourselves.'

How much did Christianity contribute to Frank's moral theism, intensely felt if confusedly expressed? On the side of its other-worldliness, nothing. Having rejected mystery in religion, and with it the central miracle of the resurrection, on rationalistic grounds, he also rejected belief in immortality of any kind. Admittedly he oscillated over the years, mainly because a belief in immortality as being *possible* might have for some 'a specific influence on spiritual thought and feeling'.[1] Such belief is pernicious, however, if the effect is to disparage this life, and 'divert good people from tearing up the roots of Evil'. For 'our best preparation for another world, if we expect another world, is by working for Justice and Mercy in this'. (*Life After Death?*, 1886.) The compensatory belief that evil and suffering in this world make immortality a matter of God's justice was in Frank's view infantile. Perfecting social justice, like perfecting individual virtue, is a salutary pain and labour, 'a stern necessity imposed by a wise God'. To rest one's faith on a certainty of immortality, an opinion '*possibly* disprovable by science', is as bad as to rest it on Bibliolatry or miracle. For himself, if 'final dissolution were established tomorrow, my cheerful, happy faith in God would remain undisturbed'. To try to make this world better is not 'an insufficient reward for a whole life of virtue'. Not that Frank's 'cheerful faith' or his belief in progress led him to minimize the 'heart-piercing, reason-bewildering fact' that John found insoluble in human terms. 'The increased brilliancy of our light discloses, alas! the blackness of our guilt as never before; but this is a necessary part of our shame, our repentance, and our purification.'

On the matter of Christian influence for good in the morality of this world, Frank's views underwent a transformation over the years. He did not, as his anxious biographer would have us believe, become an orthodox Christian believer just before his death. In saying that to him Paul became less and less and Christ became more and more, he was shifting to the view that Christ's teaching, seriously misrepresented in the Gospels and still more by the Church, would be a sufficient basis, when combined with the best of the Old Testament, for the moral and religious life of mankind.

---

[1] In 1886 Frank said that 'thirty years ago' he had tried in his *Theism*, ineffectually, to establish immortality by moral proofs. The attempt was evidently the subject of an exchange of letters between the brothers, concluded touchingly by Frank on February 6, 1858. 'Call me *earnest*, my dear J., but not *sensitive*. I am rather "thick-skinned." Do not fancy your letter could hurt me. It is all affectionate. If I value the doctrine of Immortality (which I hold with trembling hand, sometimes confident, sometimes with suspense of judgment) it is perhaps chiefly from the aid which it gives me to love; when I think,— "Hereafter, how all ignorances that separate us shall drop off; when we all ripen under the true sun." The *past* furnishes deep fountains of love towards such as you; but Hope added glorifies Memory.'

He took half a century to reach this conclusion, but he had to do it for himself and in his own way.

From his early attacks on the Scriptures as incredible historically, Frank had passed to an attack on them as unedifying morally, that is, when presented in both Catholic and Protestant teaching. What could be done with 'the incoherent, hyperbolic, enigmatic fragments of discourses given to us unauthoritatively as teachings of Jesus'? (*A Discourse Against Hero-Making in Religion*, 1864.) The true temptation of Jesus was the whisper, 'Are you not the Messiah?'; the fruit of heeding his 'haughty and bitter denunciations' and his extravagance about the keys of the kingdom was sacerdotalism and ecclesiasticism. That, and the 'low morality' of the Gospels, '*prevalently* an appeal to our prudence and our desire of eternal reward'. The praise of indiscriminate alms-giving; the view of chastity as continence (the sign of an elect); the indifference to freedom and rights for the under-privileged (how ironical that Christianity should claim credit for elevating women, who only now were winning freedom against the authority of Old and New Testament texts); the disparagement of secular knowledge and of beauty—where in all this is the moral education for humanity? ("The Defective Morality of the New Testament", Scott's *Theological Tracts*, 1866.) Orthodoxy has only been able to condone this 'low morality' by mystery and intolerance, by prostration before the divinity of an inferior being, and by exploiting the popular desire for poetical fancies, marvels, and hero-worship. Unitarians are really no better; in rejecting the supernatural Son and setting up the morally perfect Man, they really say 'that Jesus was mentally a dwarf and morally a God'. ("The Religious Weakness of Protestantism", Scott's *Theological Tracts*, 1866.) It says much for the gentle temper of the philosophic Martineau that, alternately shutting his eyes in pain and rubbing them in bewilderment, he retained his faith in the spirituality of his friend. One recalls his mild complaint that Frank tended to read the Scriptures with 'a curious literalness'.

It was, of course, the idea of a sacred text as authority that Frank was rejecting in these blasts, as vigorously as he had rejected the authority of priest and Church. Only free thought could help man to grow morally. 'Nothing can be less suited *to minister to the spirit* and train the powers of the human soul, than to be subject to a superhuman dictation of truth.' In his resistance to

Messianism as the source of dogma, he credited Paul with originating the 'spiritual principle'. It was more truly to be said of Paul than of Jesus that he 'first established the brotherhood of man, the equality of races, the nullity of ceremonies; that he overthrew the narrowness of Judaism; that he found a national, but left a universal religion'. The explanation is that Paul followed not books or men but an 'ideal Jesus', a 'construction within the mind'. Like many other devout Christians he glorified Jesus from other sources than the Gospels, from Isaiah and the Psalms. Had Paul been in a position to read the Gospels, we are told, he would not have followed Jesus at all!

It was not long before Frank was dissatisfied with Paul, finding him, for all his passion and spiritual power, responsible for the growth of divisive Christian doctrine, especially that of election and reprobation. His misplaced logic, a Rabbinical culture run wild, his 'smoky vision' and 'mystical imaginations', proved intoxicating to Christians, and threw into sharp relief the moral practicality of James, whose effort was 'to win his whole people by clinging to their common basis and common diction, expounding that in which they agreed, and stimulating Christians to right conduct'. The Pauline text, 'the letter killeth but the spirit giveth life', remained for Frank supreme, but nothing shows better the decline of his Evangelicalism and the growth of his humanitarianism than his harmonizing of works with faith. Paul is significantly absent from this formulation of a religion of the future. 'With the sympathy of Jesus and James for the poor, but with knowledge and economic science to them unattainable, it will inculcate Philanthropy as the ordinary duty of everyone; and will command that those precious possessions which grow by diffusion—Knowledge and Refinement—shall be made universal.' (*James and Paul*, 1869.) What motivated Frank in his attacks was the desire to separate religion from miracle and dogma, from those elements in religious faith that were to John indispensable, and to place it on a foundation of reason and morality. Only so, he felt, could it have universal appeal and point the way to the brotherhood of man. 'A Religion which is to promote union and charity among mankind must above all exclude from itself historical and legendary elements; for these will inevitably generate in different regions diverse mythologies, which, even if they be in the origin mere plausible accretions, before long will eat as a canker.' ("The Religious Mischiefs of Credulity", 1879.)

As late as 1881, in *What is Christianity Without Christ?*, Frank is severe on the gospel portrait of Jesus as revealing one who is often dictatorial, evasive, vituperative, and unjust. But this is only a gospel portrait. Not only have the *practical* precepts of Paul, Peter, and James become Europe's 'highest ideal of right'; it is also a 'rational hypothesis' that the *real* Jesus was eminently a man of great spiritual gifts, such as the Church by 'a sound moral instinct' has presented. What was needed to rescue Christianity from the Church had been set forth earlier. 'The noble moralities of the New Testament will stand out . . . when surrounding error is purged away: but until this work of criticism is performed, and the dogmatic principle disowned, the spiritual and moral will continue to be drowned by the ecclesiastical.' ("On the Historical Depravation of Christianity", *Controversial Tracts*, 1873.)

Frank's final position is one of surrender, on his own terms. 'I am now satisfied that Jesus took a humble place as a man and a Hebrew Prophet, preaching the pure Theism of the Prophets, and that Paul would not retain him in that position.' (*Hebrew Jesus*, 1895.) Paul is still 'a kindling moralist', who made 'a vast improvement on the old heathendom'. But his supernaturalism and allegorizing opened the way to Trinitarian speculations, and his 'dreadful delusion' with respect to notions of atonement and justification not only shifted faith in God to faith in Christ, but also foreshadowed Calvinistic fanaticism. Having disposed of Paul as well as the Evangelists, Frank is now able to offer us his revised version of Jesus, as one in whose religion there is no doctrine of hell; no *professing* of miracles; no claim to be God or even to be morally perfect; a pure inward faith based on communion with a God of love and trust; a loathing of hypocrisy; the exalting of moral duties over ceremonies; the genial advice to use our private judgment; and the preaching and practice of compassion. The essence of Christ's teaching is the Lord's Prayer, undoubtedly genuine, making up the deficiencies of the classical moralists and offering the best basis for union.

When he adds that the best in Christianity comes mainly from the Jews, Frank takes up no new position. In "Religion at the Bar of Ethics" (1875), an essay showing the ardent freethinker in religion dubious of the effect of free thought in morals, he had stressed the elevating power of the Church's view of marriage and of the belief in a personal God. Of his ethical and humanitarian church of the future, he said: 'A Theism akin to that of the Hebrews can alone cement Church union.' Now the teachings of the 'Hebrew Jesus', similarly freed of doctrinal distortions and restored to their primitive simplicity, can blend with Hebrew theism in a body of Scriptural truth. 'Thus only can we reach a pure and simple monotheistic faith which will satisfy alike reason, science, criticism, and piety, and find a common ground on which not Jews and Christians only, but Mohammedans also, may unite.'

In a letter of 1887 Francis Newman summarizes his creed, and his situation, more effectively than in his more formal writings. It does not suggest recantation; it does express the moral theism which over the years he had tried to expound. 'I suppose I must say, "Alas!" that the older I become [81 last June] the more painfully my creed outgrows the limits of that which the mass of my nation, and those whose co-operation I most covet, account *sacred*. I dare not (unasked) send to friends what I print, yet I uphold the *sacred moralities* of Jew and Christian [Hindoo and Moslem] with all my heart. Two mottoes, or say *three*, suffice me:—

"The Lord reigneth.
"The righteous Lord loveth righteousness.
"The Lord requireth Justice, Mercy, and Sobriety of thought, not ceremony and creed." '

He signs the letter, 'Your Vegetarian friend of old, F. W. Newman.' A letter in 1891 to the same friend more fully expresses the aims and hopes, religious and secular, which had filled so much of his life. 'The aspect on the whole is to me far more encouraging than alarming. The reign of false aristocracy is fast declining; the rising powers everywhere ask for *justice* between orders and (as never before) between the two sexes, and the power of women is about to signalize itself in most valuable directions—for the benefit of *both* sexes, and for the first time to claim nationally that moral and Christian *Right* shall be the aim of Law. But I confess if we wish to attract ancient nations to Christianity, we have first to reconsider our creed fundamentally, a terrible summons to Protestants as well as Catholics.'[1]

Other than his being Emeritus Professor from the time of his retirement, and an Honorary Fellow of his old College, Worcester, from 1883, no honours or offices marked Newman's career. His

[1] Sieveking, pp. 381, 385.

reputation for radicalism and crotchetiness offset his reputation for learning and originality. Minor positions he held included being an honorary member in 1863, along with J. S. Mill, of the London Association for the Promotion of Co-operatives; vice-president of the British and Foreign Unitarian Association in 1876 ('I have not changed towards them; they have moved towards me'); vice-president of the Land Nationalization Society in 1886. When he died at Weston-super-Mare, after some years of blindness and physical frailty, there was little the small group of devoted friends at his funeral could point to in the way of permanent achievement. An obituary notice in the *Manchester Guardian* for October 6, 1897, sketches his accomplishments and career, stresses his originality and scrupulous fairness, and concludes: 'Whether this openness of mind may not sometimes have prejudiced his influence and his reputation is a question that it is needless to debate. But there can be no doubt that his advocacy of women's suffrage, of land nationalization, of vegetarianism, of teetotalism, and other "advanced" movements gained for them a hearing with many who would have been deaf to the appeals of other men.' After the smile, let a friend have the last word. The Rev. Temperley Grey, a Congregationalist minister, spoke for those who had loved and respected the man behind the crusader and reformist for his simple goodness and complete selflessness. 'He was a true philanthropist. He championed the cause of the oppressed everywhere. . . . Above all, our friend was a truth seeker. This was the ruling passion of his life.'

CHAPTER 9

Different Worlds

THE OBITUARY notice of Francis Newman in *The Athenaeum* for
October 9, 1897, contains what must be regarded as a classic case
of understatement. 'In the seventies it used to annoy Dr Newman
to be called "F." (short for Father) Newman in the *Dublin Review*,
"whereas," he wrote to a friend, "my brother is commonly distinguished from me by this initial. I say this because, much as we
love each other, neither would like to be mistaken for the other".'
The notice is not wholly ironical. Fraternal feeling, if not love, did
permit a steady correspondence. In the 1860's religious and
political issues flare up occasionally, with exasperation on Frank's
part and a hint of weary resignation on John's. Mainly, and from
1870 on almost entirely, the tone is friendly enough on matters
that are domestic (the health of Jemima, the financial support of
Charles); autobiographical (from Frank's resignation as Latin
Professor at University College in 1863 to John's elevation to the
Cardinalate in 1879); scholarly (the value of an Oxford training
in the classics, John's critical interest in Frank's translation of
Horace and his Arabic dictionary). Nor is the note of good-nature
absent. With one of his rare touches of humour, Frank confides
that a trip to the East following his resignation is unlikely, partly
because of his wife's health, partly because 'she would be killed
with ennui, not only where she cannot talk, but where she cannot
visit poor people (& give away tracts!!)'. And with genial wit John
remarks to Frank on chimneys, 'the opprobium of this scientific
age. . . . Chimneys almost seem testimonies in favour of Darwin's
theories—for instead of being made for use as a final cause, they
seem to grow into comfortable use by using.' If, as Frank said on
November 9, 1861, they had long 'known one another only at
arm's length', they were still able to shake hands.

More than this, they could still pay significant, if qualified,
tribute, in Frank's case to John's superior literary gifts, in John's

165

case to Frank's purity of moral purpose. John's desire to write some great work is legitimate, Frank says in a letter of October 15, 1864. He is 'naturally made for a great *poet* or a great *musical composer*'. He will not, in Frank's view, write a great work on philosophy or history or theology that will appeal to both Protestants and Catholics. But to create a noble Catholic literature is a laudable aim. Such poetry will no more repel Protestants than 'the Paganism of Aeschylus or Sophocles'; it is 'most effective on religious minds and in the religious direction', and John can succeed in this if anyone can. If Frank's bias qualifies this tribute somewhat, a statement recorded by Holyoake in *Bygones Worth Remembering* shows John setting down his own testimony with semantic precision. When Frank's name was raised in the House of Commons, John wrote that 'for his brother's purity he would die'. Considering their differences, Holyoake adds drily, this was 'very noble in the Cardinal'.

No amount of familial chit-chat or circumscribed compliment, however, could obscure the fundamental divergence or bring about a true reconciliation. In his letter of March 2, 1863, Frank remarked to his brother, not for the first or the last time, on the nature of this divergence. It amused him, he said, to note the disparity between their agreement, on details of thought and sentiment, and the utterly different conclusions they reached. With respect to the importance and the interpretation of facts, 'We seem to look out on different worlds.' No truer statement could be made. We have seen Frank's wrath at those who cause or permit the suffering of animals for any reason whatever. Such 'cruelty' not only hardens the heart of man against 'his distant kinsfolk', it also risks 'serious damage to his own higher nature'. In a sermon on "The Crucifixion" in 1842, John tells his listeners that we can only feel Christ's sufferings, as we ought, 'by *dwelling* on the thought'. The image of the Lamb can so stir us, when we 'consider how horrible it is to read the accounts which sometimes meet us of cruelties exercised on brute animals', whether these be 'the wanton deed of barbarous and angry owners' or 'the cold-blooded and calculating act of men of science'. The facts are the same; the moral judgments on man are the same; the spiritual (or psychological) application differs completely.

Again, we have seen Frank's unremitting attacks on imperialism for unprovoked aggression and wars of conquest, for an im-

JOHN HENRY NEWMAN IN OLD AGE
from the portrait by W. Coleridge

FRANCIS NEWMAN IN OLD AGE
from a photo by John Davies

morality exceeding even the general immorality of war, together
with his hope that 'a time will come when men will look back in
wonder and pity on our present barbarism'. A second sermon by
John in 1842 is called "The Christian Church an Imperial
Power". After showing the Church to be, from Old Testament
texts, the visible kingdom of the invisible Lord, John compares it
with the far-flung British Empire. 'It is the peculiarity of an imperial state to bear rule over other states; and it is another
peculiarity, not indeed essential, but almost necessary, that it
should be always in movement, advancing or retiring, never
stationary, aggression being the condition of its existence. Conquest is almost of the essence of an empire, and when it ceases to
conquer, it ceases to be.' The same historical phenomenon that
roused Frank's crusading zeal on moral and humanitarian grounds
was for John a useful analogy to illustrate and justify the growth of
ecclesiastical power.

His Saviour and his Church were the supreme realities that
filled John's imagination, governed his reasoning, and focused his
emotions. Logic and semantics were tools he manipulated with
almost contemptuous ease in the service of a faith that was the
expression of his will and his need. Knowledge and power, private
friendship and public influence, all gave satisfaction. But if they
threatened to obscure by pride (or by disappointment) the
mystical religious truths dogmatically defined and sacramentally
realized, they could be regulated to their proper ends by self-
criticism (or by self-justification) in the pages of the *Journals*. The
merely human could be interpreted as serving the other-worldly
ideal; or could be modified to serve it; or could be condemned as a
betrayal of it, in the case of the wickedness that was a sign of man's
alienation from God and the suffering that was his just punishment. For all his involvement in activities that shaped his career,
John had marked the vital distinction in his *Journals* on September 16, 1824. 'Those who make comfort the great subject of their
preaching seem to mistake the end of their ministry. *Holiness* is the
great end.' And holiness is not of this world.

To Frank the idea of God could best be realized within the
human situation by following, however imperfectly, the injunc-
tion, 'Be ye perfect.' The mystical object of contemplation was an
hypostasized Highest in man's nature, not a mysterious revelation
confirmed by miracle, expounded by authority, and enshrined in

institutions. To suspect that these traditional sanctions of religion were intellectually jejune or morally deficient was not, in Frank's view, to discredit reasoning or to discipline moral judgments. It was rather to apply rational and moral criteria even more rigorously. It was, in short, to find nothing 'sacred'. With something of a child's directness and simplicity, Frank not only shocked his contemporaries by pointing out that Victoria needed new clothes, he shocked them even more by finding no man under the episcopal robes, and then by finding no Son of Man within the ecclesiastical shell. Where John's imagination gave power to his vision, his rhetoric allowing his reason to defend the irrational, Frank's literalism and logic led him into over-simplifications and into a prosaic discursiveness. Scepticism, as Bishop Thirlwall saw, was the bent of both brothers, but whereas John cultivated credulity to preserve intact the early vision of himself and that other 'luminously self-evident' being, Frank often risked absurdity by equating the true with the logical or the philological.

Other observers than Thirlwall remarked on the similarity and the difference. In 1849 the acidulous Whately wrote to Dr Thomas Arnold's widow: 'It is curious to observe how the brothers Newman, starting east and west, have gone so far that they have nearly met. Both have come to the conclusion that there is nothing of what is commonly called evidence for Christianity; the one resting his belief (if he has any) of that and of the silliest monkish legends alike on the Church; and the other on the infallible oracle within him. The disparagement of evidence among persons who are professed believers is characteristic of the present age.'[1] John's one-time curate, the poet Isaac Williams, draws attention rather to that difference in the brothers that shaped the response of reader or listener. Observing the 'same basis of constitutional character in both', Williams says: 'While our Newman, the eldest, has so much poetry, love of scenery, and associations of place and country, and domestic and filial affection, these qualities appeared to me wanting in his brother, who would have passed by Jerusalem and Nazareth without turning aside to look on them, or the most beautiful object in Nature.'[2] The comment is exaggerated, but perceptive. Between two men of intellectual power and passionate conviction, a major difference is the creative imagination and

[1] Life and Correspondence of Richard Whately, D.D., v. 2, p. 154.
[2] Autobiography of Isaac Williams, ed. G. Prevost, London, 1892, pp. 59–60.

emotional subtlety that produced John's *Dream of Gerontius* and his novel *Callista*, and gave such power to his sermons. These qualities won George Eliot's admiration and held Matthew Arnold's respect. Arnold's attitude, indeed, is so revealing of why many 'liberals' and 'radicals' were more sympathetic to John than to Frank, that it is worth our while to examine the gospellers according to Matthew.

On the face of things, Arnold should have welcomed Francis Newman as a kindred spirit. In dismissing miracle and legend as unscientific, in applying rationalistic criteria to the Bible, in finding both dogma and metaphysics alien to the spirit of true religion, Frank was no more iconoclastic than Arnold was to be. The famous Arnoldian definitions of God as 'the Eternal that makes for righteousness', and of religion as 'morality, touched with emotion', could have been his; and his hardest blows at orthodoxy could hardly surpass Arnold's airy reference to the Trinity as 'the fairy-tale of three Lord Shaftesburys', or his summary of Catholic teaching as a 'pseudo-scientific apparatus of superannuated dogma'. Even the phrasing is at times similar, as when Frank says of his first difficulties with the Athanasian Creed, 'If we lay down anything about it *at all*, we ought to understand our own words.'

Arnold, however, found Frank impossible. One extravagant outburst at *Phases of Faith* in the letters to Clough describes him as a 'beast', who 'bepaws the religious sentiment so much that he quite effaces it to me', and who writes as though 'enquiries into articles, biblical inspiration, etc. etc. were as much the natural functions of a man as to eat and copulate'. Even in the privacy of correspondence this tone does not recur. What irritated Arnold, one may suspect, was Frank's uncompromising attack on positions which he was himself intellectually abandoning but for which he had a nostalgic sympathy. As he was soon to say of the Carthusian monks,

> Not as their friend, or child, I speak!
> But as, on some far northern strand,
> Thinking of his own Gods, a Greek
> In pity and mournful awe might stand
> Before some fallen Runic stone—
> For both were faiths, and both are gone.

It was a matter of the poetry of religion, of tenderness for tradition, of simultaneously following 'the high white star of Truth' and cherishing the light through stained glass windows. Furthermore, in his own attempt to re-habilitate Christianity, Arnold was to emphasize the unique perfection of Jesus as the moral ideal, and to urge upon his countrymen the claims of the Anglican Church. His definition of the Church as 'a great national society for the promotion of goodness' was, it is true, hardly re-assuring to the Anglican clergy, though it would have seemed a satisfactory statement of purpose to Frank, and a matter for sardonic amusement to the future Cardinal.

It was Frank's literalness, his belief in the truth as always the shortest distance between two points, that was really the source of the trouble, whether in religious criticism or in the translating of Homer. To Arnold the truth in religion, as it affected conduct, was not to be revealed merely by the publication of critical analysis, especially before the mass of the people could adjust to new ideas in their moral significance. He attacked Bishop Colenso later for drawing attention to the inconsistencies and contradictions in the Old Testament, so confusing truth of scientific fact with truth of moral edification, and misconceiving the 'essential elements of the religious problem'. In the preface to the popular edition of *Literature and Dogma* (1873), he put this view again. 'Theology may be false, and yet one may do more harm in attacking it than by keeping silence and waiting.' He defended his own criticism by saying that the time was ripe for such disclosures, that he would (unlike Colenso) accentuate the positive, and that the fluid 'tact' of the literary critic was more helpful than the rigidities of either orthodoxy or rationalism in elucidating the essential truth of 'sacred' documents.

To Frank this was all nonsense. Truth is truth, and moral edification is only served by complete intellectual honesty, by exposing all factual error and stating every logical conclusion and answering every question. The confrontation did not occur in the area of Biblical criticism, though Frank attacked Arnold's ideas in his review of *Literature and Dogma* (*Fraser's Magazine*, July, 1873), and declared that to say the cultured 'tact' of a literary critic is necessary to discern religious truth is to pass 'a sentence of moral death on the vast majority of mankind'. It occurred instead in the famous exchange of views on the translating of Homer in 1861, when the Professor of Poetry at Oxford ridiculed the version newly offered by the Professor of Latin in the University of London.

The two main charges Arnold makes against Newman's Homer are that it is bad in diction, from the pedantic literalness of the avowed aim to 'be faithful to every peculiarity of the original', and bad in rhythm, from the unfortunate use of the ballad metre. Certainly words like *bragly, bulkin, anygait, liefly,* and *plump* for 'mass', deserve Arnold's stricture as being odd, quaint, or even grotesque; certainly too, the rhythm, of 'Nor liefly thee I would advance to man-ennobling battle' suggests an unhappy marriage of Bonnie Barbara Allan with Yankee Doodle. But the real sting lay in calling Newman's version 'ignoble', and in coining the word *Newmanise* to describe the process of writing in a vein unworthy of Homer. Frank's erudite reply overwhelms Arnold with the weight of philology and lexicography and textual criticism and scholarly authority. It condemns his specimen hexameters as impossible to scan, and angrily rebukes him for 'gratuitous rancour'. In his *Last Words on Translating Homer,* Arnold denies any intention of holding Newman's version up to scorn, protests again his sincere respect for Newman's scholarship, and apologizes for any 'vivacities' which may have given pain.

To express surprise that such a 'vivacity' as making a man's name a synonym for vulgarity should cause pain may seem somewhat disingenuous, to say the least. Nor is the doubt entirely removed when public regret is reinforced by a line in a letter to Clough. 'The one impression [Newman's pamphlet] leaves with me is of sorrow that he should be so much annoyed.' Yet Arnold does indeed have the last word, even if a modern reader may well prefer E. V. Rieu's prose translation to either Newman's jingle or Arnold's hexameters. 'I unfeignedly admire Mr Newman's ability and learning,' says Arnold, 'but I think in his translation of Homer he has employed that ability and learning quite amiss.' Why? Because 'poetical taste and feeling' will decide the value of a translation, and not merely literal fidelity to the original, or a scholar's eccentric determination to reproduce with English archaisms and coinages the presumed effect of Homer upon Sophocles. It is this matter of 'poetic truth' that is central, rather than Arnold's own crotchet about the noble or grand style.[1]

The "thing itself" with which one is here dealing, the critical perception of poetic truth, is of all things the most volatile, elusive, and

----

[1] M. Arnold, *Essays Literary and Critical,* Everyman, p. 342.

evanescent; by even pressing too impetuously after it, one runs the risk of losing it. The critic of poetry should have the finest tact, the nicest consideration, the most free, flexible, and elastic spirit imaginable; he should be indeed the "ondoyant et divers," the *undulating and diverse* being of Montaigne. The less he can deal with his object simply and freely, the more things he has to take into account in dealing with it, the more, in short, he has to encumber himself, so much the greater force of spirit he needs to retain his elasticity. . . . one often sees erudition out of all proportion to its owner's critical faculty.

Frank's early "Four Lectures on Poetry, delivered first in Wales to a select company", are hardly calculated to offset Arnold's criticisms, though in them Pope is condemned for 'corrupting Homer's simplicity'. The standards by which English poets are judged are conventional and even neo-classical, with frequent reference to Aristotle, Pope, Burke, and Reynolds. Traditional forms and figures are analysed; great tragedy is confined to Aeschylus, Sophocles, and Euripides; truth is superior to fiction; the sublime is balanced against the beautiful; pleasure is the end; elevation of diction and moral improvement are hallmarks of true poetry. The Puritan strain reaffirms that the theatre is dangerous to virtue, and the lectures conclude with a stern judgment on Byron for being, in spite of his felicity and richness, deficient in moral qualities. 'No poems will be immortal, whatever their genius, unless fitted to purify youth. Therefore Goldsmith and even Cowper will outlive many poets of far higher powers.'

Characteristically, the eccentric and the sensible mingle in Frank's pronouncements. He has a theory that we need a 'vowel of union', as in Mountebank and Handicraft, and seriously suggests that euphony would be greatly aided if we could say Steamoboat and Townowall. He proudly produces a number of passages from his version of Homer, including such lines as these:

So they on either side did fling/ —on Troians—on Achaians—
The stones thick showering; and noise/along the ramparts hooted.

His response to poetry, in fact, brings to mind a passage from *The Soul*, where the superiority of hymns over prose in 'nourishing the soul' is appreciated, but where the 'offensive' Calvinistic logic of

If one believer can be lost,
It follows, so can all,

is triumphantly set down by the 'admirable' lines of the 'glorious hymn-writer' Charles Wesley:

> To me, to all, thy bowels move,
> Thy nature and thy name is love.

The sensible and original elements blend in the pedagogical defence of the reading of English poetry in the schools, as against Dr Arnold's preference for the Latin and Greek classics, on the grounds that such elocutionary practice will develop a sense for rhythm and melody and will help form the mind and character of the pupil. Even more intelligent is a far-sighted comment on the social implications of a universal acquaintance with pure and well pronounced English. To have both a patrician and a plebian dialect, Frank tells his audience, is a mischief, a cause of heart-burning and misunderstanding. 'The poorest Turk can partake of a friendly meal without the humiliating sense of inequality occasioned by a vulgar dialect. But here the poor man is unable for five minutes to forget his essential degradation.' This is 'a gratuitous evil', to be 'subdued by proper schooling'.

A lack of imagination, a lack of feeling for style, a lack of a sense of proportion—these are the defects Arnold found in Frank's literary efforts. By implication, he may be said to extend his criticism to Frank's work as a whole, and to find him representative of the 'eccentric and arbitrary spirit' of the age. As in his religious writing, so in his social and political essays, there is much in Frank that finds an echo in Arnold—the need to reform education and politics, the need to accept democracy as inevitable and to transform it, the need to concentrate on the moral improvement of the individual as indispensable to the realizing of the good life in society. But the indiscriminate crusading zeal that carried Frank from Catholic dogma to the Contagious Diseases Act, and from social ethics to Sunday observance laws, would strike Arnold as exemplifying the distraction of his times. In the paragraph generalizing from Frank's mis-employed learning Arnold speaks of the state of literary opinion as 'a chaos of false tendencies, wasted efforts, impotent conclusions, works which ought never to have been undertaken'. To be sure, this is a judgment on the literary scene. But literature was to Arnold, as he was to say so often, a criticism of life.

When Arnold said of John Henry Newman's dogmatic

Catholicism that it was 'for the educated man today, speaking
frankly, impossible', he summed up the rejection of Newman's ideas
that he expressed firmly, if courteously, throughout his own writings
on religion. Yet the intellectual chasm was easily bridged by a temperamental imaginative sympathy, whereas the temperamental
incompatibility separating him from Francis could not be resolved by any number of shared rationalistic positions. The
phenomenon seems to offer proof for John's contention that man
reasons not with his intellect alone, but with his whole being. It
may even suggest an application, if not quite in the way intended,
of his aphorism in *The Tamworth Reading Room*: 'After all, man is
not a reasoning animal; he is a seeing, feeling, contemplating,
acting animal.' Certainly it is an interesting comment on the cross-
currents in the main religious movements of the nineteenth century that the ethical idealist Matthew Arnold should have this
ambivalent relationship with the prominent Catholic thinker, the
man who represented everything his father Thomas Arnold detested in the priestly tradition, and whom his brother Thomas
Arnold the younger, also a Catholic convert, served first as Professor of English Literature in Dublin and later as classical master
at the Oratory School in Birmingham.

The terms of the relationship are set forth in an exchange of
letters in 1871–2.[1] Agreeing with Arnold that there is nothing in
the *nature* of the Roman Catholic Church to make her anti-
democratic, Newman expresses his pleasure at Arnold's friendly
tribute, and adds: '. . . I am so sensitively alive to the great
differences of opinion which separate us. I wish with all my heart
I could make them less; but there they are, and I can only resign
myself to them, as best I may.' The tribute Arnold had paid was
indeed striking, and revealing.

> I cannot forbear adding, what I have often wished to tell you, that no
> words can be too strong to express the interest with which I used to
> hear you at Oxford, and the pleasure with which I continue to read
> your writings now. We are all of us carried in ways not of our own
> making or choosing, but nothing can ever do away the effect you
> have produced upon me, for it consists in a general disposition of

[1] *Unpublished Letters of Matthew Arnold*, ed. Whitridge, New Haven, 1923.
The relationship has been fully and ably analysed by D. J. DeLaura in his
recent "Matthew Arnold and John Henry Newman", University of Texas
Studies in Literature and Language, vol. VI, Supplement 1965, pp. 573–701.

mind rather than in a particular set of ideas. In all the conflicts I
have with modern Liberalism and Dissent, and with their pretensions and shortcomings, I recognize your work; and I can truly say
that no praise gives me so much pleasure as to be told (which sometimes happens) that a thing I have said reminds people, either in
manner or matter, of you.

The friendly exchange continues on the subject of Arnold's projected edition of Isaiah for Bible reading in the schools. To this
project Newman gives his approval, but dreads that if the Old
Testament is studied primarily for its 'literary aspect', the children
may 'never learn the secret sense of the sacred text at all'. In reply
Arnold delicately points up their different views. It might be
better to give children the 'typical side' if it were given 'rightly',
but as it is so often given wrongly, 'it is better to give them the
historical side plainly'. He then repeats and amplifies his earlier
tribute.

There are four people, in especial, from whom I am conscious of
having learnt—a very different thing from merely receiving a strong
impression—learnt habits, methods, ruling ideas, which are constantly with me; and the four are—Goethe, Wordsworth, Sainte-
Beuve, and yourself. You will smile and say I have made an odd
mixture and that the result must be a jumble: however that may be
as to the whole, I am sure in details you must recognize your own
influence often, and perhaps this inclines you to indulgence.

A general disposition of mind, ruling ideas as against particular
ideas—these terms may not bear too close analysis. Yet the gospel
of culture that Arnold opposed to the prevailing anarchy, to the
philistine obsession with 'machinery' and catchwords and clap-
trap and trivia, was conceived of as embracing religion. It would
enlarge the spirits of men as well as their minds, seeking the impossible goal of perfection by a harmonizing of all the powers and
by an inward process of moral growth. In short, Arnold gave his
allegiance to modern thought; he also attacked the thoughtless
progressivism of modern liberals. ('Progress,' said Newman, 'is a
slang term.') He rejected dogma and metaphysics and supernaturalism; he rejected equally the doctrinal rigidities of Puritanism, saying that there was more of the spirit of Jesus in St Theresa's
little finger than in John Knox's whole body.
The clue to the influence of Newman on such as Arnold is

offered in the 1884 essay on Emerson.[1] It is the Newman of
Oxford days who is praised, the eloquent preacher who has since
adopted an 'impossible' solution for 'the doubts and difficulties
which beset men's minds today', but who is 'a great name to the
imagination still; his genius and his style are still things of power'.
The famous tribute follows:

> Who could resist the charm of that spiritual apparition, gliding in the
> dim afternoon light through the aisles of St Mary's, rising into the
> pulpit, and then, in the most entrancing of voices, breaking the
> silence with words and thoughts which were a religious music,—
> subtle, sweet, mournful? I seem to hear him still, saying: 'After the
> fever of life, after wearinesses and sicknesses, fightings and despond-
> ings, languor and fretfulness, struggling and succeeding; after all the
> changes and chances of this troubled, unhealthy state,—at length
> comes death, at length the white throne of God, at length the beatific
> vision.'

A passage from another sermon is recalled.

> Again I seem to hear him: 'The season is chill and dark, and the
> breath of the morning is damp, and worshippers are few; but all this
> befits those who are by their profession penitents and mourners,
> watchers and pilgrims. More dear to them that loneliness, more
> cheerful that severity, and more bright that gloom, than all the aids
> and appliances of luxury by which men nowadays attempt to make
> prayer less disagreeable to them. True faith does not covet comforts;
> they who realise that awful day, when they shall see Him face to face
> whose eyes are as a flame of fire, will as little bargain to pray
> pleasantly now as they will think of doing so then. (See Appendix B.)

If the Cardinal read Arnold's essay, he must have found it de-

[1] M. Arnold, *Discourses in America*, London, 1889, pp. 139-41. Perhaps 'holiness' is the best name for the quality that many found in Newman, and moved
them then as now to place him among the saints. His own witty and deprecating
comment on such adulation appears in a letter of February 11, 1850. 'I have
nothing of a Saint about me as every one knows, and it is a severe (and salutary)
mortification to be thought next door to one. I may have a high view of many
things, but it is the consequence of education and of a peculiar cast of intellect
—but this is very different from *being* what I admire. I have no tendency to be
a saint—it is a sad thing to say. Saints are not literary men, they do not love the
classics, they do not write Tales. I may be well enough in my way, but it is not
the "high line." People ought to feel this, most people do. But those who are at
a distance have fee-fa-fum notions about one. It is enough for me to black the
saints' shoes—if St Philip uses blacking, in heaven.' (Dessain, v. 13, p. 419.)

pressingly ironic to be bracketed with the transatlantic trans-
cendentalist, the poet-preacher of self-reliance and optimism, as a
salutary influence, even though Emerson is praised as 'the friend
and aider of those who would live in the spirit'.

Imagination, genius, style—the terms Arnold uses here suggest
what he and others like him found in John, most of whose beliefs
they dismissed, and did not find in Francis, many of whose ideas
they shared. Sometimes it was merely a matter of taste. One recalls
Monckton Milnes's preference, unjust though the comparison may
be to all concerned, for Newman's 'gentlemanlike falsehood' over
Kingsley's 'strepitose fidgety truth'. A more meaningful contrast is
that drawn for us today by Karl Popper in *The Open Society and Its
Enemies*, between the Platonizing idealist (often authoritarian) on
the one hand, and the 'social engineer' on the other, with his
piecemeal empirical constructions. For all the spirituality of his
personal theism, Frank's moral energies were applied indis-
criminately to a multiplicity of problems, both religious and
secular. John's intense other-worldliness and Catholic absolutism
gave power and consistency to the spiritual Idea, however foreign
in its manifestations to the mind of the humanist and reformer.
Very early in life Arnold had told Clough that the poet 'must
begin with an Idea of the world in order not to be prevailed over
by the world's multitudinousness'. It is a preference for the philosophical over the logical, for the timeless over the temporary, the
bent in Arnold the critic which led him to advocate disinterestedness as an approach to establishing principles. Allied to his
pleasure in style and imagery, then, was his intellectual pleasure in
a writer who reminded the age, in its 'sick hurry' and 'divided
aims', of the need for a spiritual Idea. To Arnold, the elder
Newman, however medieval his Cause, triumphed over the world's
multitudinousness; the younger Newman, however modern his
causes, was a victim of it.

This yearning for an Absolute, or an Idea, or a unifying principle, moral or philosophical, if not theological, may be seen as a
permanent need of human nature, intensified in those who feel it
most by the post-Renaissance triumphs of science and empiricism,
and even in our own time focusing for many in the lonely crowd
their discontent with an affluent society and its unrelated special-
isms. Certainly it found frequent expression in the Victorian age.
We have seen Martineau's criticism of his friend Francis Newman

for his lack of a transcendent ideality or metaphysical basis. In the life of F. D. Maurice we have almost a parable of the dilemma facing those Victorians who would reconcile the claims of this world and the other. Saint and rebel, Evangelical in fervour but opposed to all sectarianism, a socialist concerned with practical reforms but also a metaphysician anxiously seeking the Absolute, this convert from Unitarianism to Anglicanism found Frank's *Hebrew Monarchy* and John's *Development of Christian Doctrine* equally depressing. His own painfully scrupulous search for truth led into wordy tortuosities that account for Arnold's complaint that he was always beating the bush without starting the hare. A letter of 1843 seems the pathetic cry of a 'true Christian' on the shifting and relativist scene of modern history, looking both backwards and forward. Against an 'emasculating Eclecticism', he asks, who does not long for the 'keen air' of Calvinism, or for anything that will stir to action? 'We must somewhere find a reconciliation between the comprehension or Universal which the reason of this day sighs after and the heart-stirring faith of other days.' But where? To progress beyond 'isms' we must work within them and invent the symbols of our faith, each age discarding the formulas of the last. 'The reality lies beneath them; to see that is the privilege of a few gifted seers,' who create the vesture for the multitude. So we have 'an endless repetition of half truths and half falsehoods'. Even the gifted few can hardly contemplate a time when there will be no symbols, but instead, 'a mere naked recognition of an indefinable something'.[1]

An 'indefinable something' seems an apt description of Frank's theism, as it oscillates between a vague Father-figure, the object of love and prayer, and an ideal of moral perfection towards which humanity strives, or is urged. It was either too personal a vision to be communicated, and in that sense mystical, or too secularized in action to preserve a transcendent unity. It was meaningful to Frank, and inspired the 'noble enthusiasm' which held the love and respect of Martineau and Holyoake. It expressed itself not in any intellectual formulation, however, but in moral credo and compassionate humanitarianism. Frank shared the compulsion of his contemporaries to verify the Eternal, but by the time his reason and his moral sense had disposed of the 'evidences' and the

[1] *The Life of Frederick Denison Maurice, Chiefly Told in his Own Letters*, 2 vols., ed. Frederick Maurice, London, 1884, v. 1, pp. 339-40.

authorities, the Divine and his feelings about the Divine were
virtually the same thing. He could tell Martineau in a letter of
1851 that 'Morality, Free-Will, and Theism, all three, stand or fall
together.' But the comprehensive tolerance that was the outcome
of his views led him on to praise of Holyoake as a kind and candid
man whose 'moral goodness gives power to his doctrine'. There is
no harm in such Atheism. 'It surely can only be a transition towards a new and better religion. Where the heart retains a love of
and reverence for goodness, it is essentially a worshipper, and will
find a God in due time.'[1]

There was for John no danger of the outlines of the Triune
Deity dissolving, and with them his other-worldly reality, objec-
tified as these were in creed and dogma. That 'other luminously
self-evident being' may have been just as much the reflection of
his own feelings, psychologically speaking, as in Frank's case, but
it occupied a temple of tradition which his reason buttressed with
a theory and which his imagination restored to full glory in his
sermons. With this firm commitment, and with authority to check
him in any aberration, his restless mind could safely play with
modern and liberal ideas and find a partial good in them. Even
in 1837, in an essay on the "Fall of De la Mennais", there is
sympathy for the liberal French theologian, a confessor and
martyr to the great truth that for the Roman Catholic Church
'the true basis of its power is the multitude'. Newman seems here
to accept as a matter of history that the Latin Church rose to
power by favour of the people, not of princes, 'maintaining the
freedom and equality of all men in the Gospel'. Lamennais, however, has erred in associating this truth with the cry for liberty and
the rights of man, and with the belief in 'the gradual and constant
advance of the species'. He has rightly incurred the displeasure of
the Pope, because his theology is connected with 'the popular

---

[1] That Frank's theism did not lack spirituality, at least for certain readers, is
attested by his old pupil Edward Fry, who loved 'some of J. H. Newman's
verses'. Looking back near the end of a long life, he said: 'Mr Jowett, I think,
said of Francis Newman that his book on *The Soul* contained more religion than
the writings of his Cardinal brother, and I entirely agree with that impression.
It is a most spiritual book, and contains passages of great and lofty beauty—far
nobler than anything which I have ever found in the sermons or writings of the
Cardinal, which have, I think, been greatly over-estimated by some of my
friends, such as Hutton and Lord Coleridge.' (*A Memoir of The Right Honourable
Sir Edward Fry, G.C.B.*, Oxford University Press, 1921, p. 44.)

philosophy'. Instead of following 'an invariable course of obedience', he has sympathized with the feeling of the day that 'energy, activity, bustle, extraordinary developments of intellect, are parts of the high and perfect state of the human mind'. The Anglican Newman concludes ironically, 'Such are the consequences of being wiser than one's generation,' and finds the Roman Church, in irreligious France, as much God's minister 'as if it were as pure as the primitive'.

By 1879 this question of primitive purity had long been irrelevant, the theory of development having both explained away 'corruptions' and justified later doctrinal pronouncements. His intuition of the Eternal resting safely on the dogma of infallibility, the Cardinal can grant much that is good to liberalism, in so far as it stresses 'the fundamental ethical truths of justice, benevolence, veracity, and the like', and in so far as its enthusiasm for 'natural laws' brings about improvement 'in society and in social matters'. The irony with which he views this whole shift from religious to secular, this concern with the rights and comfort of the people, is, naturally, evident throughout. He adds: 'As to religion, it is a private luxury, which a man may have if he will, but which, of course, he must pay for, and which he must not obtrude upon others or indulge to their annoyance.' The tone deepens into the gravity of prophecy, but remains calm, as he contemplates this 'great apostasy' of modern liberalism, with its evil tendency to supersede religion. It is Satan's cleverest device, catching able and virtuous men. But Christianity has survived as deadly perils. 'Sometimes our enemy is turned into a friend; sometimes he is despoiled of that special virulence of evil . . .; sometimes he falls to pieces of himself; sometimes he does just so much as is beneficial and then is removed. Commonly the Church has nothing more to do than to go on in her own proper duties in confidence and peace, to stand still, and to see the salvation of God.'[1]

When he uses the word 'commonly' one wonders whether Newman, especially in the light of his own attempt to liberalize it, foresaw a time when the Catholic Church could not 'stand still'. The question is one of compelling interest today, as ecumenical councils discuss possible doctrinal changes and moves for comprehension, as Jews are formally forgiven and Protestants tactic-

[1] "Sayings of Cardinal Newman" (a Collection of Speeches and Sermons), in *Merry England*, August, 1890.

ally tolerated, and as clergy and laity strenuously debate the over-
lapping areas of faith and mere credulity, together with such
practical matters as over-population in relation to moral teaching.
Francis Newman, noting 'the sectarianism incident to Protestants',
prophesied that a liberal Pope might yet effect the one way of
valid reform, 'to make the Church as comprehensive as Protestant Unitarians desire it to be'. ("The Future of the Roman
Church", *Fraser's Magazine*, September, 1876.) The barrenness of
conferences in this century justifies Frank's phrase about Protestants, but his prophecy that a liberalized 'Papacy and Catholicism may outlive our Protestant sects' has an all-important and
indispensable condition attached to it, the surrender of the dogma
of papal infallibility.

It is a cruel dilemma for a Church which has for so long justified
authoritarian intolerance by claiming unique possession of sacred
truth. To surrender infallibility in the hope of gaining comprehensiveness would seem to threaten, as with much of Protestantism, a gradual dissolution into pragmatical ethics and social service humanitarianism; to retain it is to go increasingly against the
rationalist and relativist thinking of modern times, and to run the
risk of facing scepticism from a splendid isolation. John Henry
Newman saw this predicament clearly, and having conquered his
own scepticism by an act of will, had no doubt where the Truth
lay. His faith assured him, as it assures those like him today, that
any isolation will be temporary. The need of men for guidance and
authority in moral and spiritual matters will bring them back
from the sterility of rationalism and the illusory promise of sub-
stitute faiths. When six young liberal radicals in the 1930's turned
to Communism, and then turned back to write *The God That
Failed*, Newman's prophecy seemed strikingly fulfilled. And his
interpretation of the Church's role in relation to man's life on
earth is in essence repeated in a chorus from T. S. Eliot's *The Rock*.

Why should men love the Church? Why should they love her laws?
She tells them of Life and Death, and of all that they would forget.
She is tender where they would be hard, and hard where they like
   to be soft,
She tells them of Evil and Sin, and other unpleasant facts.
They constantly try to escape
From the darkness outside and within
By dreaming of systems so perfect that no one will need to be good.

G

But the man that is will shadow
The man that pretends to be.

Yet the young radicals turned back because they found that new commissar was but old Czar writ large, and that the value threatened by the system was the one they most prized for the spirit, individual freedom. The slight successive relaxations of the post-Stalin era offer their own historical commentary on man's instinctive drive or spiritual need. And Eliot's contempt for any humanistic faith ignores the possibility that a humanist may appraise human weaknesses as realistically as any theologian enamoured of Original Sin. To see man's 'salvation' as dependent upon a reasoned choice among possible lines of action, it is not necessary to have illusions about human nature, or to surrender to a system-bred secular conformity. To abandon doctrinal formulas, then, need not mean abandoning human dignity or humility; it may rather mean, in Popper's words, 'to bear the cross of being human'. In this context, myths and symbols and images are not, as for Newman, the 'economical' or sacramental representation of a mysterious reality higher and truer than the world of sense, a supernatural world that offers man's fearful spirit its only home. They are on the one hand the object of scientific or critical interest, as the archetypal embodiments of man's psychological experience and mental processes. On the other hand, they are the expression of his creative imagination, not expounding infallibly the Divine Word, but clothing in fallible words those tentative intuitions that escape both laws and logic. The knowledge gained by his reason is the source of his dignity; the tentativeness of his imaginative insights is, or should be, the ground of his humility. On this ground the Catholic and the Protestant, the theist and the atheist, the humanist and the scientist, can meet in a mutual toleration, provided dogmatic rigidities either sacred or secular are relinquished.

In turning to Frank's pre-occupation with humanitarian causes, with needed social and political reforms, and to his belief that a 'spiritual faith' grows from and reveals itself in moral energies directed to the ends of human brotherhood, we may not be concerned with the charge of Pelagian heresy, but we must consider that of unrealistic optimism. His attempts to ameliorate the human condition did not ignore the caution of Thomas Hardy's lines, where such attempts to realize the best 'exact a full look at

the worst'. Yet a persistent hopefulness sustained him, a faith in
the improvability of human nature. It rested partly on the belief
common to his times, that the moral sense or conscience is innate.
Accepting this belief, a reviewer in 1851 quoted Bishop Butler to
point up its fatal defect in any scheme of naturalistic ethics. 'Had
conscience strength, as it has right, it would absolutely govern the
world.' John was sure it had no such strength without the authority
of Christian dogma and ecclesiastical power. Frank, saying that
dogmatic ecclesiasticism had distorted moral intuitions, agreed
that Christian (and other) religious teachings had assisted moral
growth, but gave as much credit to social and political developments of a progressive kind, and to the intellectual achievements of
science. As against John's pessimistic attitude towards the moral
relevance of such changes, Frank's attitude was in general
optimistic, a blend of pragmatic argument and moral idealism.

Contemplating the Hollow Men in the Waste Land, many
have agreed with Eliot that nineteenth-century liberalism and a
reasoned meliorism are broken reeds. Yet are they are broken, or
merely bruised and bent? If broken, what is there to replace them?
If a Catholic comprehensiveness is impossible without a revived
dogmatic other-worldliness, then it seems likely that man will have
only his human resources, slender and deficient as these may be.
Frank's kind of faith has taken terrible blows in two world wars,
in the appalling reminders at Guernica and Auschwitz, in the
mindless greed and jungle behaviour of our competitive civilization. It has also been sustained by the tentative gropings of the
League of Nations and the United Nations, by the young people
of the Peace Corps, and other such bodies, and by the relief
measures of organized philanthropy. The contemptuous dismissal,
by hard-headed modern 'philosophies', of evaluative judgments
as a form of semantic minuet would seem to make against such a
faith as Frank's; the attempts to marry science and humanism, or
to re-unite them, and so to produce a better humanity, would
seem to support it. Intellectual cynicism, sterile reaction, and
selfish indifference, are at least balanced by the urge to cherish
and to enhance the moral and intellectual human life so painfully
evolved. To this end it is doubtful that a transcendental and
metaphysical dogmatism would be more effective, judging by the
historical record, than such means as man in himself possesses.
The tortured modern Hamlet would enlist the rational Horatio,

and bequeath to posterity a state purified of its rottenness by frank exposure and healing measures. For the rest, as he knows, is silence.

What is here involved, as always, is the growth of knowledge into wisdom. J. A. Froude asked in 1849, through his character Markham Sutherland in *The Nemesis of Faith*: 'What is man the wiser or happier for knowing how the air-plants feed, or how many centuries the flint-stone was in forming, unless the knowledge of them can be linked on to humanity, and elucidate for us some of our hard moral mysteries.' In 1959, Loren Eiseley gave one kind of answer in *Darwin's Century*. Provided man does not confuse progress with mere mechanical extensions, with the old biological evolution of 'parts', whether armaments or gracious living, he will see that his evolution has brought the rise of mind, has brought volition into the world of nature. Turning his knowledge upon himself, he will see that transcendence of self is not to be sought in the outer world, but in 'that interior kingdom in which man is forever free to be better than what he knows himself to be'. This the great moralists have always known. This inner world 'takes its color from the minds behind it', and only when man applies to it his biologically evolved power of conscious selection will he escape 'the world which Darwin saw and pictured'.

The humanist must hope that the vast legacy of recorded experience and transmitted values from religion and philosophy and literature, from 'the best that has been known and thought in the world', scientifically assessed and imaginatively selected, may yet nourish a viable society. He must (hopefully) treat such phenomena as the theatre of the absurd or of cruelty, and the opting out of the 'beat' generation, as honest negations exacting 'a full look at the worst', not merely as signs of a collapse into moral chaos. This way lies no easy optimism, but rather the courage of the mind that can 'bear the cross of being human'.

In the task facing man, voices from the past may call him to a purposive belief and to a comprehensiveness that is neither sentimental nor flaccid. One such voice is Wordsworth's, in the last five lines of the sonnet *After-Thought*.

> Enough, if something from our hands have power
> To live, and act, and serve the future hour;
> And if, as toward the silent tomb we go,
> Through love, through hope, and faith's transcendent dower,
> We feel that we are greater than we know.

Less solemn is a reminder from Robert Frost, that 'earth's the right place for love'. In *Birches*, recalling a game of his boyhood, he would choose a high tree,

> And climb black branches up a snow-white trunk
> *Toward* heaven, till the tree could bear no more,
> But dipped its top and set me down again.
> That would be good both going and coming back.
> One could do worse than be a swinger of birches.

Perhaps at the top of our swing we may catch a whisper of the Eternal Verities from brother John, and return refreshed to join brother Francis in cultivating our garden.

Hiawatha: Rendered into Latin

SELECTIONS FROM *Hiawatha: Rendered into Latin*, by Francis W. Newman, are here offered for the delectation of latter-day Latinists. The project was undertaken to demonstrate Newman's principle that Latin is best taught by modern compositions, thus enlarging vocabulary and avoiding repetitive drill in grammar. Adding 'no ornaments', he strives for accuracy, though with some abridgement and minor alterations. Some new words, e.g. the names of birds and animals, are formed 'by strict classical analogies'.

From Caput 1: Tubulus Concordiae Fumarius

Scilicet a valle Tawasanthae
Atque Wyomingae a valle prorsum,
A memoribus Tuscalousae,
A longinquis montibus Saxosis,
A lacubus fluvisque Septentrionis,
Cunctae gentes procul dispexere
Fumi ascendentis signum
E pacifico tubulo exspirati.
'Propitius ecce fumus!'
Iniquiunt populorum vates.
'Hoc signo, tanquam virgulâ salignâ,
Quam manus innuentis vibrat,
Ad concilium serum Daemon supremus
Genteis convocat ac bellatores.'
Secundùm fluvias, per campos herbidos,
Venere gentium bellatores,
Delawāri, Mohauci, Coctavi,
Comantii, Sotsoni, Nigripĕdes,
Paunaei, Omahavi, Mandani,
Dacōtae, Hurones, Ogibbawaiae;

Pacifico tubuli signo
Omnes in unum contracti
Ad montes camporum herbosorum
Russamque tubulorum lapicidinam.

From Caput III: Hiawathae Puerita

Olim vespertino crepusculo
In diebus oblivione deletis,
In seculis memoriâ elapsis,
Plenâ lunâ decĭdit Nocōmis,
Pulcerrima Nocōmis decĭdit,
Matrona, sed nondum mater.

. . . .

Foras protenus in silvam
Solivagus incessit Hiawatha
Exsultanter, cum arcu et sagittis;
Circùmque ac suprá aves,
'Ne nos tu ferias,' cănebant.
Iterabat rubecula, cyaneda,
'Ne nos tu ferias, Hiawatha!'
Super quercum proximam juxtâ
Exsiluit sciurus erectâ caudâ,
Seque induens exuens frondibus
Tussivit, garrivit e quercu,
Ridens; atque inter ridendum,
'Ne me ferias, Hiawatha!' inquit.
Jamque e semitâ cuniculus
In obliquum prosilit: ibi longe
Natibus insĭdit erectus,
Et metuens et simul lusurus;
Isque juveni inquit venatori:
'Ne me tu ferias, Hiawatha!'

From Caput IV: Hiawathae Peregrinatio ad Occidentem

Sed gressum tardavit semel,
Semel tantummodo moratus est,
Ut a vetere sagittarum fabro
Mucrones sagittarios coëmeret
Mediâ in regione Dacotarum,
Ubi praecipites Minnehāhae
Per querceta fulgent aquae
Inque vallem ridentes desiliunt.

Ibi vetus sagittarum faber
Ex arenaceo saxo atque ex achate,
Ex silice atque iaspăre confingebat
Mucrones sagittarum acutissimos,
Eduros, usque ad aciem politos,
Impenso coëmendos pretio.
Apud eum habitabat filia
Nigris oculis decora,
Ut ipsa Minnehāha versatilis,
Mobilis inter umbram ac jubar,
Vultu arridente seu adducto,
Pedibus instar undarum rapidus,
Cincinnis instar undarum fluentibus,
Risu instar undarum canoro.
Ergo ex aquis eam nominaverit,
Ex aquis illis praecipitibus,
Minnehāham, *aquam ridentum.*

The Tree Beside the Waters

THE SERMON of which four pages are here reproduced was preached in St Mary's, Oscott, at the funeral of the Right Rev. H. Weedall, D.D., on November 11, 1859. Even this excerpt, from "The Tree Beside the Waters" (*Sermons Preached on Various Occasions*, London, 1881, pp. 243–7) will serve to show that Newman's power in the writing of sermons remained with him through the years. It may also help us appreciate the popularity of the sermon among earlier generations, to whom it was a literary form as well as a spiritual summons.

Among the many images under which the good man is described in Holy Scripture, perhaps there is none more vivid, more beautiful, and more touching than that which represents him as some favoured and thriving tree in the garden of God's planting. Our original birthplace and home was a garden; and the trees which Adam had to dress and keep, both in themselves and by the sort of attention they demanded, reminded him of the peaceful happy duties and the innocent enjoyments which were the business of his life. A garden, in its perennial freshness and its soothing calm, is the best type of heaven, and its separate plants and flowers are the exactest types of the inhabitants of heaven. Accordingly, it is introduced into the last page of Scripture as well as into the first; it makes its appearance at the conclusion of man's eventful history as in the record of its opening. As in the beginning we read of the Paradise of pleasure, with the great river and its four separate streams, with all manner of trees, fair to behold, and pleasant to eat of, and, above all, the Tree of Life,—so, in the last chapter of the Apocalypse, we are told of the river of water of life, clear as crystal, proceeding from the throne of God and of the Lamb, which he that thirsteth may drink freely; and of the Tree of Life, bearing twelve fruits, the leaves of which were for the healing of the nations.

And, in like manner, when we turn to that portion of the sacred volume which more than any other both reveals and supports the hidden life of the servants of God in every age,—I mean the Psalter,—we find, prefixed to the collection, the Psalm from which my Text is taken, in which the obedient and just man is set before us under the selfsame image; under the image of some choice specimen of the vegetable world, that innocent portion of the divine handiwork which is deformed by no fierce passions, which has no will and pursues no end of its own, and which seems created only to please the eye of man, and to be his food, medicine, and refreshment.

'Blessed is the man who hath not walked in the counsel of the ungodly, nor stood in the way of sinners, nor sat in the chair of pestilence: but his will is in the law of the Lord, and in His law he shall meditate day and night.

'And he shall be like a tree which is planted near the running waters, which shall bring forth its fruit in due season. And his leaf shall not fall off; and all whatsoever he shall do shall prosper.'

This spiritual plant of God is placed by the running waters; it is nourished and recruited by the never-failing, the perpetual, the daily and hourly supply of their wholesome influences. It grows up gradually, silently, without observation; and in proportion as it rises aloft, so do its roots, with still less observation, strike deep into the earth. Thus it determinately takes up its habitation in one place, from which death alone shall part it. Year after year it grows more and more into the hope and the posture of a glorious immobility and unchangeableness. What it has been, that it shall be; if it changes, it is as growing into fruitfulness, and maturing in its fruit's abundance and perfection. Nor is that fruit lost; it neither withers upon the branches nor decays upon the ground. Angels unseen gather crop and crop from the unwearied never-failing parent, and carefully store them up in the heavenly treasure-houses. Its very leaf remains green to the end; not only its fruit, which is profitable for eternal life, but its very foliage, the ordinary dress in which it meets our senses, its beautiful colouring, its rich yet delicate fulness of proportion, the graceful waving of its boughs, the musical whispers and rustlings of its leaves, the fragrance which it exhales, the refreshment which it spreads around it,—all testify to that majestic, serene beneficence which is its very nature, and to a mysterious depth of life which enables it ever to give out virtue, yet never to have less of it within.

Such is the holy servant of God, considered in that condition which is both his special reward and his ordinary lot. There are those, indeed, who, for the good of their brethren, and according to the will of God, are exercised by extraordinary trials, and pass their lives amid turbulence and change. There are others, again, who are wonderfully called out of error or of sin, and have experience of much conflict within or without them before they reach the heavenly river, and the groves which line its banks. Certainly history speaks much more of martyrdom and confessorship on the one hand, and of inquiry and conversion, of sin and repentance, on the other, than of the tranquil Christian course; but history does but give the surface of what actually takes place in the heavenly kingdom. If we would really bring before us what is both the highest blessedness in God's service, and also in fact the ordinary portion of good men, we shall find it to consist in what from its very nature cannot make much show in history,—in a life barren of great events, and rich in small ones; in a life of routine duties, of happy obscurity and inward peace, of an orderly dispensing of good to others who come within their influence, morning and evening, of a growth and blossoming and bearing fruit in the house of God, and of a blessed death in the presence of their brethren. Such has been the round of days of many a pastor up and down Christendom, as even history has recorded, of many a missioner, of many a monk, of many a religious woman, of many a father or mother of a family, of many a student in sacred or profane literature,—each the centre of his own circle, and the teacher of his own people, though more or less unknown to the world. This has been the blessedness of holy Job, as he sets it before us himself: 'I said, I shall die in my nest, and as a palm-tree shall multiply my days. My root is opened beside the waters, and dew shall continue in my harvest. They that heard me . . . to my words durst add nothing, and my speech dropped upon them. They waited for me as for rain, and they opened their mouth as for a latter shower.' It is expressed also in the words of the Canticle, which, though belonging in their fulness to our Lord Himself, yet in their measure apply to the benefits which any holy man extends to those who are within the range of his attraction: 'As the apple-tree among the trees of the woods, so is my beloved among the sons. I sat down under his shadow whom I desired, and his fruit was sweet to my mouth.'

Glossary of Certain Religious Terms
and References

Arian: Doctrine of Arius, presbyter of the Alexandrian Church in the fourth century, which maintained that Christ as a created being is secondary not equal to God, though as the Logos or Son he is the maker of other creatures. Condemned at the Councils of Nicaea (325) and Constantinople (381). See *Nicene Creed*.

Arminian: Teachings of Jacobus Arminius (1560–1609), Dutch Reformation scholar, who rejected the rigorous Calvinistic doctrine of absolute predestination and whose own liberal doctrines of conditional predestination and universal redemption found favour in England, especially among Wesleyans and Methodists.

Corporation Act: Act of 1661 requiring officers in municipal corporations to receive the sacrament according to the rules of the Church of England. Repealed in 1828, along with Test Act (*q.v.*), prior to Roman Catholic Emancipation Act of 1829.

Council of Trent: Sitting at intervals from 1545–63, the Council re-affirmed the Nicene Creed, and established the distinctive features of Roman Catholicism as the seven sacraments, the offering of the mass, transubstantiation, purgatory, the veneration of saints, relics, images, the efficacy of indulgences, the supremacy of the Roman Church and of the bishop of Rome as vicar of Christ. Later additions are the dogmas of the Immaculate Conception (1854), Papal Infallibility (1870), and the bodily assumption of the Virgin Mary (1951).

Disciplina Arcani: The teaching in the primitive Christian Church that the Triune Name, Creed, Lord's Prayer, and Lord's Supper were mysteries never to be divulged either to the unbaptized or to pagans, a secrecy most practised in the third to fifth centuries.

Donatist: A schismatic sect (311–431) among Christians of North Africa, following Donatus in holding that the validity of the sacraments depends on the spiritual state of the minister, that sanctity is essential for church membership, and that all who joined their sect should be re-baptized.

Erastian: Doctrine of state supremacy in ecclesiastical affairs, named after the Swiss Thomas Erastus (1524–83), who denied that the church has power to make laws and inflict penalties, maintaining that such should be left to the civil power.

Latitudinarian: Broad and liberal views in religious matters. In C. of E. a churchman favouring freedom and difference of opinion respecting government, worship and doctrine within the Church. A prominent representative was A. P. Stanley, pupil of Dr Thomas Arnold of Rugby, and Dean of Westminster from 1863.

Monophysite: A large party in the ancient Church, now represented in the Coptic and Abyssinian Churches, which maintained belief in a single nature in Christ, that the human and divine in him constituted but one composite nature.

Nicene Creed: The confession formulated at the first Council of Nicaea in 325 in opposition to Arianism, and re-affirmed at Constantinople in 381, proclaiming the Son to be of one substance or essence with the Father, the doctrinal basis of Trinitarian orthodoxy in both Eastern and Western Churches.

Pelagian: The heretical teaching of Pelagius, *c.* 400, who denied Original Sin, and hence damnation and baptismal regeneration, making man, though aided in various ways by divine grace, virtually capable of his own salvation through perfect free will.

Socinian: Doctrine of the Italian Socinus (1539–1604), who denied the divinity of Christ, though believing that Christ was a man miraculously conceived by the Virgin Mary, and who insisted that the Bible is a document to be interpreted according to human reason.

Test Act: Statute of 1673 requiring persons holding civil or military office to receive Communion according to the C. of E. and to abjure belief in transubstantiation.

Unitarian: Rejecting the doctrine of the trinity, but ranging widely in views by the principle of the right of private judgment, Unitarians have a broad basis of agreement on the doctrines of 'the fatherhood of God, the leadership of Jesus, salvation by character, and the progress of mankind onward and upward forever'.

INDEX
including selected Bibliography

(main references appear in bold type)

DATE DUE

GAYLORD			PRINTED IN U.S.A.